The Responsible Investor

The Responsible Investor is a practical introductory guide for private as well as institutional investors and financiers interested in environmental, social and governance (ESG) issues.

The authors have academia, advisory, asset management, asset owner and central bank backgrounds, bringing diverse perspectives and extensive senior-level experience in implementing Responsible Investment across different types of portfolios. Together, they have distilled what can seem a complex area into a clear guide to the topic, accessible to readers who don't necessarily have prior in-depth knowledge in the field of Responsible Investment but are interested to know more. The book presents the development of Responsible Investment, its different approaches and the drivers of Responsible Investment, as well as the implementation opportunities in different asset classes. The book introduces Responsible Investment trends that investors can take into consideration in their investment decisions. In addition, the book covers ESG data and assessment, impact and reporting for Responsible Investments.

This book suits both rookies and veterans – be they private investors, managers of investment funds or institutional investors or financiers. It is also valuable reading for students in finance, Responsible Investment and corporate social responsibility as an accessible overview of the topic.

Anna Hyrske is the Principal Responsible Investment Specialist at The Bank of Finland. She has over 20 years of finance industry experience as a credit analyst, portfolio manager, ESG specialist and Head of Asian Operations (Hong Kong). Before the Finnish central bank she worked at Ilmarinen, a multi-asset pension insurance company.

Magdalena Lönnroth is the Head of Responsible Investment at the Church Pension Fund. Magdalena has been involved in developing Responsible Investment strategies and practices across a broad range of asset classes since 2006. She was a Founder of Finsif, Finland's Sustainable Investment Forum, in 2010.

Antti Savilaakso is Head of Research at Impact Cubed in London. He has worked with Responsible Investments in the asset management and advisory industry for over 15 years and has been active in different advisory tasks internationally. Antti was a Board Member of Finsif during 2011–2015 and has been an Investor Member of the GRI stakeholder council since 2014.

Riikka Sievänen, PhD, leads Sustainable Finance services at KPMG in Finland since 2013. She has led KPMG's Global Sustainable Finance Working Group and advised the European Commission's Technical Expert Group (EU TEG) on sustainable finance. Riikka pursues post-doctoral studies at the University of Helsinki, has been on the board of Finsif and Finsif's Representative in Sitra's National Steering Group for Impact Investments.

"The book takes a simple and pragmatic approach in guiding readers from the basics through the advanced stages of the Responsible Investment process. The authors share their first-hand experience to clearly and concisely connect theory with practice in areas such as ESG-customized scoring and multi-asset sustainable allocation."

Enrico Bernardini, *Director, Climate change and Sustainability hub, Banca d'Italia [Disclaimer: The view expressed is that of the writer and does not involve the responsibility of the institution to which he belongs]*

"The book is a good introductory outline for investors seeking to understand the background to Responsible Investment, what it is, how it has evolved and where it might be heading, as well as the challenges ahead. It's also a good refresher and mind map for those already in the field. The authors are all highly experienced practitioners."

Hugh Wheelan, *Financial Journalist and Co-Founder of Responsible Investor*

"The role of global finance has never been so important. Whether it is meeting the aims of the Paris Agreement, achieving the Sustainable Development Goals (SDGs) or investing in climate change mitigation and adaptation strategies, managing geo-political risks and changing social norm are all issues that investors must consider, and responsible investors know that using an ESG framework is the best way to manage both risks and seize opportunities. This book provides a comprehensive and detailed analysis on what Responsible Investment actually is and the strategies that are used by investors to ensure that they can operate in a fast moving and evolving space. A must read for everyone wanting to understand Responsible Investment – its history, strategies and future direction."

Fiona Reynolds, *CEO, Conexus Financial*

"This book is like a driving license for modern and responsible investing, and not simply aimed at the specialists. Corporations wanting to understand the financial industry's large institutions should look no further."

Pasi Väisänen, *Director at Nordea Bank*

"The explosion of interest in Responsible Investment has resulted in numerous questions around how best to define it, which data sources to utilize or how to report on its effectiveness. This book should become the starting point for those questions and many more. Anna Hyrske, Magdalena Lönnroth, Antti Savilaakso and Riikka Sievänen have written on the topic in a thoughtful way that will be required reading for anyone interested in understanding how to develop and implement an ESG strategy in today's market environment. I highly recommend this book for laymen and practitioners alike!"

Matt Christensen, *Global Head of Sustainable and Impact Investing, Allianz Global Investors*

"This is a timely and practical contribution to the literature on Responsible Investment. It provides a comprehensive overview of key principles, trends and organizational considerations for Responsible Investment in practice. It is a valuable resource for both experienced Responsible Investment professionals and those at the beginning of their Responsible Investment journey."

Roslyn Stein, *Head of Climate and Biodiversity, AXA*

"This book provides practical definitions about responsible investing and details how this can be implemented. It informs finance professionals with a keen interest in environmental, social and governance issues why to engage with responsibility in connection with financial performance."

Bert Scholtens, *Professor, University of Groningen*

"Investing with an ESG focus is central to long-term value creation. This timely guide is essential reading for anyone looking to build a responsible investing practice and maximize long-term portfolio impact and return."

Charles Wetherill, *Former Head of Origin, Sunfunder*

"Regardless of what you want to achieve with Responsible Investments, this book will provide practical guidance for investors navigating the current Responsible Investment landscape. Based on insights from some of the most experienced Responsible Investments professionals in the Nordics."

Magdalena Håkansson, *Head of Sustainable Value Creation, AP 1*

"This book brings you up to speed on the subject of Responsible Investments. It provides a full overview of approaches and tools available in the market, and is both inspiring and practical when developing your own Responsible Investment strategy."

Heidi Finskas, *Vice President Corporate Responsibility, Kommunal Landspensjonskasse (KLP)*

"Very helpful, well and clear written guide in explaining the Responsible Investments!! Different people and organizations have different definitions of Responsible Investments that confuse people sometimes, but this book is able to use plain language to address the concerns and key considerations in mainstreams which is comprehensive and easy to follow...."

Sau Kwan, *President, E Fund*

"The authors have given the investment profession an exceptionally practical, business-like, yet inspirational and thought-provoking tool to better understand responsible investing and ESG. A must read for everyone in this industry."

Zsombor Incze, *Head of Business Development, Diófa Asset Management*

"As Responsible Investment labels, approaches and debates proliferate, this guide provides important market, regulatory and historical context for new and old practitioners alike. Recommended for anyone trying to navigate the flood of diverse and often conflicting ESG analysis and punditry."

Stuart Palmer, *Head of Ethics Research, Australian Ethical*

Responsible Investment
Series Editor: Rory Sullivan

The ground-breaking *Responsible Investment* series provides a forum for outstanding empirical and theoretical work on all aspects of responsible investment, allowing the tensions and practical realities of responsible investment to be addressed in a readable, robust and conceptually and empirically rigorous format.

Subject areas covered include:

- The financial, environmental, social and governance outcomes from responsible investment.
- Responsible investment in different asset classes.
- Responsible investment in different geographies.
- The implementation of responsible investment by different actors (e.g. pension funds, asset managers, sovereign wealth funds, private equity funds, insurance companies), and in different geographic regions.
- The role that has been played by collaborative initiatives such as the UN Principles for Responsible Investment, UNEPFI and the investor networks on climate change.
- Public policy and responsible investment.

Climate Change and the Governance of Corporations
Lessons from the Retail Sector
Rory Sullivan and Andy Gouldson

Responsible Investment in Fixed Income Markets
Edited by Joshua Kendall and Rory Sullivan

The Responsible Investor
An Introductory Guide to Responsible Investment
Anna Hyrske, Magdalena Lönnroth, Antti Savilaakso and Riikka Sievänen

For more information about this series, please visit: www.routledge.com/
The-Responsible-Investment-Series/book-series/SERI1

The Responsible Investor

An Introductory Guide to Responsible Investment

Anna Hyrske,
Magdalena Lönnroth,
Antti Savilaakso
and Riikka Sievänen

Routledge
Taylor & Francis Group

LONDON AND NEW YORK

Cover image: © Katja Kuittinen

First published 2023
by Routledge
4 Park Square, Milton Park, Abingdon, Oxon OX14 4RN

and by Routledge
605 Third Avenue, New York, NY 10158

Routledge is an imprint of the Taylor & Francis Group, an informa business

© 2023 Anna Hyrske, Magdalena Lönnroth, Antti Savilaakso and
Riikka Sievänen

The right of Anna Hyrske, Magdalena Lönnroth, Antti Savilaakso
and Riikka Sievänen to be identified as authors of this work
has been asserted in accordance with sections 77 and 78 of the
Copyright, Designs and Patents Act 1988.

British Library Cataloguing-in-Publication Data
A catalogue record for this book is available from the British Library

Library of Congress Cataloging-in-Publication Data
Names: Hyrske, Anna, author. | Lönnroth, Magdalena, author. |
Sievänen, Riikka, author.
Title: The responsible investor : an introductory guide to responsible
investment / Anna Hyrske, Magdalena Lönnroth, Riikka Sievänen,
Antti Savilaakso.
Description: 1 Edition. | New York, NY : Routledge, 2023. |
Includes bibliographical references and index. |
Identifiers: LCCN 2022018458 | ISBN 9781032257310 (hardback) |
ISBN 9781032257648 (paperback) | ISBN 9781003284932 (ebook)
Subjects: LCSH: Social responsibility of business. | Saving and
investment. | Capital market.
Classification: LCC HD60 .H97 2023 |
DDC 658.4/08—dc23/eng/20220707
LC record available at https://lccn.loc.gov/2022018458

ISBN: 9781032257310 (hbk)
ISBN: 9781032257648 (pbk)
ISBN: 9781003284932 (ebk)

DOI: 10.4324/9781003284932

Typeset in Bembo
by codeMantra

Contents

About the authors

Anna Hyrske

MSc in Economics and Business Administration
Principal Responsible Investment Specialist, Bank of Finland

Anna Hyrske is the Principal Responsible Investment Specialist at the Bank of Finland. Her duties include the development of Responsible Investment (RI) policies and targets, implementing policies in practice, supporting portfolio managers in integrating environmental, social and governance (ESG) and working in international and national working groups to enhance RI. Before joining the Central Bank, Anna was the Head of Responsible Investment at Ilmarinen, a Finnish pension insurance company. Anna has over 20 years of experience in responsible investing practices across asset classes.

Magdalena Lönnroth

MSc in Economics and Business Administration
Portfolio Manager and Head of Responsible Investment, Church Pension Fund

Magdalena Lönnroth is the Portfolio Manager and Head of Responsible Investment (RI) at the Evangelical Lutheran Church Pension Fund in Finland. She has been involved in developing and implementing the Church Pension Fund's Guidelines for RI and its climate strategy across different asset classes since 2006. In addition, since 2010 Magdalena has been contributing to both the establishment and ongoing work of Finland's Sustainable Investment Forum (Finsif). She actively supports other institutional investors in building RI portfolios.

Antti Savilaakso

MSc Economics
Head of ESG Research/Partner, Impact Cubed

Antti Savilaakso is Head of ESG Research at Impact Cubed in London. Antti was a part of the team that founded Impact Cubed in 2016 to provide innovative environmental, social and governance (ESG) data, tools and asset management. He has worked in Responsible Investment (RI) for over 15 years, mostly in asset management in both Finland and across Europe. He has held advisory positions in various countries and has written and spoken extensively on RI. Antti served on Finsif's Board of Directors from 2011 to 2015 and was an Investor Member of GRI's Stakeholder Council from 2014 to 2020.

Riikka Sievänen

PhD in Applied Economics
Director,
KPMG in Finland

Riikka Sievänen has been leading sustainable finance and Responsible Investment (RI) services at KPMG in Finland since 2013. In her daily work, she supports international and domestic institutional investors and financiers with environmental, social and governance (ESG) across the whole process. While at KPMG, she has led KPMG's Global Sustainable Finance Working Group and advised the European Commission's Technical Expert Group (EU TEG) on sustainable finance. In her spare time, Riikka is a Post-doctoral Researcher at the University of Helsinki with specialization in institutional RI, which builds on her doctoral thesis. She has been on the board of Finsif and has been Finsif's Representative in Sitra's National Steering Group for Impact Investments.

Preface

"Anyone can invest responsibly."

Few of us – as organizations or individuals – are always responsible. We constantly make choices that have both positive and negative impacts on our planet. Through our investments and financing, we create impacts just like our consumption choices do. It is, therefore, important to pay attention to how, where and what we use our assets for. Responsible investment, i.e. the incorporation of ESG issues, makes sense both from portfolio management and from a social and environmental point of view.

The core message of "Responsible Investor" is that every organization and individual can successfully invest responsibly. We want to inspire and show how each investor can choose the suitable Responsible Investment implementation for their values and overall investment strategy.

"Responsible investing means responsibility for returns."

Pension investors and asset managers have a long history as responsible investors followed by banks, insurance companies and other institutional investors. The EU has been and is currently working on regulation on many fronts to enhance sustainable finance and Responsible Investment. All investors and financiers can benefit from our practical book.

"Responsible Investor" defines Responsible Investment as an investment activity that maximizes long-term return while incorporating ESG. It has the potential to increase positive and reduce negative impacts. Increasing uncertainties and market shocks unlock the value of ESG incorporation as it allows investors to have a broader view on their investments and market risks. Better risk management and identification of potential investment opportunities are some of the benefits Responsible Investment can offer to investors and financiers.

Anna, Magdalena, Antti and Riikka
Helsinki, March 15, 2022

Acknowledgements

We would like to thank everyone who participated in this project. There have been many of you, both near and far – subject matter experts, colleagues, friends and family members. Each one of you has had an important role to play, whether submitting materials, granting interviews, fact-checking, commenting on the texts or providing support. We also thank our employers and those close to us who have made it possible to write the book. All your support has been of such importance to us. The reports prepared by the PRI have served as important background material in a number of chapters. A special thank-you goes to our editor Dean Bargh for helping us finalize the book. We would also like to make it clear that we, the authors, are solely responsible for the interpretations presented herein and any possible errors.

Acknowledgements

Abbreviations

AIFMD	Alternative Investment Fund Managers Directive
AIMA	Alternative Investment Management Association
AuM	assets under management
BICS	Bloomberg Industry Classification System
BREEAM	Building Research Establishment Environmental Assessment Method
CASBEE	Comprehensive Assessment System for Built Environment Efficiency
CDP	formerly known as Carbon Disclosure Project
CDSB	Carbon Disclosure Standards Board
CO_2e	carbon dioxide equivalent (different GHGs converted to CO_2)
CPI	Corruption Perception Index
CSDDD	Corporate Sustainability Due Diligence Directive
CSRD	Corporate Sustainability Reporting Directive
CTB	Climate Transition Benchmark
EFRAG	European Financial Reporting Advisory Group
EITI	Extractive Industries Transparency Initiative
EMIR	European Market Infrastructure Regulation
EPBD	Energy Performance and Buildings Directive
ESG	environmental, social and governance
FAIRR	Farm Animal Investment Risk and Return
FoF	fund of funds
FSC	Forest Stewardship Council
GAAP	Generally Accepted Accounting Principles
GBI	Green Building Initiative
GBP	Green Bond Principles
GHG	greenhouse gas
GICS	Global Industry Classification System
GIIN	Global Impact Investing Network
GLP	Green Loan Principles
GRESB	formerly known as Global Real Estate Sustainability Benchmark
GRI	Global Reporting Initiative

GSIA	Global Sustainable Investment Alliance
HLEG	High-Level Expert Group
ICB	Industry Classification Benchmark
ICMA	International Capital Market Association
IDD	Insurance Distribution Directive
IFRS	International Financial Reporting Standards
IIGCC	The Institutional Investors Group on Climate Change
IIRC	The International Integrated Reporting Council
INREV	European Association for Investors in Non-Listed Real Estate
IORP II	Institutions for Occupational Retirement Provision Directive
IRMA	Initiative for Responsible Mining Assurance
ISIC	International Standard Industrial Classification
ISSB	International Sustainability Standards Board
IUCN	International Union for Conservation of Nature
LEED	Leadership in Energy and Environmental Design
MFI	Microfinance institution
MiFID	Markets in Financial Instruments Directive
NABERS	National Australian Built Environment Rating System
NACE	Nomenclature statistique des activités économiques dans la Communauté européenne
NAICS	North American Industry Classification System
NFRD	Non-Financial Reporting Directive
NGBS	National Green Building Standard
OTC	over-the-counter
PAB	Paris Aligned Benchmark
PAI	Principle Adverse Impact
PCAF	Partnership for Carbon Accounting Financials
PIE	Public Interest Entity
PRB	Principles for Responsible Banking
PRI	Principles for Responsible Investment (also known as UN-supported Principles for Responsible Investment)
PSI	Principles for Sustainable Insurance
RBICS	Revere Business Industry Classification System
RI	Responsible Investing, Responsible Investment
SASB	Sustainability Accounting Standards Board
SBAI	Standards Board for Alternative Investments
SBG	Sustainability Bond Guidelines
SBP	Social Bond Principles
SBT	Science Based Targets
SBTi	Science Based Targets Initiative
SDG	Sustainable Development Goals
SFDR	Sustainable Financial Disclosure Regulation
SMCR	Senior Managers and Certification Regime
SSE	Sustainable Stock Exchanges Initiative
TCFD	Task Force on Climate-related Financial Disclosures

TI	Transparency International
TNFD	Taskforce on Nature-related Financial Disclosures
UCITS	Undertakings for the Collective Investment in Transferable Securities
UN GC	United Nations Global Compact
UNDP	United Nations Development Programme
WEF	World Economic Forum

Introduction

Responsible Investment (RI) is mainstream. No questions, no debate. The number of PRI (the UN-supported Principles for RI) signatories, the volume of assets following RI principles and the number of investors committed to national or international pledges and initiatives – these all evidence RI's popularity and its development over the past two decades. Climate initiatives such as Net Zero pledges are becoming increasingly popular among asset owners, asset managers, banks and insurers. This development encourages organizations that are not (yet) part of this development to start questioning why not.

Considering environmental, social and governance (ESG) issues is a mark of approval for investments. Investing responsibly is also part of institutional investors' social licence to operate. However, discussions remain ongoing as to what RI is or is not, notwithstanding all the debates about approaches and tools. So far, each investor, each company and each stakeholder has been able to define what responsibility means to them and how they implement it in their activities. This has been one of RI's success factors but also a source of criticism due to this lack of a universal definition for responsibility.

This book introduces the main investment philosophies that take ESG into account and explains their differences. RI is about looking more broadly into company conduct – and the products and services offered – to evaluate the risks, opportunities and impacts created, both positive and negative. Investors and stakeholders are showing an increasing interest in understanding the impacts on society and the environment created by investments, as well as how these impacts in turn affect the investments. Businesses and investors are bringing ESG issues into the centre of strategy and decision-making because ESG is now seen as a driver for value creation. Businesses and investors who fail to understand ESG issues are, in turn, risking value erosion.

Alongside the responsible or sustainable investment, the term "sustainable finance" has also become common in Europe as a result of new regulations. This book uses the term "Responsible Investment" but acknowledges that financiers may prefer to use "sustainable finance" according to the nature of their operations. The definition of "sustainable finance" is very similar to that of "Responsible Investment."

DOI: 10.4324/9781003284932-1

There are a multitude of drivers behind RI. This book will help RI professionals to identify these RI drivers and the barriers within organizations, and aims to support practical RI implementation. The RI drivers can be divided into three categories: values, financial return and operating environment. *Values* impact how individuals and organizations frame and how they implement RI. *Financial return* is at the core of any investment activity. Responsible investors review how companies take ESG issues (i.e. their sustainability or corporate responsibility) into account in their operations for the benefit of both long-term profitable business and sustainable outcomes, with the expectation that this positively impacts the financial return. There is no conclusive academic evidence that RI harms investment returns. The *operating environment* has a significant impact on the development of RI and the RI approaches taken. Culture, the market characteristics, regulations, other organizations and stakeholders all set requirements and expectations for investors, especially institutional ones.

RI can be applied across the whole investment portfolio. This is best achieved by the investor formulating an RI policy, defining what RI means for the investor and what the overall objectives are. Next, the practical details of the policy are formulated: what RI approaches and tools are to be considered, and how these will be implemented across the different asset classes used by the investor. Investors have many RI approaches to choose from, including active ownership, ESG integration, screening, impact investing and thematic investing. This array of approaches means all types of investors can take ESG issues into consideration when making investment decisions without having to sacrifice returns. The different RI approaches can be applied extensively and simultaneously across asset classes.

Processes for monitoring and reporting should also be included in an RI policy. When putting the policy into practice, investors can benefit from having drawn up a separate roadmap for implementation, which sets timelines and targets for different tasks while allocating resources and responsibilities across the organization. RI is a continuous process, constantly evolving and expanding alongside societal developments, new regulations and emerging ESG issues and trends. This book aims to capture the state of the art of this constantly evolving field.

Each chapter begins with a short list of key questions that will be answered as the chapter progresses. Concise answers to these questions can be found at the end of each chapter. Chapters 1–3 describe the philosophy, background and drivers of RI, which are important in forming an understanding of what RI is today and how it is likely to evolve in the future. Chapters 4 and 5 look into the first practical steps for a responsible investor: how to formulate an RI policy and practical roadmap, and how to consider material ESG issues, megatrends and trends to be included in investment decision-making. Chapters 6 and 7 continue to guide the reader through the next practical steps by reviewing the different RI approaches and how these can be implemented across asset classes, while taking into account asset-class-specific characteristics. Extensive insights into ESG data and ratings are provided and we see how these can be applied on a practical level to assess both the responsibility of asset managers and funds (Chapters 8–10). Chapter 11 examines RI reporting, which ultimately demonstrates the outcomes of the RI policy and the related investor activities. Reporting may be the subject of the final chapter, but it also represents the phase that initiates the following round of reviewing and updating of RI policies and practices, thereby ensuring a continuous development process.

The purpose of this book is to provide detailed yet easily understandable definitions of RI and related activities so that investors, both institutional and retail, can confidently navigate across multiple and sometimes seemingly confusing concepts. It explains in a clear manner *what* RI is all about, *why* investors are interested in ESG, *who* can make use of ESG, *which* asset classes RI is suitable for and *how* to implement RI policies in practice.

1 What is Responsible Investment?

Key questions in this chapter

- What is Responsible Investment?
- What is the difference between ethical, responsible and traditional investments?
- Who is interested in Responsible Investment?

1.1 What is Responsible Investment?

On the surface, Responsible Investment (RI) seems an obvious and straightforward concept: taking ESG into account when making investment decisions. Yet the term consists of two independent and, to some extent, even contradictory ideas. These two components need to be defined – or at least understood – because the definition is essential. "Investment" is often perceived as a cold, analytical process, with an almost mechanical reliance on hard numbers, while "Responsible" is commonly seen as being something softer and more "human" that takes the environment and society into account. How can you combine cold analytics and hard numbers on the one hand with a range of soft non-standardized opinions, human views and analysis on the other? To address this, we will first consider the term "investment."

"Investment" is defined as an activity that generates profit by trading or holding various types of assets and financial instruments. The critical factor is the requirement for a return balanced against the risk. In other words, the investor intends to acquire a return on the investment while aware that the activity involves the risk of a partial or total loss of the initial capital. Thus, in its basic form with no additional attributes, investing is not a question of either charity or philanthropy, which rarely necessitate monetary return or even capital repayment.

The definition becomes more complex, however, with attributes such as "ethical," "impact," "responsible," "sustainable" and "philanthropic." Today, there are potentially hundreds of different versions of "Responsible Investment." Given the many definitions of RI, defining unambiguously who and

DOI: 10.4324/9781003284932-2

what is actually responsible is a challenge. There are currently a variety of service providers, surveys, reports, certifications and metrics which, all in their own way, attempt to answer the question of how to evaluate responsibility.

1.1.1 Defining Responsible Investment

There is no universal and detailed definition of RI. The UN-supported Principles for Responsible Investment (PRI) defines RI as "a strategy and practice to incorporate environmental, social and governance (ESG) factors in investment decisions and active ownership." This broad definition allows for multiple interpretations of concrete ESG implementation. As the sheer number and diversity of the various types of investors incorporating ESG has increased, so have RI approaches and numerous tools evolved to help investors on this journey. All investor types are interested in RIs: pension funds, sovereign wealth funds, endowments, charities, asset managers and family offices are just some examples of investors that have publicly committed to RI policies. Retail investors, too, are increasingly demanding ESG investment products as they follow their own personal values.

As the journey of a thousand miles begins with one step, so does building an RI policy. Investors typically consider the following elements:

- Investment strategy
- ESG investment philosophy
- Responsible Investment approaches
- Target setting and tools
- Monitoring and reporting

The investor's overall investment strategy is at the heart of all subsequent decisions. An investment strategy includes topics such as risk tolerance, time horizon, available asset classes and choices between internally or externally and actively or passively managed investments. Clarifying the overall investment strategy helps to steer the investor towards the most suitable investment philosophy.

All investment philosophies are based on individual or organizational values. These values might simply be about financial returns, or about employees' satisfaction and their commitment to the organization's vision. An investor can choose to reject the traditional investment philosophy and instead adopt philosophies that incorporate ESG issues. The main ESG investment philosophies are categorized under the headings "ethical investing," "impact investing," "responsible investing" and "philanthropic investing." The chosen philosophy will form the basis of decision-making alongside the overall investment strategy. Choosing an investment philosophy isn't always a conscious decision but a response to organizations' stated values, vision and mission statements. An ESG investment philosophy is usually embedded within an RI policy rather than being a stand-alone document.

Only once the overall investment strategy and the ESG investment philosophy have been defined can the investor select the suitable RI approaches. Possible approaches are: active ownership, ESG integration, impact investments, screening and thematic investments. This is followed by a selection of the appropriate tools, among which are ESG indices, ratings and scores, ESG databases, and ESG labels and certifications.

Figure 1.1 illustrates how the investment strategy, the ESG investment philosophies, the RI approaches and the tools are interlinked with policy development, implementation, monitoring and reporting.

This chapter is interested in the investment philosophies that take ESG into account (i.e. ethical, impact, philanthropic, responsible), with an emphasis on responsible investing. Traditional investment philosophies with no ESG component will not be considered in detail here. RI approaches will be dealt with in more detail in Chapter 6; tools will be covered in Chapters 8–10; and reporting in Chapter 11.

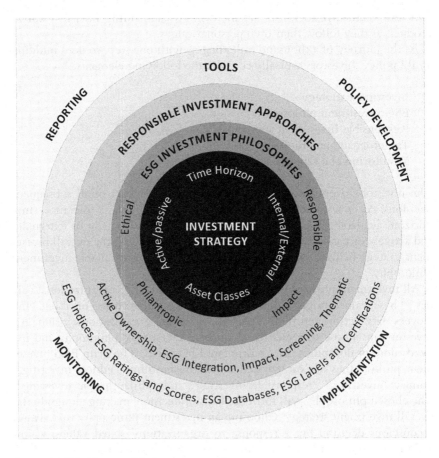

Figure 1.1 The Responsible Investment sphere

1.2 ESG investment philosophies

Investors have a variety of investment styles (e.g. "quantitative," "fundamental," etc.) and factors at their disposal (e.g. "value," "growth," etc.) in building their overall investment strategies and philosophies. Taking ESG into account offers another dimension beyond simply reading backward- and forward-looking financial statements and analysis. Investor drivers for incorporating ESG into investment decisions vary, and range from seeking a social licence to operate to enhancing their risk-adjusted returns. These drivers are discussed more in detail in Chapter 3.

ESG incorporation is not necessarily a style in its own right but rather something that can be done within various philosophies. It could be compared to creating a dish. Everyone has access to a kitchen (investment strategy), various pots and pans (investment philosophy), an array of ingredients (RI approaches) and a selection of spices (investment tools). There is no universal recipe for everyone to follow but rather a book full of different recipes leading to different outcomes. The RI recipe will be described later in terms of reporting and disclosure of RI activities. An investment philosophy guides the investor's decision-making process using a set of beliefs and principles. An ESG investment philosophy simply means that ESG is incorporated into these beliefs and principles. An investor can also apply more than one philosophy across the portfolio, as needs and requirements vary between asset classes and investment products.

Table 1.1 provides a summary of the main investment philosophies (in alphabetical order). They are distinguished according to their approaches to financial return, exclusion, impact and primary investment decision driver. Values are the foundation for all investment philosophies.

Table 1.1 demonstrates that different investment philosophies have different features with regard to return, exclusion and impact. Therefore, it is crucial for an investor to identify the most appropriate philosophy to fit the needs of their own investment strategy. These different philosophies are not mutually exclusive and can be used simultaneously in different sections of an investment portfolio.

1.2.1 Ethical investing

In ethical investment, the investor excludes industries and companies that conflict with their values and morals – even to the point where long-term returns might be negatively impacted. The notion of potentially lower returns is consistent with modern portfolio theory, whereby limited diversification leads to higher risk and lower returns. In the light of current knowledge, a strong exclusion policy (i.e. large industries as a whole or a large number of more targeted exclusions) would be required to negatively impact long-term returns. Minor exclusions on otherwise diversified portfolios tend not to lead to a material impact on portfolio returns.

Table 1.1 A summary of the main investment philosophies

Investment philosophy	Approach to investment return	Approach to exclusion	Approach to impact	Primary driver for investment decisions	Example of investor
Ethical investing	Willingness to forgo some returns as values are the driving force	Negative screening based on ethical values as the main RI approach	The significance of impact varies between investors	Personal or organization's ethical values	A religious organization that excludes several sectors based on its beliefs and values
Impact investing	Important part of investment decision-making, although some investors are willing to forgo some returns over positive, measurable impact	Strong negative exclusion policy if there is an adverse impact on the desired environmental or social outcome	The primary driver for investment decisions	Measurable positive environmental or social impact combined with acceptable levels of return	An NGO investing donations to create positive impact based on that NGO's objectives and values
Philanthropic investing[a]	Return is secondary to impact	Strong negative exclusion policy if there is an adverse impact on the desired environmental or social outcome	The primary driver for investment decisions	Environmental, social or governance impact	A foundation supporting its main objectives through investments
Responsible investing[b]	Maximizing long-term return while incorporating ESG	Risk-based exclusion	The significance of impact varies between investors	Risk-adjusted returns combined with ESG issues	A pension fund with a diversified client and beneficiary base, and with requirements for returns and positive environmental, social or governance outcomes
Traditional investing (no systematic ESG considerations)	Maximizing returns over different time periods	No exclusions, as changes in market conditions can also generate positive returns in short time periods	Impact is not considered a factor as it is not easily quantifiable in monetary terms	Risk-adjusted returns	A generic fund in which clients see no value in ESG issues

[a]If there is no requirement to return the capital, it should be classified as charity or philanthropy, not as investment.
[b]Responsible Investment, sustainable investment and sustainable finance are considered synonyms throughout this book.

The most common exclusions tend to reflect centuries-old societal values and relate to the production and distribution of alcohol, gambling, tobacco, weapons and adult entertainment, as well as religiously unacceptable products and services such as pork, beef, financial institutions (interest payments) and some pharmaceuticals (e.g. birth control).

Values change over time, albeit sometimes slowly, which makes ethical investing – like any other investment philosophy – change and evolve. A better understanding of environmental issues has led to an increase in environmental exclusions, such as coal and other fossil resources. Exclusions can also be made on a financial basis, when in the investor's view, certain industries will not be profitable enough in the long run to be included in the portfolio. If an exclusion is made on a financial basis, it is not considered an ethical investment philosophy but rather an RI approach. More details about different exclusion approaches are provided in Chapter 6.

1.2.2 Impact investing as a philosophy

All investments inherently create positive and negative impacts. However, the term "impact investing" specifically refers to investments that intentionally seek to create measurable positive societal impacts. In this type of investment activity, it is vital for the investor to gain economic returns along with such impacts.

The term "impact investing" has two meanings. It is a philosophy, but it is also one of the RI approaches. As a philosophy, the emphasis is on the impact and its measurement relative to returns, sometimes to the point that below-market-rate returns or above-market-rate risks are acceptable. As an RI approach, on the other hand, impact investing targets market returns.

The positive measurable impacts can vary from reduced disease and environmental burden through the construction of a new sewage system to improved mental health through preventative child welfare services. The examples are very different yet they all lead to improved quality of life.

Measurement of the impact is a key characteristic of impact investing. The investor needs to consider the investment's positive and negative impacts and how the impacts might be measured as realistically as possible. The positive impacts should not be exaggerated nor the negative ones downplayed, lest the investor be susceptible to the charge of "impact washing." The UN-supported PRI uses what it calls "sustainability outcomes" to discuss impacts created through investment activities.

Impact investment as an RI approach is described in detail in Chapter 6.

1.2.3 Philanthropic investing

Philanthropic investing lies somewhere between charity and investment. Some activities could be squarely classified as charitable, where the investments are not required to generate financial returns, or else any potential financial return is to be retained within the organization to finance subsequent projects. Nonetheless, targets are valued using financial ratios, as with traditional investment. Yet under this philosophy, the main emphasis when making investment decisions is on societal impacts, such as poverty eradication or environmental benefits, rather than on economic returns.

1.2.4 *Responsible investing*

In responsible investing, the investor considers ESG issues as a means of improving the portfolio's risk and return profile. Practices and definitions vary between investors as the same considerations do not apply to all investors on account of, for example, organizational differences. Each investor has their own set of principles about how responsibility manifests itself and how the ESG issues are weighed in their portfolios. Notwithstanding these differences, responsible investors should consider ESG as an indivisible set and avoid focusing on one dimension only (E, S or G). Responsible investing does not simply contrast returns against ESG factors. Rather, they are combined to better identify the risks and opportunities associated with investments. This combining of ESG, return and risk can be illustrated using a triangle (see Figure 1.2). All three sides of the triangle are of equal importance for a balanced outcome.

Responsible investing has its roots in ethical investing and offers an opportunity to combine ethical considerations with return-oriented investment activities. For example, many asset managers and asset owners have excluded certain companies or sectors on ethical grounds, such as companies failing to adhere to international norms[1] or tobacco producers. Nonetheless, these limited exclusions notwithstanding, the main focus of these investments is on incorporating ESG into investment decision-making and daily portfolio management. A limited number of ethically excluded sectors and/or companies does not hinder diversification, and thus the potential negative impact on investment return is marginal at most, especially in the long term.

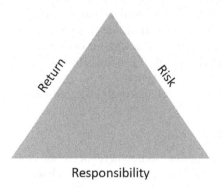

Figure 1.2 Responsible investing: return, risk and responsibility in balance

The responsible investing philosophy allows for multiple RI approaches to be incorporated within investment decision-making, such as active ownership (including engagement), ESG integration, impact investing, screening (positive and negative) and thematic investments. These will be discussed in Chapter 6. Furthermore, a responsible investing philosophy can be applied in all asset classes. Chapter 7 goes into more detail on responsible investing opportunities in different asset classes.

1.2.5 Combining philosophies

An investor does not need to commit to a single philosophy but can apply different combinations to achieve investment objectives. For example, part of a portfolio may be invested according to an impact investing philosophy, part of it using exclusions based on ethical considerations, and another part under a responsible investing philosophy. The important thing is that the investor is aware of the philosophy used in each situation and is selecting the most appropriate RI approaches and tools to achieve the outcomes set out in the investment strategy.

1.3 An introduction to Responsible Investment approaches

Having defined their investment strategy and RI philosophy, the investor selects the RI approaches that fit the strategy. The main RI approaches can be classified into broad categories, the most common of which are listed in Table 1.2 (also see Chapter 6).

1.4 An introduction to Responsible Investment tools

Investors can make use of various RI tools to support their investment processes and decision-making. RI tools can be classified into broad categories, and the typical ones are listed in Table 1.3.

Table 1.2 The most common Responsible Investment approaches

RI approach	Short definition
Active ownership (including engagement)	Using ownership rights to exert power and/or to generate change
ESG integration	Systematically integrating ESG research, outcomes and impacts within the investment decision-making process
Impact investing	Creating measurable positive societal impact through investments
Screening (both positive and negative)	Using predetermined filters to define the investable universe or to tilt portfolio weights
Thematic investments	Selecting holdings that actively contribute to the chosen theme; all holdings must be linked to the theme

Table 1.3 The most common Responsible Investment tools

ESG tool	Short definition	Further details
ESG certification and label	Third-party validation of the ESG qualities of the investment product	See Chapter 10 (Section 10.2)
ESG database	A database containing ESG data points, factors and indicators as well as ESG ratings and scores	See Chapters 8 and 9
ESG index	An index/benchmark containing ESG qualities	See Chapter 9 (Section 9.5)
ESG rating and score	An evaluation using ESG qualities to assign a comparable value (rating or score) to unit of analysis, e.g. portfolios, companies and countries	See Chapter 9 (Sections 9.2 and 9.4)

In addition to investment approaches and tools, investors typically also consider target setting, monitoring and reporting as part of the development of the overall RI policy. These topics are discussed in detail in subsequent chapters.

Chapter 1 key Q&As

Here are the answers to the key questions posed at the start of this chapter.

What is Responsible Investment?

Responsible Investment is an investment philosophy that incorporates ESG issues into investment decision-making. Responsible investors seek to improve the portfolio's risk and return profile, or at least achieve market-level returns. Each investor chooses suitable RI approaches and tools based on their overall investment strategy and philosophy.

By incorporating ESG issues, investors potentially reduce the negative social and environmental impacts and increase the positive impacts.

What is the difference between ethical, responsible and traditional investments?

In ethical investing, investor values guide decisions to the extent that investment returns are secondary. Such values might be related to religious beliefs, for example, or a strong conviction about environmental protection.

In responsible investing the investor incorporates material ESG issues into investment decision-making, thereby increasing knowledge about the risks and opportunities related to the investment portfolio. Incorporating ESG factors can reduce portfolio risk and/or increase the return potential. Prioritizing responsibility over investment returns is a critical element within responsible investing.

Traditional investing does not factor any information other than financial in the investment decision-making process. The philosophy here is that all relevant material information can be found in financial statements, valuation models and security pricing.

See Table 1.1 for a breakdown of the main investment philosophies.

Who is interested in Responsible Investment?

Responsible investments are made by different types of investors across all asset classes. Increasing numbers of institutional investors, asset managers and retail investors are defining, following and using RI policies or approaches as part of their investment processes.

Note

1 Examples of what investors consider as international norms are the UN Global Compact, the OECD Guidelines for Multinational Enterprises, the ILO core convention on workers' rights and international treaties on controversial weapons.

Bibliography

Hyrske, A. (2003). *Non-Financial Aspects in Investment Decision-Making.* Hanken

Hyrske, A., Lönnroth, M., Savilaakso, A., & Sievänen, R. (2020). *Vastuullinen sijoittaja.* Helsingin kauppakamari.

Hyrske, A., Lönnroth, M., Savilaakso, A., & Sievänen, R. (2012). *Vastuullinen sijoittaja.* Finva.

Principles of Responsible Investment. (2022). *An Introduction to Responsible Investment.* Retrieved 21 February 2022 from https://www.unpri.org/investment-tools/an-introduction-to-responsible-investment

Putnam-Walkerly, K. (2018, February 7). "Philanthropy: The Forgotten Investment Asset." *Forbes.* Retrieved 21 February 2022 from https://www.forbes.com/sites/krisputnamwalkerly/2018/02/07/philanthropy-the-forgotten-investment-asset

2 Responsible Investment is mainstream

Key questions in this chapter

- What is the role of Responsible Investment in the financial markets?
- How has Responsible Investment evolved and how will it continue to evolve?

Responsible Investment (RI) is a relatively young term, but its predecessors – that is to say, mainly ethical investing – have a much longer history, dating back to the seventeenth century. RI has taken its time to hit the mainstream, but recent statistics clearly show that it is crucial to many investors. One indication of its mainstreaming is the increased number of significant associations and initiatives in the sector and their growth in membership. Various market surveys have identified increased investor interest in incorporating environmental, social and governance (ESG) issues into investment decision-making. According to the Global Sustainable Investment Alliance (GSIA)'s Global Sustainable Investment Review 2020, over 35% of global assets are invested using RI approaches. This implies a 2.5 percentage point growth compared to the previous report in 2018 (Table 2.1). However, it should be noted that data between the different trend reviews is not fully comparable, as regional data collection and the definitions used are continuously evolving.

Table 2.1 Sustainable investment share

	2016	2018	2020
Total AuM of regions (USD billions)	81,948	91,828	98,416
Total AuM, sustainable investments[a] only (USD billions)	22,872	30,683	35,301
% Sustainable investments[a]	27.9%	33.4%	35.9%
Increase in sustainable investments[a] (in percentage points, compared to prior period)		**5.5%**	**2.5%**

[a]Sustainable investments in the GSIA (Global Sustainable Investment Review) includes Responsible Investment approaches and therefore the terms "sustainable" and "responsible" can be used as synonyms.

DOI: 10.4324/9781003284932-3

Europe has traditionally been a key market for responsible investing. Stricter industry standards and increased legislation in Europe have significantly impacted what can be classified as sustainable, according to GSIA. This development explains the negative growth rate in European sustainable assets, with US assets under management (AuM) surpassing European levels (Table 2.2). Similar tightening in definitions and slower, or even negative, growth can be expected in other markets in the future.

Another perspective from which to analyse RI growth is the number of investor signatories to the UN-supported Principles for Responsible Investment (PRI). A rise from fewer than 200 signatories in 2006 to nearly 4,000 by mid-2021 clearly indicates the growth in investor interest in RI. Also, the AuM by PRI signatories have grown significantly in 15 years, reaching US$120 trillion in 2021 (Figure 2.1). This figure, part of mandatory reporting by PRI signatories, surpasses the global reported AuM in the GSIA review mentioned above, although this may be partially explained by the fact that the PRI signatory base exceeds the regional coverage of the GSIA.

Table 2.2 Sustainable investment assets regionally

	2016	2018	2020
Europe[a,b]	12,040	14,075	12,017
USA	8,723	11,995	17,081
Canada	1,086	1,669	2,423
Australasia[b]	516	734	906
Japan	474	2,180	2,874
Total (US$ billions)		30,683	35,301

[a]European coverage does not include all European countries.
[b]Europe and Australasia have enacted significant changes in how sustainable investment is defined in these regions, so direct comparisons between regions and previous versions of this report are not easily made.
Source: Global Sustainable Investment Alliance (Global Sustainable Investment Review 2020).

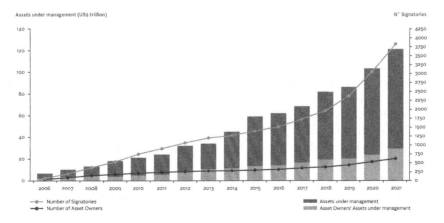

Figure 2.1 PRI signatory growth (2006–2021)
Source: PRI (2021)

2.1 From ethical to responsible

Although responsible investing itself is very young, there are historical examples where investors have used criteria other than traditional financial information when making investment decisions.

A knowledge of the past allows us a better understanding of current approaches, ESG issues and trends within responsible investing. Ethical investment can be seen as the ancestor of RI. Traditionally, ethical investment has excluded sectors or economic activities defined as unsuitable by religious communities, which citizens of that community should eschew in their investment activities and in their lives more broadly. Examples of such proscribed areas are pharmaceuticals (birth control for a Catholic investor), the food industry (pork for an Islamic investor, beef for a Hindu investor) and finance companies (interest payment for an Islamic investor).

The Quakers are often considered the first ethical investors. They were against slavery which for them meant avoiding sugar, cotton or any products linked to the slave trade. The first recorded actions go back as far as the late seventeenth century. Quakers also excluded alcohol and, of course, the arms industry from their investments, and even refused to pay taxes supporting the ongoing war with France in the eighteenth century. They founded banks and were actively involved in trade, significantly influencing the development of ethical investment. In fact, the roots of the first ethical fund in the UK can be traced to a life insurance company founded in 1832 by the Quakers (see Table 2.3).

Social justice emerged as a matter for investments in the 1950s and 1960s in the US, via health care and housing projects funded by companies and trade union pension funds. In the 1970s, opposition to the Vietnam War and the anti-apartheid movement gained support globally. Investment exclusions by a few US universities demonstrated their students' desire not to support racial segregation in South Africa.

In sum, in many countries, religious communities were the first to follow ethical guidelines in their investment activities, which led to the development of investment funds and strategies that better suit their needs.

2.1.1 The first ethical funds

New investment funds were founded across various markets, especially in the 1980s and 1990s, to cater for a growing desire to incorporate ethical values into investments. The earliest ethical funds were usually established in countries with a strong community-based investor background based on mutual trust, as in the US and the UK. The US still has a very strong tradition of ethical investing, while in other countries ethical investing has given way to responsible investing.

Table 2.3 lists the first ethical funds across a range of countries (grey shading). The first climate-focused funds are also included (white shading). It is

Table 2.3 The first ethical and climate-focused funds across a range of countries

Year established	Country/ domicile	Founder/asset manager	Fund name
1965	Sweden	Aktie-Ansvar	Ansvar Aktiefond Sverige
1971	USA	Pax World Investment	Pax World Fund
1983	France	Meeshaert AM	Nouvelle Stratégie 50
1984	UK	Friends Provident	Stewardship Unit Trust
1986	Canada	North Shore Credit Union	Ethical Growth Fund
1988	Norway	Vesta	Vesta Miljöinvest
1988	Sweden	Carlson	Världsnaturfonden
1989	Australia	Australian Ethical	Australian Ethical Balanced Fund
1989	UK	Jupiter Asset Management	Jupiter Ecology
1989	Scotland	Scottish Equitable	Ethical
1990	Netherlands	ABF	Het Andere Beleggningsfonds
1990	Luxemburg	Amundi	Amundi Funds Global Ecology ESG
1990	Germany	Invesco	Invesco Umwelt und Nachhaltigkeits Fond
1992	Belgium	KBC	KBC Eco Fund World
1993	Norway	Orkla	Orkla Finans Nordic
1997	Finland	OP AM	OP-Climate
1998	Denmark	Alm. Brand Bank	Miljö
1999	Spain	MSDW	Fondo Etico
1999	Finland	Gyllenberg	Forum
1999	Denmark	Sparinvest forening	Globale Vaekstemarkeder med Etiske Hensyn
1999	Singapore	UOB Asset Management	United Global Unifem Fund
2000	France	MAM Société Générale	MAM Transition Durable SG Actions Europe ISR
2000	Ireland	Green Effect Investments	Green Effects NAI-Wertr Fonds
2001	Netherlands	ASN	ASN Milieu & Waterfonds
2002	Italy	Banca Popolare de Milano	Investietico
2005	Israel	Altshuler Shaham Mutual	Altshuler Shaham Green Fund
2006	China	Bank of China Investment Managers	Sustainable Growth Equity Fund
2006	Taiwan	Allianz	Allianz Global Eco Trends
2007	Austria	ERSTE	ERSTE WWF Stock Environment
2008	Estonia	Limestone	New Europe SR Fund
2008	China	Industrial Fund Management	Social Responsible RMB Mutual Fund
2013	Spain	Microbank	Microbank Fondo Ecólogico
2019	Switzerland	UBS	UBS Global Climate Awareness

Source: Hyrske et al. (2020, 2012); Krosinsky, Sparkes, Bengtsson

clear from the table that in many countries ethical funds act as precursors to climate funds, which mostly came into being in the 2000s.

2.2 The rise of responsibility

In the late 1990s and early 2000s, some (mainly non-religious) pension investors began to adopt ethical guidelines that were not solely based on traditional exclusionary strategies. These investors, which included asset managers, had a diverse customer base and organizational backgrounds and hence did not find mere faith-based (ethical) exclusion appropriate. The preference was rather to factor in aspects such as human rights and governance to their investment activities alongside traditional economic considerations. For most investors, this impulse arose internally from staff or direct client contacts. Investment decision-makers began to take into consideration investing's broader societal impact. These societal effects could also have direct or indirect economic implications, such as fines, penalty payments or reputational risks potentially leading to asset price distortions. At this time, however, there was, in general, very little external pressure to take responsibility into account. Non-governmental organizations (NGOs) and other stakeholders did not interrogate investor action as closely as they do today. It would be at least another decade before investors found themselves the focus of closer attention.

The vocabulary of the nascent RI industry was not fully developed in the late 1990s and early 2000s. Ethical investment was still being discussed in investor statements and reports, even though the policies and approaches used did not correspond to the definition of ethical investment. This era is also characterized by misconceptions about the subject, both on the investor side and from various stakeholders, including academia. The misinterpretations gave investors a rationale for avoiding ESG topics: while it was all under the "ethical investment" umbrella, the religious connotations remained, deterring many investors. Such religious philosophical connotations – exacerbated by potentially inferior returns on account of limited diversification opportunities – sullied the reputation of ethical investing, all the more so because some academic studies supported the misconceptions.

2.2.1 Norm-based screening as the first step

Despite such misconceptions and communication challenges, certain investors nevertheless sought to increase their understanding of responsibility considerations, having noticed ESG-related impacts on investment returns and risks. As ESG issues were not well analysed or understood at the time, the associated risks were often unquantifiable and only observable reactively through corporate scandals, for example. The assumption here was one of the potential reputational risks, despite very little, if any, pressure from stakeholders. The ESG considerations of these investors, who were mainly European, were based on international norms such as human rights, respect for the environment and labour standards. They wanted portfolios that incorporated at least some ESG considerations but without the diminishing returns. The aim was to eliminate the "worst offenders," i.e. companies that did not comply with international human rights and environmental standards and norms.

In addition to these basic exclusions, some investors sought to add more proactive approaches to the overall responsibility review. Rather than react to past or current events, they looked for positive outcomes and favoured companies with a strong ESG performance. This RI approach grew in popularity in the early 2000s and is known as positive screening or "best-in-class."

Responsible investing emerged from this desire to more systematically incorporate responsibility issues (or ESG) into investment decision-making while achieving market returns. The term "Responsible Investment" broke through internationally in 2006 when the UN-supported Principles for RI were launched.

2.2.2 Active ownership and other emerging approaches

Screening can be a blunt instrument: a company is either in or out. Excluding a company doesn't necessarily lead to positive change, as an investor can no longer assert ownership rights or exert pressure based on investment holdings. Investors wanted more alternatives in their toolbox. We have seen individual examples from the 1970s of active ownership and putting forward shareholder resolutions, but engagement and the active use of investor power only became mainstream post-2000 – due among other things to corporate malpractice and poor corporate governance.

With increased resources going into the incorporation of ESG into investment decision-making, it was inevitable that questions about returns, cost–benefit and impacts began to emerge. ESG integration can be seen as an answer to questions of accountability. It has been a natural progression to include ESG along with financial analysis in a cost-effective and meaningful way rather than manage two different teams researching the same names but from different angles. In the 2020 GSIA Trends Review, ESG integration surpassed screening to become the most common approach.

Impact investing has gained increased traction internationally, especially post-2006 when Muhammad Yunus and Grameen Bank won the Nobel Peace Prize for the pioneering use of microcredit and providing access to finance for previously "unbankable" customers. Impact investing is seen as a way of generating positive impact while diversifying portfolios and generating returns in a low-interest-rate environment.

To begin with, a basic exclusion policy – whether of individual companies or sectors – was the favoured approach for investors. As alternatives developed – such as active ownership, ESG integration and impact investing – investors increasingly turned to these more active approaches. However, this trend seems to be currently reversing: thematic investing, especially climate-related negative screening, is leading to exclusions, with an increasing number of investors committed to "Net Zero" or "Paris-aligned" climate targets. It is quite probable, though, that simple exclusions represent only the first phase, with active ownership or other more complex RI approaches to follow. Thematic investing may well traverse the same path as responsible investing did before.

Despite the development of RI approaches, there is still a demand for screening. Norm-based screening is still applied by many institutional investors to the extent that one could argue that it sets a minimum standard for RI. Along with the basic screens, investors are incorporating other approaches across asset classes. The ESG focus has spread over time from equity investments through fixed-income investments to other asset classes. The RI approaches are discussed more in detail in Chapter 6, and the various asset classes are presented in Chapter 7.

2.2.3 Responsible investing developing alongside corporate responsibility

The development of RI from simple exclusions to more holistic approaches seems to be aligning closely with the development of corporate responsibility. Companies have been reporting for years now according to international reporting standards such as GRI, and reporting initiatives such as CDP. This increased level of disclosure is now encompassing investors, too. New mandatory legislation is being introduced in many jurisdictions to cover both corporates and their investors.

It is hard to say who preceded whom among the various market participants in considering their own responsibility and consequently driving companies towards more systematic responsibility. Investors, for example, seem to have been eager to demand change at the portfolio-company level before turning attention to their own operations. Consumers have been demanding greener products or social responsibility in production or the supply chain. In other cases, company employees have been active in developing policies and processes. Neither should we overlook the expertise of non-governmental organizations in bringing issues to the fore. Often NGOs have deep local and topic-level know-how which an investor would be wise to acknowledge.

Whatever the catalyst in foregrounding ESG issues, whether at a corporate or investor level, responsibility is now a major trend. In the best cases, it is visible at all organizational levels, affecting strategy, operations, R&D and so forth. The current consensus is that responsibility has a financial impact. An increasing number of investors are therefore encouraged to familiarize themselves with ESG and find new ways to incorporate it into investment decision-making.

Chapter 2 key Q&As

Here are the answers to the key questions posed at the start of this chapter.

What is the role of Responsible Investment in the financial markets?

Responsible Investment has grown in significance over the last decade. This is evident in the increase in PRI signatories and in AuM invested using

RI approaches. It is estimated that RIs account for somewhere between 35% and over 50% of all global AuM.

How has Responsible Investment evolved and how will it continue to evolve?

Responsible investing has roots in ethical investing. The term Responsible Investment emerged in the 2000s and became a familiar concept in 2006 when the UN-supported Principles for RI were launched.

Previously, only simple exclusionary approaches were available for investors. The market has since developed to allow investors to incorporate multiple and more complex approaches into their investment policies. RI approaches are not just for equity investments but can be incorporated across all asset classes. It is safe to assume that, going forward, RI will continue to attract innovation and further increase its significance in the overall investment markets.

Bibliography

Bengtsson, E. (2007). "A History of Scandinavian Socially Responsible Investing". *Journal of Business Ethics*, 82(4), 969–983. Retrieved 21 February 2022 from https://doi.org/10.1007/s10551-007-9606-y

Boffo, R., & Patalano, R. (2020). *ESG Investing: Practices, Progress and Challenges.* OECD Paris. Retrieved 21 February 2022 from https://www.oecd.org/finance/ESG-Investing-Practices-Progress-Challenges.pdf

Global Sustainable Investment Alliance (2020). *GSIA Trends Review 2020.* GSIA. Retrieved 21 February 2022 from http://www.gsi-alliance.org/trends-report-2020/

Hyrske, A., Lönnroth, M., Savilaakso, A., & Sievänen, R. (2012). *Vastuullinen sijoittaminen.* Finva.

Hyrske, A., Lönnroth, M., Savilaakso, A., & Sievänen, R. (2020). *Vastuullinen sijoittaja.* Helsingin kauppakamari.

Krosinsky, C. (2012). *Sustainable Investing: The Art of Long-Term Performance.* Earthscan.

Nobel Prize. (2006). *The Nobel Peace Prize 2006.* NobelPrize.org. Retrieved 21 February 2022 from https://www.nobelprize.org/prizes/peace/2006/yunus/biographical/#:~:text=Muhammad%20Yunus%20and%20Grameen%20Bank, Yunus%20was%20the%20bank%27s%20founder

Quakers in the World. (2022). *Anti-slavery in North America.* Quakers in the World. Retrieved 21 February 2022 from https://www.quakersintheworld.org/quakers-in-action/56/Anti-Slavery-in-North-America

Sparkes, R. (2002). *Socially Responsible Investment: A Global Revolution.* John Wiley & Sons.

3 Drivers of Responsible Investment

Key questions in this chapter

- What are the key drivers and barriers for Responsible Investment? How can we understand and classify them?
- How might these drivers and barriers impact Responsible Investment in an organization?

Whenever policies, processes or activities are introduced inside an organization, there are always drivers behind them that can be identified, as well as barriers to their implementation. Both of these can be either internal and/or external. Within Responsible Investment (RI), the drivers and barriers can be categorized under values, financial return and operating environment. These three factors interact with and influence one another (see Figure 3.1).

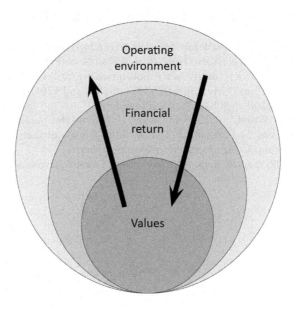

Figure 3.1 Factors influencing Responsible Investment

DOI: 10.4324/9781003284932-4

An understanding of these factors can help investment professionals in a number of ways:

- Defining one's own opinions, methods and procedures regarding RI
- Recognizing how the investment team and other colleagues can work together on RI
- Developing RI processes within the organization both domestically and internationally
- Enhancing assessment and analysis of potential partners and investment targets
- Increasing understanding of client needs and regulatory requirements

3.1 Values

Values serve as guiding principles both for individuals and organizations. Values are relatively permanent phenomena, which tend to stay the same or evolve only slowly over time (or, more pertinently, over an organization's strategy period). According to Schwartz's value theory, there are ten universal values that fall into four dimensions, as indicated in Table 3.1. Self-transcendence values are concerned with the willingness to care for others and the environment and thus link well with ESG issues. Hedonic values seem more closely connected with financial profit.

Values evolve as societies change. They are also linked to attitudes and intentions to behave in a certain way.

Both private and institutional investors have values, which are reflected in their investment activities. They might include considerations about the suitability of investing in companies utilizing child labour or companies making no effort to reduce their operations' CO_2 emissions. Values are thus at the core of RI and influence the investment decisions made.

Organizations that have clearly stated their values usually find them helpful in supporting their RI practices. The definition of RI forms the basis for selecting suitable RI approaches and relevant ESG criteria. Institutional investors such as pension funds and asset managers prefer to describe RI broadly, which enables them to respond to a diverse group of stakeholders and diversify the portfolio without too many restrictions. Although some institutional investors are defined as values-based investors (e.g. ethical investors who prefer investments that pursue their mission and impact targets with less focus on financial profit), it is to be noted that considering only financial profit is also a manifestation of particular values. Responsible institutional investors combine financial, altruistic and biospheric values (Table 3.1) in their RI policy and implementation.

From a portfolio diversification and risk–return ratio perspective, adding values – i.e. ESG (whatever the definition used by the investor in question) – means in practical terms selecting suitable investment objects by making use of values. Seen from an RI perspective, this may mean less diversification

Table 3.1 Schwarz's ten universal values and the links to Responsible Investment research

Value	Dimension of the value	The connection to responsible investing from the point of view of academic research
• Tradition and conformity • Security	Conservation	–
• Achievement • Power • Hedonism (50%)	Self-enhancement	Responsible investors act as active owners and impact the sustainability of their investment targets.
• Hedonism (50%) • Self-direction • Stimulation	Openness to change	Academic research has connected hedonism with financial profit-seeking
• Benevolence • Universalism	Self-transcendence	Responsible investors act as universal owners. Altruistic and biospheric value orientations (willingness to help and willingness to care for the environment) relate to Responsible Investment.

and higher risk, if the investment universe becomes too restricted. The same caveat applies to positive screening, thematic investments and impact investments if the focus is on too few companies.

Examples of institutional investors that might want to connect their altruistic or biospheric value orientations with their investments include: a health research foundation that wants to avoid alcohol or tobacco companies; a trade union that seeks to avoid companies that are quick to terminate employment contracts during challenging economic times; or an environmental foundation that favours investments in renewable energy.

It is important for asset managers to understand their (both institutional and retail) clients' values so that suitable investment solutions can be provided. In addition to altruistic and biospheric value orientations, investors may require transparency in investments and risk management, something typically associated with RI. Institutional investors, such as pension funds and asset managers, may also be interested in international norms because of their diversified stakeholders and beneficiaries.

Changes in values lead to changes in behaviour by companies, policymakers and consumers. It is reasonable to expect that institutional investors will face increasing demands with regard to sustainability. Here, investors and financiers with global portfolios have a powerful role to play in financing targets that are in alignment with sustainable development, and in acting as active owners to foster change across markets.

3.2 Financial return

Financial return is at the core of all investment activities; without it, these activities would be classified as a charity. As such, RI seeks at least the same level of return as a traditional investment – but with a long-term perspective. Some responsible investors aim to obtain overperforming financial returns in the long run. It is a point worth noting that the primary source of financial return for a multi-asset investor tends to come from allocation decisions between asset classes rather than allocation decisions within an asset class.

Responsible Investment and level of financial return

So far, researchers investigating the question about the level of financial return for RI have largely done so using historical data sets. In brief, the majority of academic studies found RI to deliver at least the same financial returns as a conventional investment. A significant minority of academic studies report a lower financial return and likewise some a higher return. This heterogeneity of findings may be explained by, among other things, data sets focusing on different time periods, geographical areas, asset classes or products. The definition of a responsible company may also vary.

Modern portfolio theory asserts that diversification is essential in obtaining maximum returns and managing risks. Yet academic studies indicate that excluding certain sectors, such as fossil fuels, in the short run (and under normal market conditions) does not negatively impact financial return. This is an important finding for climate-aware investors. What, then, are the key reasons for the enormous growth in RI over the last decade, if data on the level of return is still awaiting more clarity? The answer lies in RI's characteristics of an expected delivery of a better risk–return ratio. This supplies us with three explanations for RI's popularity.

First, expecting at least the same level of return with less risk is appealing for all investors. Second, companies with high ESG performance seem to be less volatile and attract long-term shareholders. Third, markets may not yet be fully pricing in ESG-related risks or opportunities, which appeals to investors from a financial-upside perspective.

As an example, a company discloses its greenhouse gas emissions reduction targets. This signals to the investor that the company has evaluated the climate-related risks and impacts of its operations. Addressing climate change, along with many other ESG issues, is linked to long-term societal development and difficult-to-anticipate policy decisions. It is not always easy for investors to combine this information with short-term financial reporting and incentives, as there is both personal and external pressure (from a range of stakeholders) to succeed both with regard to financial returns and ESG performance.

Aiming for short-term targets may be a recipe for only short-term profit optimization. Long-term RI, however, can be pursued by aligning the expectations and objectives of all relevant parties: the investment target, the organization making the investment (e.g. an asset manager), the investment professionals making the investment decisions, and the clients and beneficiaries of the institutional investor. This requires more public discussion, improved guidance for investments, additional research and, above all, an increased level of understanding among the various parties involved. Thus, patience and a longer-term investment horizon are needed.

Although RI is typically associated with a long-term view, ESG issues should not be overlooked in the short term. A responsible investor accounts for ESG in every investment decision. An investee company's industry as a whole may show much potential, but the valuation of the company and appropriate timing *vis-à-vis* internal and external factors will have a significant impact on an investment or divestment decision. Relevant factors here might include an increase in the share price above a set price target, changes in corporate management or altered market conditions.

3.3 The operating environment

The operating environment significantly impacts an organization's RI practices and how they develop. Local culture, market characteristics, legislation and reputational pressure – these all set expectations, as well as create opportunities for investors. The European Union (EU)'s sustainable finance regulation is an example of lifting minimum requirements to a new level. Stakeholders' expectations can also influence investors' RI choices.

3.3.1 Culture

Broadly, culture as a concept includes everything related to a particular country, region or community. Cultures can be divided into those in which individualism is central and those that emphasize communality. Our values, attitudes and practices reflect the characteristics of the culture in which we live. The culture of the host country impacts a company's operations and also how responsible investors see ESG. Culture is one factor that explains why there are differences in sustainability and RI across countries.

One example is the use of child labour – something that persists in many regions and markets. In some societies, children may work hard to survive and to support their families, which, in cultures that emphasize community, can be normalized in the absence of better alternatives. Yet investors from developed countries will typically refuse to be involved in anything associated with child labour, which violates the United Nations Convention on the Rights of the Child and furthermore poses a reputational risk for the investor. Almost every country has ratified the convention, although we are some way from seeing the elimination of child labour worldwide. The convention does not prohibit all work done by children and allows geographic and age-specific variation. Investors should be aware of possible ESG issues that may contravene their values and their public RI commitments. To address this, an investor could identify those geographical areas in which there is a higher likelihood of child labour and see if a company has operations and/or supply chains in any of these higher-risk countries.

3.3.2 Market development, economics and finance

A common assumption is that the ESG risks associated with investment are lower in developed markets compared to developing markets. In Europe, for example, standards of living are higher than in developing countries and European countries are typically considered to have lower country-level and regulatory risks. This makes developed markets more attractive to investors from a lower risk perspective. Academic research finds that a country's regulations, institutions, as well as its economic and financial sectors, seem to have a bearing on RI implementation.

So why, then, do responsible investors invest in higher-risk markets? The main reasons are portfolio diversification and higher return expectations. Large countries such as China and India are important markets on the world stage. Economic growth in these countries may be a source of new investment opportunities. No matter where the investment is located, compliance with international norms is a key question for investors, and these norms include the UN Convention on the Rights of the Child and the ILO Declaration on Fundamental Principles and Rights at Work. This commitment applies to activities in all regions, including material supply chains.

3.3.3 Institutions and regulation

Across the world, RI remains widely unregulated by national institutions. Soft regulation – such as guidelines and recommendations – until recently has been the dominant means by which investors' activities have been steered. Disclosure requirements and taxonomies have been published or are being developed in various jurisdictions around the globe to curb green washing and encourage green financing. This is similar to the way corporate sustainability has progressed, with guidelines and recommendations ultimately becoming incorporated into legislation. In Europe, the Non-Financial Reporting Directive (NFRD) has been in force since 2016, requiring large companies to report on their corporate responsibility. The Netherlands, the UK and France are regulatory pioneers in their national contexts. The US Securities and Exchange Commission's statements, as well as the Australian Securities and Investments Commission's operating and financial review, both expressly acknowledge the importance of sustainability risks and of reporting on them. In South Africa, compliance with the King Code requirements, including disclosure, is a listing rule for local companies. Globally, the Sustainable Stock Exchanges (SSE) initiative encourages its member stock exchanges to publish guidelines for voluntary sustainability disclosure. Some of these member stock exchanges, across several continents, even require sustainability reporting as a listing rule. Increased regulation for companies benefits investors when analysing companies and when reporting on their investment activities.

3.3.4 Case: EU sustainable finance regulation

Responsible Investment and sustainable finance regulations are developing apace in Europe. One outcome of the financial crisis (2007–2009) was that higher investment transparency is seen to support economic stability. In 2016, the European Commission set up the High-Level Expert Group on sustainable finance (HLEG) to advice the Commission on how to direct more public and private capital towards sustainable investments, how to make the financial system more robust in the face of risks relating to the environment, and how to implement these on a pan-European scale. As a result, a ten-step action plan was created. The HLEG's successor in 2018 was the Technical expert group on sustainable finance (TEG), which advised the Commission on the implementation of the ten-step action plan and the development of a classification system for sustainable economic activities (the EU Taxonomy), an EU green bond standard, methodologies for low-carbon indices and metrics for climate-related disclosure. The European Commission has also launched unique EU sustainable finance regulations and updated existing financial services legislation, such as the UCITS Directive, AIFMD, Solvency II, MIFID II, IDD and IORP II, which contribute to the prevention of greenwashing and the consideration of sustainability risks in investment decision-making.

These sustainable finance activities will enable the EU to deliver its policy objectives under the European Green Deal. They will also contribute to the EU's climate and energy targets, including the EU Paris Agreement climate targets to be achieved by 2030, including a 40% reduction in greenhouse gas emissions. The EU's climate and energy targets for 2030 are achievable only if an additional €180 billion annual investment is made into sustainable development.

Examples of EU sustainable finance regulations and other corporate sustainability regulations are described in Table 3.2 (see also Table 7.4 in Chapter 7). When these regulations are implemented, sustainability and ESG practices of investors and companies will be taken to a new level.

Although the EU is a pioneer in sustainable finance regulation, the development of this phenomenon is nonetheless happening around the world. For example, China has issued the green bond catalogue, a "Guiding catalogue for the green industry" and Green Credit guidelines. A voluntary Sustainable Development Goals (SDG) Finance Taxonomy also exists for China, developed together with experts from various organizations and the UN Development Programme (UNDP). Green taxonomies are being developed or have already been launched in Russia, South Korea and South Africa.

Regulation	Target and status	Impacts
Taxonomy regulation	The aim is a harmonized classification system for what is sustainable. In force since 2020.	Various financial market actors will need to make use of the Taxonomy, while complying with other sustainable finance legislative requirements, both EU and national.
		Large non-financial-sector companies with over 500 employees (i.e. companies that are regulated by the Non-Financial Reporting Directive [NFRD], public interest entities [PIEs]) need to report on Taxonomy-eligible economic activities for the financial year 2021, regarding climate change mitigation and adaptation. For the financial year 2022 and beyond, Taxonomy alignment needs to be disclosed for the remaining four environmental objectives (situation in June 2022). Similarly, large financial-sector companies with more than 500 employees gradually report on their Taxonomy eligibility and alignment, by making use of relevant specified KPIs (the Green Asset Ratio, the Green Investment Ratio, the Green Insurance and Underwriting Ratio, the Green Asset Ratio for Financial Guarantees, and KPI for Fees and Commission Income).
		Social Taxonomy development is in progress (as of 2022).
Sustainable Finance Disclosure Regulation (SFDR)	The purpose is to increase the openness and transparency of financial market participants, financial advisers and financial products from an ESG and accountability perspective. In force since 2021.	This regulation introduced disclosure obligations for how financial market participants and financial advisers integrate ESG into their risk management and investment decision processes, and for disclosures.
		These actors have had to disclose information on their websites about how they evaluate sustainability risks, prepare a principal adverse impact (PAI) statement, and explain how their remuneration policy is aligned with a consideration of sustainability risks.
		The regulation also requires classification of products into those that promote ESG ("Article 8"), make sustainable investments ("Article 9") or have no such characteristics ("Article 6"). Information about this must be disclosed in pre-contractual documents and in periodic reports.
		For Article 8 and 9 products, detailed Regulatory Technical Standards need to be followed from 1 January 2023 (situation in 2022).

(*Continued*)

Regulation	Target and status	Impacts
Non-Financial Reporting Directive (NFRD)	The aims are: to provide investors and other stakeholders with information regarding how large companies manage sustainability; and to encourage large companies to develop their sustainability practices. In force since 2014, with national implementation by 2016 at the latest.	Companies that are large and of public interest (PIEs) must report on their sustainability, in a separate statement. The Taxonomy regulation requires these large companies to report on the taxonomy jeligibility and alignment of their economic activities. The NFRD will be replaced by the Corporate Sustainability Reporting Directive (CSRD).
Corporate Sustainability Reporting Directive (CSRD)	The aim is to revise and strengthen reporting requirements and the target group. Proposal published in 2021.	The CSRD will initially apply to all companies that fulfil at least two of the following three characteristics: over 250 employees, a turnover over €40 million or a balance sheet of over €20 million; and, starting from 2026, it will apply to all listed companies excluding micro-companies (if the proposal is implemented as per the current draft), and may be extended to larger unlisted entities. Provisions include a requirement for the company to report on impacts on the environment as well as risks to the company posed by the environment (including climate change), and to provide a description of the process of selecting the most relevant sustainability risks and impacts. The reporting must comply with EFRAG EFRAG sustainability reporting standards, be in electronic format, be assured and part of the board of directors report (thereby implying that the board is directly responsible for the information given).
Corporate Sustainability Due Diligence Directive (CSDDD)	The aim is to advance sustainable and responsible corporate behaviour such that human rights and environmental considerations become an integral part of companies' operations and corporate governance. Proposal published in 2022.	The target group is: (a) large EU limited liability companies with over 500 employees and a net turnover of over €150 million worldwide; (b) two years later, large EU limited liability companies in high-impact sectors (textiles, agriculture, extraction of minerals) with over 250 employees and a net turnover of over €40 million worldwide; (c) third-country companies active in the EU whose generated turnover in the EU is greater that the turnover thresholds in (a) and (b). Small and medium companies may be indirectly impacted. The regulation implies a corporate due diligence duty for companies, i.e. they will take responsibility for negative human rights issues and environmental impacts throughout their operations. The identification of, elimination of, prevention of, mitigation of and accounting for negative human rights and environmental impacts are steps laid out the proposed regulation, and cover the company's own operations, as well as its subsidiaries and its value chain. This implies that certain large companies will need to align their businesses with the Paris Agreement limiting global warming to 1.5°C. These goals will be supported using incentives. Directors will be responsible for, among other things, designing and monitoring the due diligence and

Low Carbon Benchmarks	The aim is to enable the creation of benchmarks as tools for investors to support low-carbon investment strategies. In force since 2019.	Amendments to the Benchmarks Regulation specify two low carbon benchmarks: the EU Climate Transition Benchmark (EU CTB) and the EU Paris-aligned Benchmark (EU PAB). Administrators of the benchmarks will have to provide an explanation of how the key elements of the methodology reflect ESG factors, with reference to the Taxonomy regulation. The benchmarks are tools for investors to support low-carbon investment strategies. The low carbon benchmarks (EU CTB) may be created by decarbonizing a standard benchmark. The underlying stocks are selected based on their reduced carbon emissions compared to stocks constituting a standard benchmark. The positive-carbon-impact benchmarks (EU PAB) align with the objectives of the Paris Agreement. The underlying stocks are selected on the basis of their carbon emission savings exceeding the stocks' residual carbon footprint.
EU Green Bond Standard (GBS) Regulation (voluntary)	The aim is to support the growth of the green bond market and to achieve the EU's climate targets by enabling issuers and investors to assess the sustainability of the bond. Proposal published in 2021.	The Regulation is voluntary – i.e. issuers will not be required to issue green bonds, but any green bonds they do issue will have to comply with the GBS. The regulation will impact issuers of green bonds that are traded in the EU, as well as EU bond issuers. The GBS has four elements: - alignment with the Taxonomy Regulation; - the bond framework confirms alignment with the GBS, explains how the issuer's strategy aligns with the environmental objectives, and provides details on use of proceeds, reporting and other key aspects - mandatory reporting on use of proceeds (allocation report) and environmental impacts (impact report) - mandatory external review by an accredited party.
Guidelines on reporting climate-related information (voluntary)	The aim is to support companies to report on climate-related information. Published in 2019.	The guidelines are voluntary. They take into account the NFRD and the recommendations of the TCFD (Task Force on Climate-related Financial Disclosures).
EU Ecolabel for retail financial products (voluntary)	The aim is to encourage investments in sustainable economic activities. Final report by the project team published in 2021; input to be adopted under the EU Ecolabel regulation	It is expected that the regulation will require many types of retail financial products (including investment funds, insurance-based investment products and bank structured products) to comply with certain requirements if they wish to use the ecolabel. The underlying investments will have to be sustainable activities.

3.3.5 Organizations

Credible RI throughout an organization requires top-management and board-level commitment. Otherwise, it will remain a marginal activity. As a best practice, RI policy implementation in an organization is supported by a roadmap or an action plan (see Chapter 4 for more details) and this should include, among other things, targets, guidance, metrics, monitoring and reporting. The pioneers in this area have incorporated ESG into their incentive systems.

It is also worthwhile for an organization to review any of its other guidelines, policies and processes that might be relevant to RI and ESG. Organizations domiciled in the EU, or marketing their products there, will also need to keep the regulatory requirements in mind and organize their operations and policies so that sustainability risks and principal adverse impacts are considered. Another useful step is to identify barriers, i.e. which organizational structures could potentially complicate RI implementation, such as competition between departments or teams, short- and long-term financial targets that neglect to cover ESG and organizational values that fail to align with the overall RI objectives. Other potential barriers include: practical difficulties in rolling out RI practices, lack of relevant skills and fear of failure and public criticism.

3.3.6 Reputation

The development of RI globally has been driven mainly by local initiatives and by investors demanding sustainable business activities from companies. Questionable business practices in a portfolio company, such as inadequate supply chain management, can damage an investor's reputation. Unsustainable business practices by investee companies may lead to weaker financial figures, which in turn increases investors' interest in the responsibility of operations. Also, investors themselves may be the cause of reputational damage: a financial adviser may lose customers by giving poor-quality investment advice.

Questionable activities are readily reflected in the organization's public image, brand and overall reputation. Stakeholders will hear of these via the media and react accordingly. How and how quickly an organization responds is critical in preserving credibility. In the financial markets, trust and reputation are crucial. A clear RI policy coupled with related process descriptions give an organization the leeway to defend itself in the teeth of negative media attention.

Institutional investors proactively develop their operations in pursuit of cultivating a positive public image. In practice, this also applies to RI activities. Investors seek to build portfolios with no questionable investments as the portfolio may be of interest to the media, NGOs or other stakeholders. If certain investments fail to meet the desired ESG criteria, this is when communication by investors of their RI processes becomes important, and how these processes affect the management of investments. To support the analysis of their investments, investors may procure ESG data, or they may find

NGOs a useful source of information. Proactivity is almost always easier and less harmful than reacting after the fact.

Responsible investors should aim for a sufficient level of transparency in their operations. This includes disclosure of the RI policy covering all asset classes and the practical implementation of their chosen RI approaches. Depending on the operating environment, this transparency may endow them with a competitive edge over their peers, or possibly it already represents a minimum standard in that market. It should be noted that, by disclosing information about their RI practices, investors are inviting public scrutiny.

Transparency also provides good communication opportunities. The organization's actions can be explained and misunderstandings avoided. Reporting on responsible investing requires truthful examples of how the RI policy has been implemented in practice, backed up with qualitative and/ or quantitative data. Reporting opportunities depend on the organization's available resources and also the stage of RI development. Reporting should always be immune from charges of greenwashing. In many of today's markets, RI reporting is considered a minimum standard.

Chapter 3 key Q&As

Here are the answers to the key questions posed at the start of this chapter.

What are the key drivers and barriers of Responsible Investment? How can we understand and classify them?

It is possible to classify the drivers and barriers into: values; level of financial return; and operating environment. Values are guiding principles for both individuals and organizations. Investment decisions reflect the values of the investor. Financial return is essential in investments. Operating environment covers culture, market development and the economic and financial sector, institutions and regulation, organizations and reputation.

How might these drivers and barriers impact Responsible Investment in an organization?

It ought to be recognized that, in addition to organizational values, the values of individuals play a role in an organizational setting. Among the key drivers are the commitment by top management and the inclusion of ESG into remuneration. Internal competition between departments or teams, or short-term incentives that fail to cover ESG, can act as barriers.

Bibliography

Alda, M. (2019). "Corporate Sustainability and Institutional Shareholders: The Pressure of Social Responsible Pension Funds on Environmental Firm Practices". *Business Strategy and the Environment*, 28, 1,060–1,071.

Australian Securities & Investments Commission. (2013). *Effective Disclosure in an Operating and Financial Review*. Retrieved 17 January 2022 from https://asic.gov.au/media/1247147/rg247.pdf

Berkhout, T., & Rowlands, I.H. (2007). "The Voluntary Adoption of Green Electricity by Ontario-Based Companies. The Importance of Organizational Values and Organizational Context". *Organization and Environment*, 20, 281–303.

De Groot, J.I.M., & Steg, L. (2009). "Mean or Green: Which Values Can Promote Stable Pro-environmental Behavior?" *Conservation Letters*, 2, 61–66.

Ervin, D., Wu, J., Khanna, M., Jones, C., & Wirkkala, T. (2013). "Motivations and Barriers to Corporate Environmental Management". *Business Strategy and the Environment*, 22, 390–409.

European Commission. (2019). *Guidelines on Reporting Climate-Related Information*. Retrieved 17 January 2022 from https://ec.europa.eu/finance/docs/policy/190618-climate-related-information-reporting-guidelines_en.pdf

European Commission. (n.d.). *Corporate Sustainability Due Diligence*. Retrieved 27 February 2022 from https://ec.europa.eu/info/business-economy-euro/doing-business-eu/corporate-sustainability-due-diligence_en

European Commission. (n.d.). *JRC Technical Reports. Development of EU Ecolabel Criteria for Retail Financial Products*. Retrieved 17 January 2022 from https://susproc.jrc.ec.europa.eu/product-bureau/sites/default/files/2021-03/2021.03.05-EUELfinancial products-TechnicalReport4FINAL.pdf

European Commission. (n.d.). *Overview of Sustainable Finance*. Retrieved 17 January 2022 from https://ec.europa.eu/info/business-economy-euro/banking-and-finance/sustainable-finance/overview-sustainable-finance_en

European Parliament. (n.d.) *Legislative Train for Corporate Sustainability Reporting Directive*. Retrieved 17 January 2022 from https://www.europarl.europa.eu/legislative-train/theme-a-european-green-deal/file-review-of-the-non-financial-reporting-directive/05-2021

Gond, J.P., Kang, N., & Moon, J. (2011). "The Government of Selfregulation: On the Comparative Dynamics of Corporate Social Responsibility". *Economy and Society*, 40, 640–671.

Hawley, J., & Williams, A. (2000). *The Rise of Fiduciary Capitalism: How Institutional Investors Can Make Corporate America More Democratic*. University of Pennsylvania Press.

Hawley, J., & Williams, A. (2007). "Universal Owners: Challenges and Opportunities". *Corporate Governance*, 15, 415–420.

Influence Map. (2021). *Policy Alert: The Korean Sustainable Finance Taxonomy (K-taxonomy)*. Retrieved 17 January 2022 from https://influencemap.org/report/Investor-Intervention-Opportunity-The-Korean-Sustainable-Finance-Taxonomy-K-taxonomy-15855

Johannesburg Stock Exchange. (n.d.). *JSE Limited Listings Requirements*. Retrieved 17 January 2022 from https://www.jse.co.za/sites/default/files/media/documents/2019-04/JSE Listings Requirements.pdf

OECD. (n.d.). 9. *Sustainable Finance Definitions and Taxonomies in China*. Retrieved 17 January 2022 from https://www.oecd-ilibrary.org/sites/5abe80e9-en/index.html?itemId=/content/component/5abe80e9-en

Patterson, J. (2022). Personal Communication on EU Sustainable Finance. 1 March 2022.

Rakkolainen, E. (2022). Personal Communication on EU Sustainable Finance. 24 February 2022.

Scholtens, B., & Sievänen, R. (2013). "Drivers of Socially Responsible Investing: A Case Study of Four Nordic Countries". *Journal of Business Ethics*, 115, 605–616.

Schwartz, S.H. (1992). "Universals in the Content and Structure of Values: Theoretical Advances and Empirical Tests in 20 Countries". In M. Zanna (Ed.), *Advances in Experimental Social Psychology*. Academic Press.

Schwartz, S.H. (1994). "Are There Universal Aspects in the Structure and Contents of Human Values?" *Journal of Social Issues*, 50, 19–45.

Sjöström, E. (2010). "Shareholders as Norm Entrepreneurs for Corporate Social Responsibility". *Journal of Business Ethics*, 94, 177–191.

South Africa Sustainable Finance Initiative. (n.d). *Taxonomy Working Group*. Retrieved 17 January 2022 from https://sustainablefinanceinitiative.org.za/working-groups/taxonomy/

State Development Corporation VEB.RF. (n.d.). *Green Finance*. Retrieved 17 January 2022 from https://xn--90ab5f.xn--p1ai/en/sustainable-development/green-finance/

Steg, L., Perlaviciute, G., van der Werff, E., & Lurvink, J. (2014). "The Significance of Hedonic Values for Environmentally Relevant Attitudes, Preferences, and Actions". *Environment and Behavior*, 46, 163–192.

Stern, P.C. (2000). "Toward a Coherent Theory of Environmentally Significant Behavior." *Journal of Social Issues*, 56, 407–424.

Stern, P.C., & Dietz, T. (1994). "The Value Basis of Environmental Concern". *Journal of Social Issues*, 50, 65–84.

United Nations Development Programme. (2020). *Technical Report on SDG Finance Taxonomy*. Retrieved 17 January 2022 from https://www.cn.undp.org/content/china/en/home/library/poverty/technical-report-on-sdg-finance-taxonomy.html

US Securities and Exchange Commission. (2021). *Statement. Public Input Welcomed on Climate Change Disclosures*. Retrieved 17 January 2022 from https://www.sec.gov/news/public-statement/lee-climate-change-disclosures

US Securities and Exchange Commission. (2020). *Statement. Regulation S-K and ESG Disclosures: An Unsustainable Silence*. https://www.sec.gov/news/public-statement/lee-regulation-s-k-2020-08-26

Williams, S., & Schaefer, A. (2013). "Small and Medium-sized Enterprises and Sustainability: Managers' Values and Engagement with Environmental and Climate Change Issues". *Business Strategy and the Environment*, 22, 173–186.

4 Becoming a Responsible Investor

Key questions in this chapter

- How can an organization implement Responsible Investment credibly?
- Why implement Responsible Investment into investment processes?
- What should always be considered when developing Responsible Investment in an organization?

This chapter guides investment professionals through the relevant steps for developing Responsible Investment (RI) policies and practices in order to become a responsible investor. These steps form a process of continuous development which seeks to establish a credible plan for RI, evolving in line with (or surpassing) leading practice, regulation and environmental, social and governance (ESG) trends. This process, as portrayed in Figure 4.1, consists of four main phases:

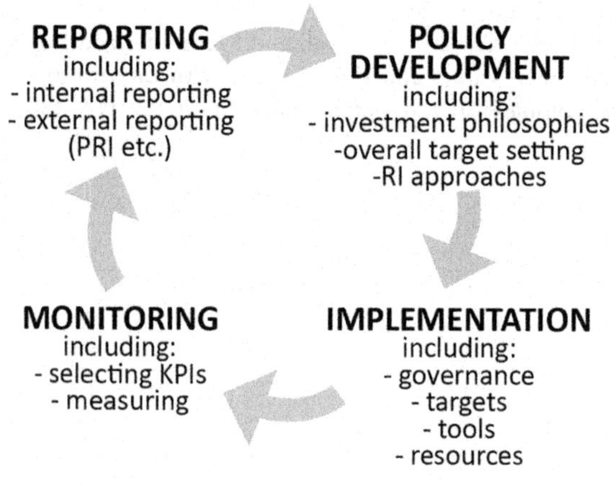

REPORTING
including:
- internal reporting
- external reporting
(PRI etc.)

POLICY DEVELOPMENT
including:
- investment philosophies
-overall target setting
-RI approaches

MONITORING
including:
- selecting KPIs
- measuring

IMPLEMENTATION
including:
- governance
- targets
- tools
- resources

Figure 4.1 The four phases of Responsible Investment
Note: PRI: Principles for Responsible Investment; KPI: key performance indicator

DOI: 10.4324/9781003284932-5

- Developing relevant RI policy documents
- Implementing the policy
- Monitoring progress
- Reporting on the practices and results

4.1 Strategy and policy document requirements

In developing an RI policy, the starting point is defining what RI actually means to the investor: not just establishing what it is but what is to be achieved by it – what is the level of ambition?

4.1.1 Defining Responsible Investment

Developing a definition basically means deciding which kinds of investments are acceptable and which are not, simply because unacceptable investments run counter to the values of the investor or investment organization. Are all sectors and products investable? Some investors will not be comfortable with, for example, controversial weapons, tobacco, alcohol, gambling or adult entertainment. The criterion might, alternatively, be around minimum standards of corporate responsibility, for which many investors look to international norms for guidance.

Establishing acceptability may seem like a difficult, abstract exercise. A helpful rubric is: would a potential investment sector, product or practice tolerate closer scrutiny? In other words, would the investor encounter reputational risk if these investments faced public exposure?

Different institutional investors have different legal obligations, organizational objectives and stakeholder perspectives. What institutional investors have in common is that they invest and manage assets on behalf of others and have a fiduciary duty to act in the best interest of their beneficiaries. Asset owners such as pension funds are likely to favour a broad definition because they invest the assets of a wide group of beneficiaries. Asset managers seek to serve a variety of clients and may therefore also prefer broad definitions, but they may also develop specific products with an ESG focus. Foundations, trade unions and family offices are generally less regulated and can therefore use RI to pursue their societal objectives.

The choice of RI approaches – ESG integration, screening, thematic and impact investing, or active ownership – will have a strong bearing on how RI is defined, as well as its practical implementation. The Principles for Responsible Investment (PRI) is one source of definitions.

The definition of RI together with the chosen RI approaches form the very core of the RI policy.

4.1.2 Aligning a Responsible Investment policy with overall objectives

The key guiding question when setting the scope of an RI policy is: what do we want to achieve with RI? Do we want to follow minimum standards in compliance with regulation or do we want to be more ambitious? Here, an iterative process may be useful, i.e. start with a draft and then consider whether the chosen definition and approach support the objectives.

Some organizations name their guiding document "Responsible Investment Principles" or "ESG Strategy," depending on both its role in the organization and its structure. Smaller organizations might prefer to embed ESG considerations directly into the investment strategy. Investors can select a name and format that best fits their organizational needs.

Describing the overall RI objectives is central. The policy also needs to establish which asset classes are covered, and it can include a practical description of how RI approaches are applied in each asset class. Strong governance is key in bringing RI considerations into the investment process in a structured and controlled way. It should be based on clear procedures and responsibilities that are either laid down in the policy or in a separate document. Key RI commitments and initiatives, such as PRI, are also pertinent and warrant inclusion in the policy document, as do any possible legal restrictions. If an investor is to include information on an initiative, they should not do so without first gathering information and becoming a signatory or member – or else signalling in the policy the intention to do so.

An RI policy must align with such documents as the ownership policy, the investment strategy and the sustainability strategy. Once the RI policy is ready, approval and sign-off by the board strengthens the document's credibility. A recent development is a consideration of ESG across all three lines of defence (business, risk management and internal audit). Climate, for example, represents a significant risk for the organization by potentially impacting both physical assets and, more importantly, the investment portfolio's risk–return prospects. Risk management is therefore always a relevant factor.

4.1.3 Ownership policy

If an organization selects active ownership and engagement as an RI approach, it becomes relevant to define what kind of an owner the organization is. Active ownership through voting requires the organization to be a shareholder. Nowadays, many investors' active ownership of companies is manifested through engagement, which is the case in fixed-income and other asset classes. Engagement is also a practice directed towards external funds and asset managers.

An ownership policy describes what the key objectives are for the organization as an owner and how these objectives are to be reached. It will typically also delineate focus areas, such as climate change, or board independence, diversity and remuneration.

4.2 Implementing Responsible Investment

Credible RI implementation requires, at a minimum, the following: governance, targets, practical guiding documents, resources (both human and financial) and, most likely, incentives.

To take the first point, RI needs to be well governed. A reputational risk is posed if the organization does not act according to its RI policy, which is of concern for the board and top management. A guiding rule is that the board approves the RI policy and has overall responsibility for its implementation. Top-management commitment is essential and helps to establish a high level of ambition. Not only are organizational resources to be deployed: financial resources have a role to play in acquiring tools and external services.

Target setting enables the organization to steer towards the aims outlined in the RI and ownership policies. Target setting can be supported by an RI roadmap (described in Section 4.5). Targets are important, as they reflect the level of ambition and also set a benchmark for monitoring RI activities.

Targets can be qualitative or quantitative by nature. Examples of targets that relate to the organization itself are: implementing RI in a new asset class; number of companies engaged with; and yearly ESG training. An example of a qualitative target that focuses on the investee is encouraging portfolio companies to formulate human rights policies.

Recently, climate change-related targets – such as "Net Zero" or "Paris Aligned" – have become increasingly popular with asset owners and managers. Such targets can relate to entire portfolios or sections thereof. Investors often begin with scope 1 (direct emissions) and scope 2 (emissions from purchased energy) before adding emissions from up- and downstream activities (scope 3). Some investors even prepare separate documents for climate change governance and climate change policy.

RI and ownership policies warrant practical guidance or provision of further information to enable all professionals to understand what is meant in practice. RI practices vary from one asset class to another, so it may be worthwhile to prepare asset class-specific policies and guiding documents. Not all documents need to be publicly available, but the RI policy and ownership policy are expected to be.

ESG incentives can assist in reaching targets. They are preferably set for the entire investment organization but are more typical for just top management. Broad ESG incentive schemes are seen as evidence of a high level of ESG incorporation.

4.3 Monitoring

Monitoring allows the investor to assess whether the direction of travel is towards the set targets. It is an essential part of RI implementation and enables RI reporting.

Agreement should be reached on how progress towards the targets is measured: will it be via indicators or descriptions, for example? Monitoring, like the targets, can be quantitative or qualitative. Consensus on measurement methods provides a common language for monitoring RI.

Monitoring can take place at different levels of the organization. The board and top management need regular updates. Depending on the organization's level of ESG incorporation, role descriptions and responsibilities may include RI-related tasks and measuring. Incentives can also be linked to these responsibilities.

4.4 Reporting

It is useful to understand the distinction between corporate responsibility reporting and RI reporting. The former explains how an organization makes use of sustainability to support its business activities and what role the organization plays as a responsible actor in the society. The latter focuses on the portfolio side. Naturally, there are overlaps between the two, and some organizations report on their RI practices as a part of their corporate responsibility report. External RI reporting could mean reporting to the PRI, to the Principles for Responsible Banking (PRB) or to the Principles for Sustainable Insurance (PSI), for example. Both external and internal reporting require resources, but at the same time reporting supports organizations in learning, implementing and monitoring their RI practices. The appearance of a report marks the time to start anew the iterative process of developing RI and to revisit the RI policy to assess its relevance.

4.5 Developing a Responsible Investment roadmap

Credible RI requires a systematic approach. As in running a marathon: the achievement is easy to promise, but if one is not already a runner, success will require setting targets, planning and carrying out the planned exercises consistently over time. One needs to start by running shorter distances. Similarly, an investor can get started with one asset class or product but with the aim of ultimately covering the entire investment portfolio.

4.5.1 Important dimensions of the roadmap

Often, RI competes with other daily business tasks for attention. This is why a roadmap can be a useful tool (Figure 4.2). A roadmap typically consists of topics and sub-topics that the organization wants to develop. A topic could be, for example, the development of policy-level documents with relevant sub-topics being the definition of RI and the selection of appropriate RI approaches.

It is recommended to set targets for every topic and sub-topic, as they represent the status that the organization wants to reach and its level of ambition. It can also be helpful to document the current status with respect to every topic to understand where the organization currently is and to provide support in defining the actions needed to move towards the targets.

	TOPIC	TARGET	CURRENT SITUATION	ACTIONS TO BE TAKEN	RESPONSIBLE PERSON(S)	TIMING
DEVELOPMENT OF RI POLICY	**Define what RI means**	Definition that considers our organizational values	No definitions yet in place	....	....	Q4 2022
	Select RI approaches	....	....	....	....	....
	....	....	....	....	....	....
IMPLEMENTATION	**Asset class-specific guidance**	Easy-to-understand guidance in place	Not yet in place	....	....	Q1 2023
	ESG data procurement	....	....	....	....	....
	....	....	....	....	....	....
DISCLOSING RESULTS / REPORTING	**Plan for PRI reporting**	Preparation of a project plan containing roles	Not yet in place	....	....	....
	Following up internal KPIs	....	....	....	....	....

Figure 4.2 An illustrative roadmap for the development of Responsible Investment
Source: KPMG

To make the roadmap more tangible and easier to understand, it should include timelines for all actions. And allocating responsibilities for implementation means having a task list readily available. It is up to the organization to decide what level of detail is appropriate.

4.5.2 *Well begun is half done*

It is worthwhile to acknowledge that organizations consist of people with differing individual values, drivers, capacity to undertake tasks and ways of working. Hence, a carefully prepared roadmap can save a lot of time and be pivotal in the success of RI. The roadmap might take into account the company's business strategy, its culture, how different teams work together or how they are incentivized. Organizational commitment is essential. RI should not be a topic or task that one person alone is taking care of. It is better allocated to a team or committee and they should have clear targets.

A roadmap helps to transform limited resources and objectives into concrete actions, reducing the risk of accusations of greenwashing. If a few essential interim objectives are selected and workable actions established to achieve them, this is infinitely preferable to an overly ambitious plan that cannot realistically be implemented alongside the daily responsibilities.

Last but not least, it is important to acknowledge that people have different levels of expertise in RI. To establish a credible and aligned view of what RI is and how it is implemented in an organization, regular training opportunities are needed. Involvement in the working groups of RI initiatives such as PRI will build an organization's RI capacity.

Chapter 4 key Q&As

Here are the answers to the key questions posed at the start of this chapter.

How can an organization implement Responsible Investment credibly?

First, define what RI means for the organization, including objectives and the level of ambition. A guiding document, typically called a Responsible Investment policy, must be developed, as well as an ownership policy, if active ownership and engagement is being practised. These two documents need to be aligned with each other and with the investment strategy.

Governance increases the credibility of RI, as does target setting, practical guidance, a sufficient allocation of resources and incentives.

Why implement Responsible Investment into investment processes?

ESG issues have financial significance and as such need to be incorporated into investment processes. An analysis that considers ESG issues – and, at a more detailed level, the material ESG risks and opportunities of the sector in question, as well as company specifics – provides a more granular view than one that doesn't. Markets may not yet have fully priced in ESG-related risks and opportunities, which is appealing to an investor from a financial upside perspective.

What should always be considered when developing Responsible Investment in an organization?

In an organizational setting, planning is recommended, rather than hastily taking action in an uncoordinated way. Don't make the plan too ambitious but select a few things to develop and stick to them. Organizational buy-in is important, at different levels of the organization. It is therefore useful to recognize organizational drivers and barriers.

Bibliography

Carbon Action Tracker. (n.d.). "Glasgow's 2030 Credibility Gap: Net Zero's Lip Service to Climate Action". Retrieved 17 January 2022 from https://climateactiontracker.org/publications/glasgows-2030-credibility-gap-net-zeros-lip-service-to-climate-action

Juravle, C., & Lewis, A. (2008). "Identifying Impediments to SRI in Europe: A Review of the Practitioner and Academic Literature". *Business Ethics – A European Review*, 17, 285–310.

KPMG. (2021). "Can Capital Markets Save the Planet?" Retrieved 17 January 2022 from https://home.kpmg/xx/en/home/insights/2021/10/can-capital-markets-save-the-planet.html

Otterström, T. (2022). Personal Communication on ESG roadmaps. 15 February 2022.

Sievänen, R., Rita, H., & Scholtens, B. (2017). "European Pension Funds and Sustainable Development: Trade-Offs between Finance and Responsibility". *Business Strategy and the Environment*, 26, 912–926.

Sustainable Development Solutions Network (SDSN) & Bertelsmann Stiftung. (2021). *Sustainable Development Report 2021*. Retrieved 17 January 2022 from https://s3.amazonaws.com/sustainabledevelopment.report/2021/2021-sustainable-development-report.pdf

5   Materiality and megatrends

Key questions in this chapter

- How can we assess the material ESG issues of an investment?
- How do we consider megatrends and other rising trends in investment decision-making?

Investment decisions are based on a number of different factors, including environmental, social and governance (ESG). The importance of each of the various factors is determined by the investor's values, investment strategy, investment philosophy, selected Responsible Investment (RI) approaches and the tools used to assess the investment target. Relevant factors to consider in each investment decision include: macroeconomic and sector-specific outlooks, issuer-specific details such as turnover, cash flow and demand projections, as well as the capabilities of a company's management.

Similarly, ESG issues should be broken down in an investor's overall assessment and the relevant ESG issues prioritized. An investor may wish to emphasize human rights or the environment, for example, or possibly smaller more specific concerns – or even a broader set of ESG issues without going into detail. In reality, choices are investment-specific and decisions are based on a combination of variables around ESG and finance. This chapter will discuss the financial materiality, i.e. the importance of ESG issues at both a company and a sector level, and then review those issues that have an effect on a global scale – issues that are also known as megatrends.

5.1 The three-pillar ESG model and the selection of material ESG issues

There can be no universal list of ESG issues, as relevant issues vary according to investor, company and sector. In addition, ESG regulatory environments differ across countries. Figure 5.1 presents examples of well-established ESG issues typically considered by responsible investors. These are identical to the issues addressed by companies as part of corporate responsibility.

DOI: 10.4324/9781003284932-6

RESPONSIBLE INVESTMENT
Considering ESG as part of investment
decision-making

Environment
- Biodiversity
- Circular economy
- Climate change
- Deforestation
- Energy efficiency
- Environmental impacts of investments
- Environmental technologies
- Pollution
- Resource depletion
- Standards, certificates, programmes
- Waste

Social
- Communities impacted by investments
- Human rights (including modern slavery; diversity, equality, inclusion; child labour; working conditions)
- Personnel policy, well-being at work
- Population growth
- Product responsibility
- Social cohesion erosion
- Standards, certificates, programmes

Governance
- Anti-fraud and anti-corruption
- CEO and steering committee
- Code of conduct
- Digitalization (including cyber-security)
- Selection, independence and remuneration of the board
- Tax payments

ESG as a basis for long-term financial return

Figure 5.1 The three-pillar model of responsible investing: examples of ESG issues relevant to investors

5.2 Company-level materiality

Company-level materiality means issues that are significant within the operations of a specific company. Companies often identify significant ESG issues in their operations using materiality analysis.

Materiality analysis begins with a long list of potential ESG issues which is then narrowed down. The company's key stakeholders, such as management, board, employees and customers, play an important role in this by assessing the importance and priority of ESG issues, typically by means of interviews and surveys. The significance and impact of each of these ESG issues are subsequently assessed. A materiality analysis therefore addresses both the issues and their economic impact. Double materiality analysis, as mentioned in the forthcoming EU Corporate Sustainability Reporting Directive (CSRD), requires companies to identify and report the impacts the company creates but also the impacts the company faces.

Results of materiality analyses are often disclosed in annual corporate responsibility reports, which is useful for investors, who can assess the risks and opportunities. However, as a portfolio can sometimes include hundreds of companies, concentrating on sector-specific material issues might be more efficient.

5.3 Sector-level materiality

Sector-level materiality means issues that are significant within a specific sector. What is a material ESG issue varies considerably from one sector to another. Customer welfare, product safety and water management are material in the health care sector, whereas in the financial sector fair marketing and systemic risk management are crucial (see Table 5.1).

Sector-specific data sources and related tools are commonly used, one of which is the Value Reporting Foundation's SASB Standards, which classifies relevant ESG issues by sector. SASB has defined 26 specific ESG issues, which are scored per sector for materiality, e.g. "material in more than 50% of industries of the sector" or "material in less than 50% of industries of the sector" (see Table 5.1).

5.4 Megatrends

Megatrends are powerful forces reshaping the global economy, business and society. The outcomes of megatrends may have opposing impacts. For example,

Table 5.1 Examples of material ESG issues classified by SASB Standards in selected sectors

Financials		
Environment	*Social[a]*	*Governance[a]*
Zero out of seven (0%) environmental factors are material	Six out of 12 (50%) social factors are material:	Five out of 11 (42%) governance factors are material:
	Material in more than 50% of industries of the sector:	Material in more than 50% of industries of the sector:
	– Fair marketing and advertising	– Lifecycle impacts of products and services
	– Diversity and inclusion	– Systemic risk management
	– Compensation and benefits	– Business ethics and transparency of payments
	Material in less than 50% of industries of the sector:	Material in less than 50% of industries of the sector:
	– Access and affordability	– Environmental and social impacts on core assets and operations
	– Customer welfare	– Competitive behaviour
	– Data security and customer privacy	

Health care

Environment	Social[a]	Governance[a]
Four out of seven (57%) environmental factors are material:	Eight out of 12 (67%) social factors are material:	Seven out of 11 (64%) governance factors are material:
Material in more than 50% of industries of the sector: – Energy management – Water and wastewater management – Waste and hazardous materials management	Material in more than 50% of industries of the sector: – Access and affordability – Customer welfare – Recruitment, development and retention	Material in more than 50% of industries of the sector: – Lifecycle impacts of products and services – Product quality and safety – Business ethics and transparency of payments
Material in less than 50% of industries of the sector: – Fuel management	Material in less than 50% of industries of the sector: – Human rights and community relations – Data security and customer privacy – Fair disclosure and labelling – Fair marketing and advertising – Employee health, safety and well-being	Material in less than 50% of industries of the sector: – Environmental and social impacts on core assets and operations – Product packaging – Materials sourcing – Supply chain management

a The classification of ESG issues used by SASB differs from that used in this table. In the table, "social capital" and "human capital" are presented as social factors; "business model," "innovation" and "leadership and governance" are presented as governance.

higher average temperatures caused by climate change prolong the agricultural growing season in certain geographical areas – whereas intolerable heat and drought are experienced elsewhere.

Megatrends can also be linked to other megatrends and other individual ESG issues. Some ESG issues, such as taxation, can also be classified as megatrends because of the high level of global interest in the topic. There is no all-encompassing list. However, there are some useful existing frameworks. The UN's 17 Sustainable Development Goals (SDGs) can be seen as megatrends. The World Economic Forum, on its part, lists global risks, many of which have names that match those of megatrends. Academic research by scientists has its own take on megatrends. Table 5.2 looks at how megatrends, global goals and issues compare according to how they are framed by these aforementioned sources. Despite the variations in outlook and nomenclature, it is possible for investors to identify commonalities and overlaps in megatrends.

Table 5.2 Examples of megatrends as identified by selected sources

ESG dimension	Megatrend	The megatrend is part of global issues/goals listed by the following sources:		
		UN SDGs	Academic research ("Planetary Boundaries" only)	World Economic Forum: "global risks"
Environment	Climate change	x	x	x
	Biodiversity	x	x	x
	Sustainable use of natural resources and sustainability of the earth	x	x	x
Social	Peace	x		x
	Equality and justice	x		x
	Sustainable societies	x		x
Governance	Economy and finance	x		x
	Successful governance	x		x
	Digitalization	x		x

Of the 17 SDGs, five relate to the environment: clean water and sanitation (Goal 6), affordable and clean energy (Goal 7), climate action (Goal 13), life below water (Goal 14) and life on land (Goal 15). Scientists have identified ten megatrends related to the sustainability of the earth, which they refer to as "Planetary Boundaries" (see Table 5.2 and the Appendix). The classification implies that the most concerning is the loss of biodiversity, followed by the nitrogen cycle and climate change.

The World Economic Forum annually gathers views from global leaders on global risks, and the trend over the last decade is that environmental risks have increased in importance relative to other risks. As many as four out of the five most likely global risks (or megatrends) in 2021 were environmental: extreme weather, climate action failure, human environmental damage and biodiversity loss. The remaining top-five risk is infectious diseases.

Because megatrends can be seen as comprising individual, smaller trends, an investor can analyse them from several ESG perspectives. For example, climate change is related not only to the environment but also to societal issues and to governance.

5.4.1 Climate change

Climate change is the result of human activity in which greenhouse gases are released into the atmosphere over a long period of time resulting in global warming. For investors, climate change means both risks and opportunities. It is relevant to analyse physical and transition risks for investee companies, as these may result in either appreciation or depreciation of investments.

The Task Force on Climate-related Financial Disclosures (TCFD) classifies physical climate risks as either acute or chronic. The former refer to event-driven risks such as increased severity of extreme weather events (e.g. hurricanes or floods). The latter refer to changes in longer-term climate patterns causing e.g. chronic heat waves. Businesses located in areas prone to any of these physical climate risks, may face increased costs from damages to their assets.

According to the TCFD classification, there are also transitional risks, which can be related to policy, regulation, technology, market and reputation. An example of a transitional risk relating to regulation is a tightening of fuel taxation, which may adversely affect the profitability of a company's business – a logistics company that operates trucks, for example.

Climate change mitigation and adaptation can also present business opportunities for companies such as renewable energy producers and those in the value chain that provide materials and components for solar panels and windmills. The EU Taxonomy focuses on those sectors that are key in climate change mitigation and adaptation (see Table 5.3). Technologies and solutions

Table 5.3 EU Taxonomy sectors for climate change mitigation and adaptation

Sector	Climate change mitigation	Climate change adaptation
Forestry	x	x
Environmental protection	x	x
Manufacturing	x	
Energy	x	x
Water supply, sewerage, waste management and remediation	x	x
Transport	x	
Information and communication	x	x
Construction and real estate	x	
Financial and insurance activities		x
Professional, scientific and technical activities	x	x
Education		x
Human health and social work activities		x
Arts, entertainment and recreation		x

The situation as of January 2022

that support sectors to become Taxonomy-aligned are especially interesting for responsible investors.

So, apart from the environment, how does climate change relate to social issues and good governance? According to one study, global warming will expose up to 340 million people to annual floods by 2050, particularly in Asia in China, Bangladesh, India, Vietnam, Indonesia, Thailand, the Philippines and Japan. Insufficient global environmental governance may be a key underlying reason for the failure to arrest global warming. Table 5.4 presents examples of E, S and G outcomes of climate change.

5.4.2 Biodiversity loss

Biodiversity describes the richness and variability of genes, species and ecosystems in land, air and water – within each environment and across them.

Table 5.4 Climate change as environmental, social and governance factors

Climate change	Background	Outcome/impact
As an environmental factor (E)	The volume of industrial activity, building and construction, as well as transport, have significantly increased during the last two centuries.	Global warming results in melting glaciers, a decrease in snow-covered areas and permafrost and rising sea levels. Numbers of extreme weather events increase.
		Nature adapts, and plants and animals migrate to new areas. Biodiversity declines.
	The volume of greenhouse gases in the atmosphere has multiplied.	Changes in companies' physical operating environment due to increased acute and chronic physical climate risks. Insurance premiums rise or the policies are terminated altogether. Construction companies are expected to benefit from increased business.
		Transition risks also create challenges and opportunities. For example, highly polluting sectors may be subject to further regulation to reduce emissions leading to significant cost increases. Companies that provide new reduced-emission technology or renewable fuels may benefit from transition risks.
		Climate change mitigation and adaptation provide business opportunities such as new technologies, heat-resistant plant varieties and plant-based protein.

Climate change	Background	Outcome/impact
As a social factor (S)	Global warming is impacting people's abilities to pursue their professions in some sectors and geographical areas, e.g. farming in hot and dry climates. People migrate to new areas and even new countries. The "climate refugee" is already an established concept.	The arrival of large numbers of refugees in a country requires substantial efforts from the receiving society, as well as from refugees themselves. On the other hand, for many industrialized countries, young refugees and immigrants present an opportunity to correct a distorted age pyramid and grow the labour force. The Just Transition Declaration, agreed at COP26, is an important commitment by over 30 nations to support communities and workers globally who may be impacted by climate change or decarbonization.
As a governance factor (G)	Awareness around the impact of human activities on climate has been limited. As awareness has increased, actions have nevertheless remained insufficient and driven by country-specific political and economic impacts. One reason for this, among others, has been the limited pricing of emissions. Insufficient attention has been paid to greenhouse gas emissions at international, national or company levels.	To mitigate climate change, the Paris Agreement on limiting global warming to 1.5°C took place in 2015. This legally binding international treaty entered into force in 2016. Almost 200 countries have endorsed the agreement, and almost all of these have solidified their support with a formal approval. The EU has established an action plan and a number of regulations, including a Taxonomy to define what is sustainable, in order to direct more capital towards sustainable investments and to manage climate risk. Examples are described in Chapter 3. Institutional investors are increasingly making decarbonization commitments in their investment portfolios. How well companies and nations succeed in their climate commitments is relevant to investors.

According to scientists, biodiversity loss is at a more concerning level even than climate change is. Key drivers for biodiversity loss are overuse and pollution of both land and marine resources, impairing the balance in nature and causing domino effects, the impacts of which can still not be fully understood. To provide a clear example of the potential economic consequences of biodiversity loss: as a result of human impacts, 40% of the world's insect species are threatened with extinction, and pollinating insects, e.g. bees, are essential for 35% of the production of food crops such as coffee, tomatoes and cocoa.

Biodiversity loss is closely related to the climate change megatrend because a warmer climate impacts species' natural habitat. Another interlinking megatrend is population growth, as growing food demand requires more arable land.

Biodiversity loss has not been on the agenda for decision-makers, companies and investors simply because the focus has been on extracting economic wealth from nature rather than protecting these assets in the long term. Another factor keeping it off the agenda is that actual attributable economic losses remain unclear although the impacts are becoming increasingly evident. This implies a governance problem and a lack of internalization of the environment- and biodiversity-related risks. A consensus on how to measure and price biodiversity loss is only just emerging, without which it has been difficult to make biodiversity loss tangible from a business and investment perspective. According to a World Bank estimate, the cost of biodiversity loss may result in an annual decline in the global gross domestic product (GDP) of US$2.7 trillion by 2030.

According to the Taskforce on Nature-related Financial Disclosures (TNFD), over 50% of economic activities depend on nature, with a direct or indirect relationship with biodiversity loss. Some would argue that this estimation is low, as all human activities ultimately depend on nature. Forests are important for biodiversity and climate change mitigation but they are being cut down across the world to provide land for agriculture, buildings, mines and industrial areas, among other things. Further complicating matters are a growth in timber use and unsustainable forest management. We are already seeing the effects of overuse and pollution of marine resources.

Scientists have tried to communicate their findings, but this has been frustrated by a lack of a common language merging ecology and finance. The TNFD is currently developing a risk management and disclosure framework to support companies and investors in taking action on nature-related risks and thereby direct capital flows to nature-positive outcomes. Other international organizations helping to concretize biodiversity loss to companies and investors are the World Economic Forum, the World Business Council for Sustainable Development, the Science-Based Targets Network and the Intergovernmental Science-Policy Platform on Biodiversity and Ecosystem Services.

A responsible investor should analyse possible impacts companies and their business activities have on biodiversity loss. Relevant questions include:

- What is the business's dependency on natural resources?
- How does the business impact biodiversity and vice versa?
- What are the concrete actions taken by the company to prevent biodiversity loss?

Because lack of data has been a barrier for a more extensive inclusion of biodiversity in investors' ESG assessments, engagement with companies and ESG data providers is important.

5.4.3 Population growth

The global population is growing rapidly, making it one of the key challenges for planetary sustainability. At the end of 2021, it was 7.9 billion and forecast to reach 9.8 billion in 2050, potentially peaking at nearly 11 billion around 2100. These increases will be more marked in developing countries: a salient figure in population estimates is how Africa's population is set to grow from 1.4 billion in 2021 to 2.5 billion in 2050, also with concomitant changes in consumption patterns.

Population figures depend on birth and death rates and migration. Higher government spending on health care and education leads to lower child mortality, longer life expectancy and a reduction in family size.

Population growth creates opportunities, such as a larger workforce for developing-country economies, and challenges, such as pressure on available space, food and income (see Table 5.5). As economies in developing countries grow, and parts of their population reach middle-class levels of income, consumption and land demands increase. More people will have electricity, televisions and smartphones. Although the middle class is growing, in-country income inequality has increased in many developing countries. Higher-income levels and a growing middle class mean reductions in poverty and increases in justice, well-being and equality.

At the same time, increased consumption requires more resources: higher efficiency and less food waste are called for in agriculture and food production and supply. This means adequate infrastructure and technological innovation as well as more power – preferably renewable electricity (see Table 5.5). Technology will improve and expand (e.g. in health care and digital services). Responsible investors can consider how companies that benefit from this growth are responding to essential ESG issues. The key question is: how can growth and production take place in the most sustainable way? Such companies will present the best opportunities for the investor.

5.4.4 Digitalization

Digitalization means the increase and spread of digital solutions. States, businesses and consumers benefit from digitalization as it brings efficiency to everyday life (see Table 5.6). Because of digitalization, information becomes increasingly available and can be easily used and updated. However, these benefits are only partially reflected in economic statistics: for example, free services, changes in quality of services or intangible capital transfers between countries are not fully reflected in GDP.

Table 5.5 Population growth as an environmental, social and governance factor

Population growth	Background	Outcome and impact
As an environmental factor (E)	Increased population puts pressure on the environment. More natural resources are needed to cover the needs of a larger population.	People migrate to new areas and more land is allocated for agriculture. In existing urban areas, population density increases. Vehicle use increases. The natural habitat of numerous species is destroyed or reduced. Companies either increase their use of natural resources or else recycle or use more efficiently. New technologies lead to new production methods and enable businesses based on a "circular economy."
As a social factor (S)	Access to health care has risen globally and a wider selection of health care services are available. Access to education has increased. More children make it to adulthood. People live longer and healthier lives. Better education levels lead to decreasing birth rates.	Larger and wealthier populations consume more, which requires more efficient and innovative solutions from agricultural and food sectors, as well as from closely related sectors such as logistics and trade. Climate change is accelerating the need to develop activities across sectors. Renewable energy technologies and decentralized energy production bring opportunities for access to electricity in rural areas in developing countries. Efficient and innovative production methods and technologies, e.g. plant protein products, represent global business opportunities in the context of a growing global demand for food. In developing countries, improvement in the status of women and a strengthening of institutions play a crucial role in enabling a better future.
As a governance factor (G)	According to the UN Declaration of Human Rights, everyone has the right to start a family. Means for birth control are available in several countries.	Issues related to population growth and ageing are being addressed both internationally and nationally. As a result of better education and availability of birth control, families are better equipped to choose a suitable family size. For companies offering birth control products, managing population growth is a business opportunity.

Table 5.6 Digitalization as an environmental, social and governance factor

Digitalization	Background	Outcome and impact
As an environmental factor (E)	Investing in digitalization may address megatrends related to the environment; it also enables better data gathering. Yet some digital services are electricity-intensive, and the power may not be from renewable sources. Examples of positive solutions are: smart grids, intelligent transport, energy efficiency in buildings (and related data control), environmental protection (and related data), "circular economy" solutions, health technology and ICT infrastructure.	Digital solutions make it possible to respond to megatrends and to concretize outcomes and impacts. Commuting may decline as a result of remote working. This would reduce vehicle use and hence emissions. However, one outcome of the pandemic might be increased use of cars and decreased use of public transport. Online shopping decreases vehicle use by consumers but increases delivery transportation. Self-driving cars and electric cars will increasingly represent a significant proportion of road vehicles.
As a social factor (S)	Traditional, analogue methods are slower and more prone to errors. Digitalization saves time. Information is transferred at high speed. Communication and information sharing is effortless. Remote working has now not only become possible but is a new normal in many sectors.	Societies become more efficient. Regional disparities may decrease with information, services and goods being available digitally. Digitalization enables companies located in small towns and remote areas to go international and reach a wider market. Consumers and businesses increasingly order goods and services online. Investments are needed for transport, storage and packaging of goods, which benefits those sectors. Various technologies, such as devices and applications, are an intrinsic part of the digitalization infrastructure and may be of interest to responsible investors from an impact perspective (e.g. health technologies). Employees may have more freedom to choose the geographical location of their employer and their status.

(*Continued*)

Digitalization	Background	Outcome and impact
As a governance factor (G)	As digitalization increases, products and services become more efficient.	Although digitalization provides many opportunities, threats such as cybersecurity and information breaches have emerged as important issues. This presents opportunities for companies providing solutions in this field.
	The number of electronic services available has grown exponentially. Online banking, taxation, health-related information, and many other services that concern sensitive personal data, are online. This requires governance, security and a minimum level of quality of systems.	Digitalization also improves the efficiency of societal and corporate functions as it frees time for other revenue-generating activities.

Digitalization has underpinned the development of many companies and provided new opportunities – sensor technologies, robotics, artificial intelligence and digital platforms are some examples. It has expanded companies' reach from local markets to global ones, presenting huge growth opportunities. Remote working (wholly or partially) is becoming the new normal across a number of sectors, making it possible to work from geographically distant locations. Once established, remote working may enable companies to reduce their business premises and related costs, and employees may spend less time and expense on daily travel and business trips – which is also beneficial from an emissions point of view. On the other hand, digitalization raises questions about the transformation of our societies: to what extent do we need to – and indeed should we – re-skill people to work in digital solutions? There are also ethical questions around robotics and artificial intelligence.

5.5 Rising trends

New ESG issues emerge as developments take place in society or scandals come to light. Some trends may turn into established ESG issues whereas some remain less important or even disappear. In the following sections, some selected trends are discussed.

5.5.1 Animal rights

Animal rights form the underlying basis for animal protection and welfare. However, attitudes to the welfare of production animals vary from one jurisdiction to another. In many EU countries, and elsewhere, prophylactic mass treatment of production animals with antibiotics is common. This is deemed necessary as animals often have insufficient space to exhibit their normal behaviour, and therefore become stressed and prone to illnesses. Those interested in animal rights will question whether current levels of animal welfare are sufficient, regardless of legality. Currently, the EU is revising its animal welfare legislation (proposal in 2023), as per its commitment in the Farm to Fork Strategy.

Integration of animal rights considerations in investments is supported by organizations such as Cruelty Free Investments, a California-based non-profit organization that provides investors with information on US-listed companies implicated in the deprivation of animal rights. It evaluates companies using publicly available information such as company websites. Examples of proscribed behaviour include:

- The production or retail of food and drink of animal origin
- The manufacture and sale of clothing of animal origin (such as leather and fur products)
- The manufacture and sale of products that have relied on animal testing
- Animal breeding for food production and animal testing

The key drivers for vegan and vegetarian lifestyle choices include personal health, respect for animal rights and climate awareness. In addition to these consumer-level drivers, there is increasing pressure at the macro level for sustainable and efficient food production throughout the value chain, with the negative impacts of animal-based protein production evident from a climate perspective. Not just meat but dairy products also have vegan alternatives, and companies producing them range from local startups to large multinationals. In the cosmetics industry, vegan and cruelty-free options are expanding. The current global vegan food market size is estimated at around US$25–30 billion and is forecast to grow to around US$160 billion by 2026. Estimated growth figures for the coming decades are strong.

The world's first animal rights exchange-traded fund (ETF) – US Vegan Climate ETF (VEGN) – was launched at the New York Stock Exchange in September 2019. In addition to companies breaching animal rights standards, the ETF excludes tobacco, fossil fuels, weapons and companies violating human rights. There is also a growing number of funds specializing in sustainable food and agriculture innovations.

5.5.2 *Cannabis*

The number of companies linked to cannabis – and their sizes – has grown significantly. This has attracted investor interest in the topic.

Cannabis is a hemp plant that contains different types of cannabinoids, which are responsible for both its health and intoxicating effects, THC (tetrahydrocannabinol) and CBD (cannabidiol) being the best known. THC has an intoxicating effect; CBD does not, but it is the cannabinoid typically referred to with regard to health and medical benefits.

The results of cannabis-related research are partly contradictory, and it is also hampered by the illegality of the product. Regulation on intoxicant cannabis (THC) varies greatly from one jurisdiction to another.

The increase of cannabis, or products containing cannabis, in the market, means that listed companies are also getting involved. As a result, investors are now presented with a number of issues around such products, and these depend on the country in question. For screening purposes, investors might differentiate between recreational and medical uses of cannabis, allowing the latter while excluding the former.

The main environmental impacts associated with cannabis are energy consumption, greenhouse gas emissions, the use of pesticides and water consumption. Products with a high THC content may violate international norms and agreements. It is also relevant for an investor to consider legal aspects, social acceptability and impacts from the consumption of THC. Governance is also a relevant aspect for high-growth companies.

5.5.3 Taxation

Recent years have seen increasing scrutiny on business taxation, with opprobrium for those companies seen not to be paying their fair share. The context is one in which large multinationals especially have paid very little tax in relation to their turnover and financial profit. Some companies have registered their profits in countries with lower taxation or have contrived to show a loss in their country of origin when the profit has in fact been transferred elsewhere (i.e. transfer pricing). This is perceived as unfair because it gives internationally operating companies the advantage over those operating nationally, and the same applies for countries: those with high taxation are more likely to be stable operating environments for companies when there is an educated workforce available; in countries with lower taxation companies may not enjoy similar operating conditions.

A key problem has been the lack of information and transparency, something that has been addressed by an information exchange agreement among OECD countries from 2014. Today, nearly 100 countries exchange their tax information based on automatic information exchange. In 2021, country-by-country tax disclosure saw progress through new EU reporting requirements, and the G20 adopted a global minimum tax rate reform prepared by the OECD.

A tax footprint refers to different kinds of taxes paid by a company. By reporting their tax footprint, companies show a commitment to the transparency of their operations. Responsible investors often follow the corporate tax footprint as part of their ESG assessments. This can raise questions about a company's tax performance, especially if the tax footprint is low in comparison to similar companies in the same jurisdiction. Tax planning is part of normal business practice, but in some cases, the investor may find it appropriate to have a more detailed dialogue with the company.

5.5.4 Human rights

Every person is entitled to their basic human rights, and not to be discriminated against on account of, for example, their nationality, sex, national or ethnic origin, colour, religion or language. In reality, societies, businesses and investors all have work to do to see this basic right applied, as it is not yet a common practice in many jurisdictions.

At the core of human rights is the International Bill of Human Rights which comprises a number of declarations and rights, and the International Labour Organization (ILO)'s Declaration on Fundamental Principles and Rights at Work. Documents that build on these and which are relevant to investors and businesses are the United Nations Guiding Principles on Business and Human Rights (UNGP) and the OECD Guidelines for Multinational Enterprises.

Human rights are relevant for investor consideration as they have both direct and indirect financial impacts. Human rights risks can materialize just as other ESG risks do. The investor's reputation – and business – is also at stake, so this issue is relevant from a stakeholder perspective. Indirectly, addressing human rights risks allows investors to manage megatrends such as climate change and digitalization as enablers of equality and justice.

When assessing investment targets in practice, investors can make use of the UNGP or OECD Guidelines for Multinational Enterprises or they can buy relevant data from ESG data providers. Typical aspects relating to human rights include employee relations, health and safety, modern slavery such as forced labour, and diversity and inclusion. As active owners, investors can also benefit from consideration of these issues by taking action to manage and remediate human rights risks relating to their investments. Through impact investments, investors can contribute to the SDGs, each of which has a bearing on human rights.

5.5.5 Modern slavery

Modern slavery is intrinsically a human rights issue. It means work or services that an individual has to perform under the threat of punishment but which the individual has not offered to do voluntarily. According to ILO estimates, over 40 million people are victims of modern slavery globally, 71% of them women and girls. About 25 million of the victims are in forced labour and 15 million in forced marriages.

Poverty and inequality form the backdrop of modern slavery, with indebtedness associated with around 50% of cases: the debtor must work to pay off the creditor. Debt imprisonment is linked to human trafficking, child exploitation and forced prostitution. It is believed that modern slavery mainly affects paperless immigrants in developed countries who resort to the "grey economy" to survive.

Relevant here for responsible investors is the supply chain of investee companies: does the company have the necessary responsibility policies for its own operations, those of its suppliers, and of those suppliers further along the value chain? It is important that companies have policies and practices that seek to address problems and their root causes. Termination of cooperation or subcontracting agreements does not solve the problem but potentially just externalizes it to others. If a company becomes aware of modern slavery in its own operations or in the supply chain, the prime directive is to take the proper remedial action and address the root causes to ensure that human rights are protected going forward. Investors play an important role in engaging with companies on modern slavery: they can address the issue by developing human rights policies in tandem with companies.

5.5.6 Diversity, equality and inclusion

Diversity, equality and inclusion are also concerns linked to human rights. In an ideal world, companies would have an equal relative distribution of gender, nationality, national or ethnic origin, colour, religion, language and so on in their boards, management and workforce.

This topic is relevant for an investor as there is growing evidence of financial implications. For example, companies with diverse boards seem to provide a better financial return.

In practice, responsible investors can address diversity, equality and inclusion at a policy level, and bring these considerations into investment decision-making – thereby contributing to the SDGs. This can be done by analysing companies' sustainability reports, making use of external ESG data and through best practice as active owners.

Chapter 5 key Q&As

Here are the answers to the key questions posed at the start of this chapter.

How can we assess the material ESG issues of an investment?

A consideration of ESG issues and their financial implications is, ultimately, investment-target specific and comprises a sum-total of the issues under assessment. The starting point is deciding which ESG issues are important for the investor, as outlined in the Responsible Investment policy. These are then compared with the ESG issues relevant both to the investment target and to the sector.

How do we consider megatrends and other rising trends in investment decision-making?

Megatrends are broad global issues that are changing our operating environment. They often consist of individual, smaller trends. For companies, megatrends can represent business opportunities, or they may force companies to update their business models. A responsible investor can consider how megatrends affect different sectors: is growth a likely path as a result of that megatrend (or rising trend), or will the opposite be true? Potential future regulation can also impact a sector's prospects.

Bibliography

Ahlroth, P. (2022). Personal Communication on Biodiversity. 18 January 2022.

Bloomberg Intelligence. (2021). "Plant-Based Food Sales to Increase Fivefold By 2030, BI Says". Retrieved 16 January 2022 from https://www.bloomberg.com/news/articles/2021-08-11/plant-based-food-sales-to-increase-fivefold-by-2030-bi-says

Cruelty Free Investing. (n.d.). "Cruelty Free Investing". Retrieved 16 January 2022 from http://crueltyfreeinvesting.org

Euromonitor. (n.d.). "The Rise of Vegan and Vegetarian Food". Retrieved 16 January 2022 from https://www.euromonitor.com/the-rise-of-vegan-and-vegetarian-food/report

European Commission (n.d.). "Animal Welfare". Retrieved 16 January 2022 from https://ec.europa.eu/food/animals/animal-welfare_en

European Commission. (n.d.). "Animal Welfare in Practice". Retrieved 16 January 2022 from https://ec.europa.eu/food/animals/animal-welfare/animal-welfare-practice_en

European Commission. (n.d.). "The Just Transition Mechanism: Making Sure No One Is Left Behind". Retrieved 16 January 2022 from https://ec.europa.eu/info/strategy/priorities-2019-2024/european-green-deal/finance-and-green-deal/just-transition-mechanism_en

Expert Market Research. (n.d.). "Reports". Retrieved 16 January 2022 from https://www.expertmarketresearch.com/reports/vegan-food-market

Goda, T., & Garcia, A.T. (2017). "The Rising Tide of Absolute Global Income Inequality During 1850–2010: Is It Driven by Inequality within or between Countries?" *Social Indicators Research*, 130, 1,051–1,072.

HM Treasury. (2021). "The Economics of Biodiversity: The Dasgupta Review". Retrieved 16 January 2022 from https://assets.publishing.service.gov.uk/government/uploads/system/uploads/attachment_data/file/962785/The_Economics_of_Biodiversity_The_Dasgupta_Review_Full_Report.pdf

Hytti, J. (2022). Personal communication on Human Rights. 17 January 2022.

Intergovernmental Panel on Climate Change (IPCC). (n.d.). "AR6 Climate Change 2021: The Physical Science Basis". Retrieved 16 January 2022 from https://www.ipcc.ch/report/ar6/wg1

International Labour Organization. (2021). "ILO Welcomes COP26 Just Transition Declaration". Retrieved 27 February 2022 from https://www.ilo.org/global/about-the-ilo/newsroom/news/WCMS_826717/lang--en/index.htm

Laaksonen, M. (2022). Personal communication on Digitalization. 17 January 2022.

McKinsey & Company. (n.d.). "Delivering through Diversity". Retrieved 16 January 2022 from https://www.mckinsey.com/~/media/mckinsey/business functions/organization/our insights/delivering through diversity/delivering-through-diversity_full-report.ashx#:~:text=Ethnic%20and%20cultural%20diversity%27s%20correlation,likely%20to%20experience%20higher%20profits.

Mijs, J.J.B. (2021). The Paradox of Inequality: Income Inequality and Belief in Meritocracy Go Hand in Hand". *Socio-Economic Review*, 19(1), 7–35.

OECD. (2020). "International Community Continues Making Progress against Offshore Tax Evasion". Retrieved 16 January 2022 from https://www.oecd. org/newsroom/international-community-continues-making-progress-against-offshore-tax-evasion.htm

Sumelius, J. (2022). Personal Communication on Population growth. 14 January 2022.

Swedish Foundation for Strategic Environmental Research MISTRA. (2021). "Background Paper: Aligning Markets with Biodiversity". Retrieved 16 January 2022 from https://www.mistra.org/wp-content/uploads/2021/06/mistra-bp-aligning-markets-with-biodiversity-2021.pdf

Taskforce on Nature-related Financial Disclosures. (n.d.). "TNFD Proposed Technical Scope". Retrieved 16 January 2022 from https://tnfd.global/publications/

United Nations. (n.d.). "The Paris Agreement". Retrieved 16 January 2022 from https://www.un.org/en/climatechange/paris-agreement

United Nations Populations Fund. (n.d.). "World Population Dashboard". Retrieved 16 January 2022 from https://www.unfpa.org/data/world-population-dashboard

World Bank. (2021). "Protecting Nature Could Avert Global Economic Losses of $2.7 Trillion Per Year". Retrieved 16 January 2022 from https://www.worldbank. org/en/news/press-release/2021/07/01/protecting-nature-could-avert-global-economic-losses-of-usd2-7-trillion-per-year

World Business Council for Sustainable Development. (n.d.). "What Does Nature-Positive Mean for Business?" Retrieved 16 January 2022 from https:// www.wbcsd.org/contentwbc/download/13439/196253/1

World Economic Forum. (2020). "Nature Risk Rising: Why the Crisis Engulfing Nature Matters for Business and the Economy". Retrieved 16 January 2022 from https://www.weforum.org/reports/nature-risk-rising-why-the-crisis-engulfing-nature-matters-for-business-and-the-economy

World Economic Forum. (2022). "The Global Risks Report 2022". 17th Edition. Retrieved 16 January 2022 from https://www3.weforum.org/docs/WEF_The_Global_Risks_Report_2022.pdf

World Economic Forum. (n.d.). "75% of Crops Depend on Pollinators: They Must Be Protected". Retrieved 16 January 2022 from https://www.weforum.org/agenda/2019/12/protect-pollinators-food-security-biodiversity-agriculture/

Worldometer. (n.d.). "Current World Population". Retrieved 16 January 2022 from https://www.worldometers.info/world-population/

6 Responsible Investment approaches

Key questions in this chapter

- What are the main Responsible Investment approaches?
- How do you choose the right approaches?

The incorporation of Responsible Investment (RI) into overall investment processes has to be done in phases. Having defined the investment strategy, the relevant philosophy and the key drivers for the integration of environmental, social and governance (ESG), the next step is to choose the suitable RI approach (or approaches) (see Figure 6.1).

The main RI approaches are: active ownership (including engagement and voting); ESG integration; impact; screening (including positive, negative and norm-based); and thematic investments. Each approach has both benefits and challenges which must be carefully considered. This chapter presents these main approaches in alphabetical order, although ESG integration, screening and active ownership are far more commonly used compared to impact and thematic (see Table 6.1 later in this chapter).

6.1 Active ownership

The French literary artist Honoré de Balzac famously wrote in 1835 that *"noblesse oblige."* One could translate that as "with wealth, power and prestige come responsibilities." This is equally applicable to ownership rights. Investing in company shares quite literally means owning a share of a company. This ownership creates the potential for return on investment but, it is argued, also confers responsibility for that company's actions and impacts. Investors can choose to proactively use their ownership rights to create a positive impact, reduce risks, improve investment returns and/or better understand the entities in which they are invested. Investors can use their voting rights, company meetings and engagement as means to achieve their stated goals. All this behaviour falls within the active ownership approach.

Active ownership does not mean confrontation with the company management, in a way that is often associated with shareholder activism. Rather,

DOI: 10.4324/9781003284932-7

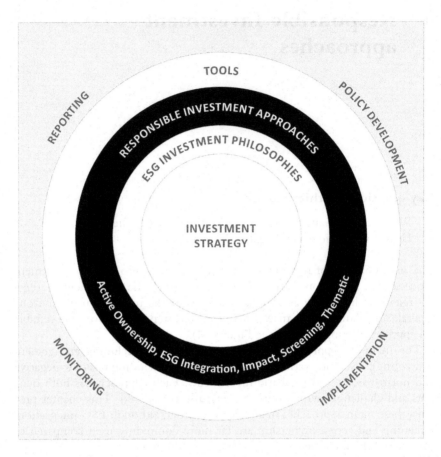

Figure 6.1 Responsible Investment approaches as a next step after investment philosophy

active ownership typically involves private action, with no media coverage, to gain trust among the parties. Investors might publish the company names, overall progress, or the themes of engagement, but not the actual details of the discussions.

A company can be evaluated according to its conduct, the products or services it provides, or a combination of the two. Figure 6.2 shows a universe of potential investment targets plotted according to how they are scored on the responsibility of both their conduct and products. In the top–right corner are companies with both behaviour and product evaluated as most responsible within its peer-group universe. In the bottom-left corner are companies that are failing to meet such responsibility requirements at both levels. Through an active ownership approach, investors can influence a company to improve its conduct- and/or product-level responsibility. The process for choosing

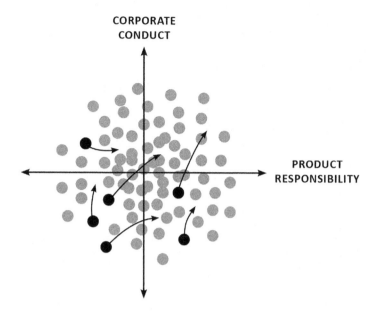

Figure 6.2 Map of the potential investment universe: an illustration of active ownership activities improving company behaviour or the responsibility of
manufactured products

active ownership activities, and companies with which to make contact, is
usually described in RI and ownership policy documents. The main activities within the active ownership approach – engagement, company meetings
and voting – are covered in the following sections.

6.1.1 Engagement

Engagement is defined as a specific activity by means of which the investor
aims to influence a company's behaviour or strategy, or to increase understanding around a particular topic or potential problem area. The engagement
process happens in phases, including but not limited to: researching the topic,
setting an agenda, formulating an engagement strategy, estimating timelines,
and planning further action. Engagement can be either proactive or reactive.

In proactive engagement, the investor seeks to improve its understanding
of a topic or to highlight potential problems without any negative incident or
event having already occurred.

In reactive engagement, some undesired incident or event has already occurred. Here, the investor persuades the company to desist from the unwanted
activities – such as breaches of international norms or local legislation –
remedy its failures and change company policy to avoid reoccurrences. Other

failures to meet investors' ESG requirements might include the continued pursuit of business activities with high dependence on fossil fuels.

Engagement is an alternative to exclusion. An investor initiates an engagement process to prevent undesirable behaviour from actually happening rather than simply excluding the company from the investment universe. Engagement can be a powerful means of creating a positive impact and remedying a negative one. As engagement is usually conducted privately, an investor may face scrutiny from stakeholders about the effectiveness of the engagement and the true motivations behind it. If no details are made available, stakeholders might struggle to view engagement as a credible tool rather than a mere gimmick of which the sole purpose is to hold on to an investment.

Successful engagement requires resources and access to extensive information. Company actions, policies, relevant legislation and international norms, market practices and stakeholder impact – these all need to be researched in advance to guarantee fruitful discussions and to allow progress to be measured. Building dialogue and a trusting relationship take time. Engagement topics vary – from human rights issues to complex production methods and supply chains – and results will not be immediate. For example, developing a human rights policy will take more time than might be imagined in order to see it fully implemented at all levels of a multinational corporation. To mitigate stakeholder concerns and to maintain the consistency of the engagement process, the process should be well documented.

Engagement can be undertaken individually or collectively. The latter, where a group of investors pool resources rather than approaching the same company individually, are referred to as "collaborative engagements." Engagement is resource-intensive, so some investors use a specialized service provider to plan, conduct and document the process on their behalf. Outsourcing like this facilitates the pooling of resources. Furthermore, when assets under management are pooled, investors' influence on the company can be enhanced.

6.1.1.1 Documenting the engagement process

A comprehensive engagement document should have, at a minimum, the following elements:

- An engagement agenda declaring the target company, the engagement topic and the reason for engagement
- The desired outcome of the engagement and an estimated timeline
- Steps taken during the engagement and planned next steps
- An evaluation of progress so far
- Steps to be taken if the desired outcome is not reached (a so-called "escalation strategy")

The documentation develops as the engagement progresses because the outcome and timeline can change in the light of further information and a deeper understanding of the topic by the investor. The documentation itself does not need to be public, but a more general communication of the process will increase the credibility of the process.

Engagement case: Nordic Engagement Cooperation

Asset owner
Area: Nordic investors, global portfolios
AuM: total €182 billion

Nordic Engagement Cooperation (NEC) is a collaborative engagement between a small number of Nordic pension investors. NEC uses a service provider to research the cases, coordinate company discussions and maintain documentation. The investors collectively choose themes to be further researched and companies with which to engage. The cases are divided between the participating investors so that there is always a lead investor responsible for each engagement strategy. NEC publishes an annual report in which it categorizes the engagements as either proactive or norm-based (reactive).

Water crises have been identified as a major risk by the World Economic Forum's 2020 Global Risk Report, and this motivated NEC to take water management as a proactive engagement theme:

NEC has chosen to initially focus its attention on two companies that were identified as being of common interest to all NEC members, with the plan to further select two companies in 2021. These companies are Anheuser-Busch InBev (AB InBev) and AkzoNobel, which operate in water-scarce regions. Both companies already acknowledge the dependence of their operations on sound water management and have been responsive to the engagement. First calls were held in 2020 and the dialogue will continue in 2021, aiming for meaningful progress in the companies' water risk management efforts and related reporting.

Previous proactive themes included sustainable cotton. The food-sector Task Force on Climate-related Financial Disclosures (TCFD) reporting engagement is ongoing at the time of writing.

The 2020 annual report names the target companies, the reasons for engaging with them, and provides information on progress and company responses. It also lays out anticipated next steps.

The chosen proactive engagement themes have been identified with contributions towards specific UN Sustainable Development Goals (SDGs), which helps report readers to appreciate the expected overall impact of engagement efforts.

Source: NEC Annual Report 2020

6.1.2 Meeting with company executives

Key channels of communication between investors and issuers are: letter writing, participation in investor initiatives, and asking relevant ESG questions at investor meetings and capital markets days (CMD). Shareholders and bondholders can meet with company executives without it entailing an official engagement process, and therefore without the need for extensive documentation. Sometimes this is how an engagement process starts when an investor sees the need for increased dialogue.

Group meetings can be convened for announcements of results or on CMDs, for example. Institutional investors and significant retail investors tend to meet companies regularly in a one-on-one format. In tandem with letter-writing campaigns, this can achieve results while using fewer resources compared to a lengthy engagement process. In these cases, however, the direct impact created is harder to quantify.

6.1.3 Proxy voting

Proxy voting usually refers to the exercise of shareholder voting rights at company annual general meetings (AGMs) and extraordinary general meetings (EGMs). Here, the investor appoints a representative (proxy) to cast a vote either at an in-person meeting or electronically. In such meetings, shareholders vote on approval of annual accounts, discharging and selecting board members and auditors, or issuance of shares or share purchase programs; they might also receive financial or other relevant information about the company's activities. All of the above are dependent on the company's jurisdiction. Rather than physically attending these meetings, which can add up to hundreds in total and sometimes involve a lot of travel, institutional investors and asset managers will often cast their votes electronically, which has to be done in advance (sometimes well in advance) of the meeting. It is therefore incumbent on companies to produce comprehensive meeting documentation in a timely manner so that investors can make informed decisions.

Going through hundreds (or even thousands) of meeting notes is time-consuming. Some investors use service providers whose voting data allows them to analyse meeting resolutions more quickly and through whose voting systems they can cast votes.

Fixed-income investors can attend bondholder meetings. Here, rather than on company strategy, board composition or other shareholder rights topics, the investor can vote on specific clauses within the bond documentation (formal meetings) and acquire information about the company (informal meetings). This is a less frequent activity compared to voting in shareholder meetings. Formal bondholder meetings are rarely held.

Other asset classes might hold unit-holder meetings or similar. Usually, voting rights are based on shareholding, unit-holding or similar metrics.

6.2 ESG integration

ESG integration is a widespread approach within responsible investing. It simply means that ESG research, objectives and outcomes are integrated within the investment decision-making process. Investors applying an ESG integration approach tend to view ESG issues as having financial impacts. It therefore makes sense to incorporate ESG research within the traditional financial analysis.

There is no universal definition of ESG integration, as each investor can define how they seek to integrate ESG into investment processes. The Principles for Responsible Investment (PRI) defines integration as "the systematic and explicit inclusion of material ESG factors into investment analysis and investment decisions." PRI uses the broader term "ESG inclusion" when referring jointly to the approaches of integration, screening and thematic (including impact).

What ESG integration does not do is exclude individual companies or sectors based on predefined criteria. This means the potential investment universe includes companies in all four quadrants of Figure 6.3. Investors select companies that fulfil investors' overall investment criteria while taking ESG issues into consideration. Companies can be found in the bottom-left quadrant although in reality they are more likely to be in the top-right quadrant. The highlighted dots in Figure 6.3 represent companies selected in a

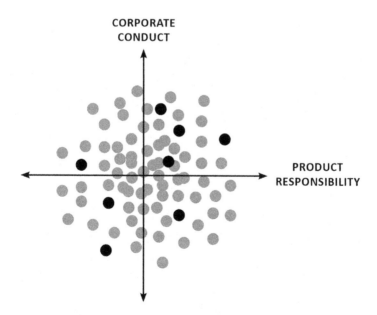

Figure 6.3 Map of the potential investment universe: an illustration of ESG integration

portfolio. Companies performing relatively poorly against their peers can be subjected to an engagement process if the investor in question also incorporates active ownership approaches into the overall investment processes.

ESG integration implies a systematic approach in evaluating ESG risks and opportunities in investment decision-making. Investors can use internal tools such as ESG fact sheets, templates and databases or external data provided by specialized service providers. What is key is how the ESG data is used alongside other information to reach an investment decision. Within the ESG integration approach, portfolio managers and analysts might have access to internal or external ESG specialists, but the ESG data is not used as an add-on or separate checklist. ESG data is an integral part of the bottom-up decision-making by portfolio managers and analysts.

The drawback of ESG integration is this lack of firm definition. It is not always clear whether an approach can be classified as ESG integration, and it is a challenge to ensure that ESG is truly integrated into investment processes not just in reporting or marketing material. The approach has practical

---

Case study on ESG integration: Boston Trust Walden

Asset manager
Area: US, developed market portfolios
AuM: $15 billion

Boston Trust Walden defines their ESG integration as follows:

ESG integration, the process of assessing the potential financial materiality (or significance) of environmental, social and corporate governance factors, is an integral part of our process to identify high quality companies. ESG analysis bolsters traditional fundamental analysis by helping us better understand and interpret a company's past performance (its profitability, growth, stability, etc.), and provides an important lens through which to assess the ability of a company to perpetuate past success. We therefore believe it is important to consider a company's management of significant ESG risks and opportunities as part of our fiduciary duty to all clients.

Boston Trust Walden's ESG integration process has three phases: "identifying potentially material ESG considerations, based on a company's business model and industry, among other factors; gathering information; and evaluating performance." The analysts assess the risks and opportunities and the impacts on revenue, expenses, assets, liabilities and overall risk of potential or existing investments using a proprietary framework.

Source: Boston Trust Walden Public PRI
Transparency Report 2020

implementation challenges, too. How can an investment organization system-atically integrate ESG not just across asset classes but also among individual portfolio managers and analysts while guaranteeing that all relevant ESG risks and opportunities are accounted for? And how are they to define the material risks and opportunities to be considered within the investment process?

These challenges can be tackled, however, by means of clear policy state-ments and process descriptions, training, internal tools, external data, port-folio ESG quality monitoring, remuneration and transparent reporting. International reporting standards are a helpful tool in identifying material ESG issues for individual companies or entire sectors. These standards and taxonomies are being constantly developed and refined.

6.3 Impact as an approach

Impact investing has already been introduced in Chapter 1 as an investment philosophy in which the financial return comes second to the measurable impact generated. However, impact investing is also an RI approach in which the investor seeks market–rate returns alongside the ability "to generate pos-itive, measurable social and environmental impact," as defined by Global Impact Investment Network (GIIN). A predefined measurable impact has become a standard feature of impact investing, even though GIIN does not include this requirement in their definition.

Impact investing as an approach involves the evaluation of the investment targets using three dimensions: risk, return and impact. Figure 6.4 shows

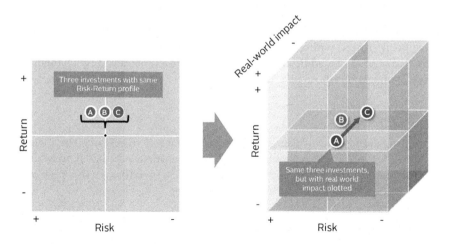

Figure 6.4 Impact investing provides a third dimension alongside risk and return
Source: PRI

how two investment targets might have similar risk–return profiles but the addition of an impact dimension allows for differentiation.

Originally, impact investing was seen as an approach more suitable for private assets because measurement of the impact and of relevant impact elements and characteristics was deemed too complex to be adequately defined and quantified for listed securities. Today, impact investing is not just limited to project financing or microloans but can be applied to both listed and non-listed securities and assets, including real assets. However, due care must be taken to avoid "impact washing," where positive societal impacts are overestimated and negative ones underestimated – whether knowingly or unknowingly. To avoid impact washing, the investor needs to keep up to date with the constantly developing market standards, frameworks and best practices. One of the most commonly used impact definitions is the one provided by GIIN.

6.3.1 Elements of impact investing

In addition to a broad definition of impact, GIIN provides a list of significant factors to help define impact investing:

1 Investors have an intention to generate a positive impact.
2 The investment is expected to generate a financial return.
3 The return on investment generated can vary between below-market rate to risk-adjusted rates and also include a wide spectrum of asset classes.[1]
4 Investors are committed to the measurement and reporting of the impacts generated and progress made, including the setting of performance targets and metrics.

Some investors will require additional impact to classify their investments as impact investing. Here, additionality means that the impact would not have been created without the investment. As an example, additionality can be calculated as the additional carbon sequestration achieved by changes in forest management post-investment.

6.4 Screening

Screening simply means using predetermined factors to research the investment universe to find investable assets. The screening can be based on a company's products and services or the way it operates. Investors use this approach to create negative or positive screens and/or tilts.

6.4.1 Negative screening

Negative screening means using predetermined factors to restrict the potential investment universe. The factors can be based on products and raw

**Case study on impact investing: Government
employees pension fund of South Africa (GEPF)**

Asset owner
Area: Africa, global portfolios
AuM: $129 billion

A proportion of the assets of the Fund will be designated for newly
formed black owned asset managers in order to encourage the development of black professionals in the investment management area, with
benchmarks and risk parameters which will be more tightly managed
than those applicable to the specialist portfolios until such time as experience has been gained.

GEPF has a developmental investment policy "whose objective is to
earn good returns for the members and pensioners of the Fund while
supporting positive, long-term economic, social and environmental
outcomes for South Africa." The developmental investment policy lists
four key themes: "Economic infrastructure, Social infrastructure, Sustainable future (green economy) and Job creation, new enterprises and
broad-based black economic empowerment."

GEPF uses key development indicators (KDIs) to measure impact
created through unlisted investments. The KDIs relate to various social
and environmental aspects such as number of minority-owned SMEs
funded, megawatts of energy sourced from renewable and clean energy,
number of farm workers with access to health care and/or education
and number of housing projects and houses built.

The Fund's approach to developmental or impact investing is to invest for a return that also provides positive outcomes by creating jobs,
addressing high levels of inequality and transformation imperatives,
providing energy security, mitigating and adapting to the impacts of
climate change and providing access to quality education and health
care. This approach is part of the GEPF's long-term thinking on Responsible Investment and forms part of their strategy and investment
beliefs.

Source: GEPF Public PRI Transparency Report 2020, Annual
Report 2020/2021, GEPF Investment Policy Statement

materials sourced and manufactured – to exclude sectors such as alcohol or
fossil fuels – or based on company behaviour to exclude individual companies
such as those that breach international norms like the UN Global Compact.
Norm-based screening is primarily a reactive approach because it recognizes
past events and their impacts. However, it does not need to be a passive RI

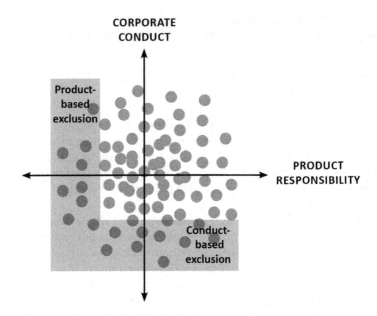

Figure 6.5 Map of the potential investment universe: an illustration of product-based and conduct-based exclusion

approach: the investor can seek an engagement process with the investee company to discourage breaches of norms as an alternative to exclusion.

The excluded companies in Figure 6.5 are those situated within the grey shading. The size of this area is dependent on the level and scope of restrictions. A company performing poorly on corporate conduct assessment would find itself near the bottom of the vertical axis irrespective of how responsible its manufactured product might be. Alternatively, a company could perform very well on conduct-based screening but its products are considered detrimental to human health, for example, leading to a high position on the vertical axis but a far-left position on the horizontal axis, resulting in exclusion. Broad exclusion policies can ultimately lead to only the top-right quadrant remaining as the potential investment universe after screening.

Exclusions can include both ethical and financial considerations. Ethical exclusions represent a negative screening approach based on the investor's beliefs or societal norms. Financial exclusions, on the other hand, are based on an understanding that the current valuation models do not price risks correctly. An investor does not want to take on such an elevated risk without financial compensation. This particular approach is often used to exclude coal or other fossil fuels.

6.4.2 Positive screening

Positive screening is the opposite to negative screening and exclusions. Companies that meet predefined criteria are *added* into the potential investment

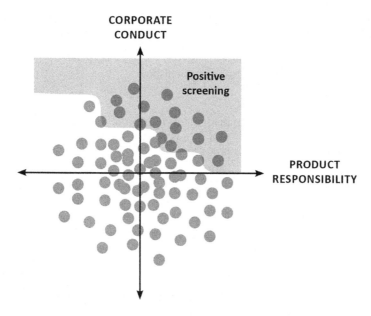

Figure 6.6 Map of the potential investment universe: an illustration of positive screening

universe. The most common positive screening method is the best-in-class approach, where an investor chooses only those companies that perform best in their peer group based on a set of predetermined factors, such as ESG ratings or scores, emissions data, energy efficiency, etc.

If we look at the map of the investment universe again (Figure 6.6), we see that only companies that are performing well enough on conduct-based or product-based screening are added into the portfolio. The size of the grey area (which in this case is positive) once again depends on the level and scope of screening criteria.

6.4.3 Tilting

Instead of exclusion or inclusion of companies or sectors based on predefined screens, there is an approach available to investors known as "tilting," whereby specific issuers or sectors are overweighted or underweighted. Excluding certain sectors can lead to unwanted sectoral biases. These biases can be reduced by limiting the sectoral exposure without having to exclude the sector in its entirety (negative tilting).

Alternatively, investors can increase portfolio weights at issuer or sector level based on predefined ESG criteria (positive tilting). Positive tilts also admit poorer-performing companies providing the overall portfolio have a greater positive performance than the selected benchmark.

Case study on ESG screening: NBIM (Norges Bank Investment Management)

Asset owner
Area: Norway, global multi-asset portfolios
AuM: $1.4 trillion

NBIM is the investment management division of the Norwegian Central Bank ("Norges Bank") and is responsible for investing the Norwegian Government Pension Fund Global. As a manager of the fund on behalf of the Norwegian people, it aims to achieve long-term returns with an acceptable level of risk as defined in the mandate laid down by the Ministry of Finance.

The Ministry of Finance has issued ethically motivated guidelines for the observation and exclusion of companies from the fund. The fund must not be invested in companies that produce certain types of weapons, base their operations on coal, or produce tobacco (product-based exclusions). Nor may the fund be invested in companies whose conduct contributes to violations of fundamental ethical norms (conduct-based exclusions). The Ministry of Finance has set up an independent Council on Ethics to make ethical assessments of companies and to send its recommendations to Norges Bank. The Executive Board of Norges Bank makes the final decision on exclusion, observation or active ownership. Excluded companies are removed from the fund's benchmark index. By not investing in companies whose products or conduct are considered unethical, the fund's exposure to unacceptable risks that could damage its credibility is reduced.

In addition to ethical exclusions, NBIM has introduced risk-based divestments which are investment decisions made by NBIM, and not decisions made on the basis of a recommendation by the Council on Ethics. The purpose of risk-based divestments is to reduce the fund's exposure to companies that operate in ways that are not considered sustainable. The scope of risk-based divestment framework was broadened in 2021 to include companies to be added by the index provider to the broad benchmark index. Through the pre-screening process, NBIM is able to identify companies with particularly high sustainability risks before they enter the fund's portfolio as the fund is expected to be invested in all companies in the index. Information gained from pre-screening may lead to risk-based divestments.

Source: NBIM press release 2021; NBIM
Ethical Guidelines 2017

6.5 Thematic

Thematic investing is an approach in which the investor chooses a theme on which the investments are based. It is a much broader approach than simply a portfolio of green bonds or sustainability bonds. Thematic investment is not an asset class: the theme can be carried across asset classes or used in a single portfolio section. All investments within the thematic portfolio need to be attributed to the selected theme(s). The theme can relate to sustainability, water, animal rights or positive societal impacts, to name a few examples.

Thematic investments and assets within the thematic portfolio can be classified as impact investing as long as the definition of predefined and measurable impact is fulfilled. In recent years, central banks have become increasingly interested in incorporating ESG into investment decision-making, with many articulating a desire to add green and sustainability bonds into their portfolios. In most cases, such investments should correctly be classified as thematic, as the positive impact achieved through, for example, emissions avoided is only measured and reported post-investment rather than being a determining factor before the investment is made.

Thematic investing shares similarities with positive tilting and screening. In thematic investing, all the investments selected into the portfolio must contribute to the chosen theme. Figure 6.7 shows how the theme might include companies that perform poorly on conduct-based assessments but qualify for

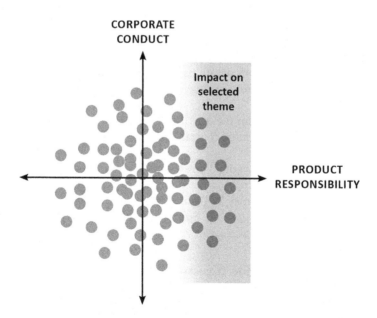

Figure 6.7 Map of the potential investment universe: an illustration of thematic investment

the portfolio because they have a strong contribution to the theme. In practice, many investors apply minimum ESG criteria to company conduct and sometimes do engagement simultaneously, leading to a more limited thematic investment universe.

Case study on thematic investment: central banks

Asset owners
Area: Global, global portfolios
AuM: N/A

According to the December 2020 progress report of the Network of Central Banks and Supervisors for Greening the Financial System (NGFS), 76% of respondents have green or other thematic SSA (sovereign, supranational and agency) bonds in their policy portfolios (portfolios used for monetary policy operations) and almost 70% hold green or other thematic SSA bonds in their own investment portfolios (investment portfolios without a monetary policy dimension). That is a significant rise in comparison to their previous survey of 2019 where just over 60% of respondents had these bonds in their policy portfolios and 40% in their own investment portfolios.

Some of this growth can be attributed to the overall growth of the green bond market and the inclusion of green bonds into market indices. However, some central banks have also highlighted thematic investment as an applicable RI approach, with targets set for allocation.

Central banks that have established a green bond target allocation point to a number of considerations for doing so, including obtaining market intelligence, helping to develop the market, and mitigating reputational risks.

However, the greenium (i.e. the lower yield due to the greenness of the product) is of concern to central banks, as expressed in the NGFS progress report:

The potential existence of a "greenium" is mentioned by other central banks as one of the reasons for being more cautious in adopting a target allocation, as this may be incompatible with their fiduciary duty.

Source: NGFS Progress Report 2020

6.6 Selecting Responsible Investment approaches

Finding the right approach can seem complicated at first as there are so many to choose from. It is important to understand that the choice is not limited to a single approach: an investor can choose multiple approaches and use them simultaneously.

Table 6.1 Assets under management (AuM) invested according to Responsible
Investment approach

Responsible Investment approach	Assets under management following this approach (US$ billion)
ESG integration	25,195
Screening (negative, norm-based and positive screening combined)	20,554
Negative screening	15,030
Norm-based screening	4,140
Positive/best-in-class	1,384
Active ownership	10,504
Thematic	1,948
Impact	352

Source: Global Sustainable Investment Alliance, *Global Sustainable Investment Review 2020*

The recent *Global Sustainable Investment Review 2020* revealed that ESG integration, closely followed by screening, is the most commonly applied RI approach. The data in Table 6.1 shows the relevant significance of each approach. Impact investing is still the least commonly applied approach in absolute numbers, although it is believed to be currently showing the highest growth rate of all approaches.

Before selecting an approach, it is essential to consider how it will affect overall investment objectives. Negative screening may adversely impact liquidity and return, if the screens applied restrict the investment universe too much. On the other hand, excluded sectors might perform worse than the overall market which may lead to better performance both in absolute terms and relative terms (compared to broad market benchmarks). Thematic investments or positive screening can lead to sectoral biases and unintentional overweights or underweights if not carefully constructed. By using thematic and impact investing, investors can gain a valuable and deep understanding of the risks and opportunities related to the theme as well as create a positive impact. Active ownership may not be suitable for investors who wish to remain passive and neutral and do not seek to influence the companies or entities in which they invest.

Availability of resources may dictate the extent to which investors can implement a given RI approach. Some approaches, especially active ownership, can be very resource-intensive and therefore not suitable for a resource-constrained investor. Others, such as negative screening, are more cost-effective in incorporating ESG issues into investment decision-making yet they may lack nuance and the more detailed analytical aspects. Rather than doing everything in-house, there are multiple possibilities for outsourcing RI approaches. Data and service providers sell ESG research, screening, voting and engagement services. External fund managers can implement – for example – ESG integration, screening and impact approaches on behalf of investors. Chapter 7 describes how the different RI approaches can be applied across asset classes.

Table 6.2 outlines the most common RI approaches and lists their benefits and challenges.

Whether or not an investor chooses one or a number of RI approaches within the portfolio, it is important that they act transparently and report regularly on them, as well as on the RI activities and processes.

Table 6.2 The benefits and challenges of Responsible Investment approaches

	Brief description	*Benefits*	*Challenges*
Active ownership, including engagement	Using ownership rights to exert power and/or to create change	Reduce risks, provide feedback to companies, act as a catalyst for change	Resource-intensive
ESG integration	Systematically integrating ESG research, outcomes and impacts within the investment decision-making process	Better overall risks and opportunities evaluation process	No universal definition of which ESG issues are to be considered or how to include them in the investment processes
Impact	Creating measurable positive societal impact through investments	Creating positive impact and change through investments	Predefinition of measurable impacts; accurate measurement of the impact attributed to the investment
Screening	Using predetermined filters to define the investable universe or to tilt portfolio weights	A simple and often cost-effective means of adding ESG into the investment processes	Liquidity and return constraints if the screens significantly restrict the investment universe; it does not easily allow for case-by-case justification and detailed analytics
Thematic	Selecting holdings that actively contribute to the chosen theme; all holdings must be linked to the theme	The ability to incorporate a meaningful theme across the investments, and create positive impact in the selected theme	Unintentional tilts and biases if the theme is used broadly across the portfolio

Chapter 6 key Q&As

Here are the answers to the key questions posed at the start of this chapter.

What are the main Responsible Investment approaches?

The main RI approaches are: active ownership (including engagement and voting), ESG integration, impact investing, screening (including positive, negative and norm based) and thematic investments. Each approach has its unique benefits and challenges which need to be carefully considered before applying it to the overall investment processes.

Investors can use multiple approaches simultaneously as the approaches can be complementary. Some approaches are only suitable for certain asset classes or for a particular section of the investor's portfolio.

How do you choose the right approaches?

Choosing suitable RI approaches is one of the steps in incorporating RI into overall investment processes. Having defined investment strategy and philosophy, and understood the key drivers for integrating ESG, an investor is ready to select one or a number of RI approaches. The key is to align values, needs and investment processes with RI approaches to build a coherent combination. Whether investments are done directly or indirectly will have an impact on the choice of approach, as will the availability of resources. Investors that mainly use external fund managers may prefer to concentrate on ESG integration and choose asset managers that are active in engagement and voting. Other investors might choose only external fund managers that allow them to exercise their voting rights directly. Each case is unique and careful consideration is needed when selecting approaches.

Note

1 If the expected return falls below market rates, this approach belongs to the impact investing philosophy rather than the Responsible Investment philosophy (see Chapter 1).

Bibliography

Boston Trust Walden. (2021). *Public PRI Reporting Framework 2020.* Retrieved February 19, 2022 from https://reporting.unpri.org/surveys/PRI-reporting-framework-2020/8D6A1223-509A-48CF-805D-8C9639627407/79894dbc337a4 0828d895f9402aa63de/html/2/?lang=en&a=1

Brest, P., & Born, K. (2013, 14 August). "Unpacking the Impact in Impact Investing". *Stanford Social Innovation Review.* Retrieved 19 February 2022 from https://ssir.org/articles/entry/unpacking_the_impact_in_impact_investing

Finsif. (2021). *Vastuullisen sijoittamisen opas 2021.* Retrieved 19 February 2022 from https://www.finsif.fi/vastuullisen-sijoittamisen-opas/

Global Impact Investing Network. (2022). "What You Need to Know about Impact Investing". Retrieved 19 February 2022 from https://thegiin.org/impact-investing/need-to-know/#what-is-impact-investing

Global Sustainable Investment Alliance. (2021). *Global Sustainable Investment Review 2020*. Retrieved 19 February 2022 from http://www.gsi-alliance.org/wp-content/uploads/2021/08/GSIR-20201.pdf

Government Employees Pension Fund of South Africa. (2021). *Public PRI Reporting Framework 2020*. Retrieved 19 February 2022 from https://reporting.unpri.org/surveys/PRI-reporting-framework-2020/07EC0B5D-08C8-4003-A5D0-ECF2A93A29B2/79894dbc337a40828d895f9402aa63de/html/2/?lang=en&a=1

Government Employees Pension Fund of South Africa. (2021). *GEPF Annual Report 2020/2021*. Retrieved 19 February 2022 from https://www.gepf.gov.za/wp-content/uploads/2021/11/GEPF-Annual-Report-2020%EF%80%A221-30-September-2021.pdf

Government Employees Pension Fund of South Africa. (2021). *Investment Policy Statement*. Retrieved 19 February 2022 from https://www.gepf.gov.za/wp-content/uploads/2019/08/GEPF_Investment_Policy_Statement.pdf

Hyrske, A., Lönnroth, M., Savilaakso, A., & Sievänen, R. (2020). *Vastuullinen sijoittaja*. Helsingin kauppakamari.

IFRS. (2021). "An Update on the ISSB at COP26". Retrieved 19 February 20222 from https://www.ifrs.org/news-and-events/news/2021/11/An-update-on-the-ISSB-at-COP26/

Network for Greening the Financial System. (2019). *A Sustainable and Responsible Investment Guide for Central Banks' Portfolio Management*. Retrieved 19 February 2022 from https://www.ngfs.net/sites/default/files/medias/documents/ngfs-a-sustainable-and-responsible-investment-guide.pdf

Network for Greening the Financial System. (2020). Progress Report on the Implementation of Sustainable and Responsible Investment Practices in Central Banks' Portfolio Management. Retrieved 19 February 2022 from https://www.ngfs.net/sites/default/files/medias/documents/sri_progress_report_2020.pdf

Nordic Engagement Cooperation. (2021). *Annual Engagement Report 2020*. Ilmarinen. Retrieved 19 February 2022 from https://www.ilmarinen.fi/media_global/liitepankki/ilmarinen/sijoitukset/vastuullinen-sijoittaminen/ulkoiset-raportit/2020-nec-report_final.pdf

Norges Bank Investment Management. (2021). "Pre-screening of Companies with Sustainability Risk". Retrieved 19 February 2022 from https://www.nbim.no/en/the-fund/news-list/2021/pre-screening-of-companies-with-sustainability-risk/

Norges Bank Investment Management. (2021). "Observation and Exclusion of Companies". Retrieved 19 February 2022 from https://www.nbim.no/en/the-fund/responsible-investment/exclusion-of-companies/

Norges Bank Investment Management. (2022). "Guidelines for Observation and Exclusion of Companies from the Government Pension Fund Global". Retrieved 19 February 2022 from https://www.nbim.no/contentassets/4702e3a1c60f-468296b8e9005ee9b46e/etikkraadet_guidelines-_eng_2017_web.pdf

Principles for Responsible Investment. (2016). "ESG Integration Techniques for Equity Investing". Retrieved 19 February 2022 from https://www.unpri.org/listed-equity/esg-integration-techniques-for-equity-investing/11.article#:~:text=The%20PRI%20defines%20ESG%20integration, alongside%20thematic%20investing%20and%20screening

Principles for Responsible Investment. (2022). "Screening". Retrieved 19 February 2022 from https://www.unpri.org/download?ac=10608

7 Responsible Investment across different asset classes

Key questions in this chapter

- Can Responsible Investment be implemented in all types of asset classes?
- In practice, how can ESG be taken into account in different asset classes?
- Can a passive investor be a responsible one?

Responsible Investment (RI) has traditionally been associated with listed equity investments. However, today, global institutional investors such as pension funds, endowments and asset managers actively take environmental, social and governance (ESG) issues into account across different asset classes. The share of RI in institutional investors' portfolios is constantly growing as investor commitments and practices evolve, alongside an expanding offering of ESG data and investment products. The Global Sustainable Investment Alliance (GSIA) reported in their latest trend review a 15% assets under management (AuM) growth in sustainable investments between 2018 and 2020.

As ESG practices continue to develop across asset classes, a responsible investor will find ways to incorporate ESG issues into every asset class in the investment portfolio. However, each asset class has its own opportunities and challenges to consider from an RI perspective, and it is the task of the responsible investor to evaluate these asset class-specific characteristics before making an investment decision. When developing objectives and practices for each asset class, it is important for institutional investors to align these with organizational values and policies. The purpose of this chapter is to introduce the central characteristics of the most common asset classes and show how these can be viewed and addressed from an RI perspective.

The starting point is to understand the return and risk profile of the asset class when building investment portfolios: the investor cannot change the intrinsic characteristics of the asset through responsible investing. For example, listed/unlisted and liquid/illiquid investments all have very different profiles. In practice, these characteristics determine how different RI approaches can be applied in different asset classes. As summarized in Table 7.1, most RI

DOI: 10.4324/9781003284932-8

Table 7.1 Opportunities for applying different Responsible Investment approaches across common asset classes

Asset class	Responsible Investment approaches					
	ESG incorporation				Active ownership	
	ESG integration	Screening (positive and negative)	Thematic	Impact[a]	Engagement	(Proxy) voting
Listed equity	◉	◉	◉	◉	◉	◉
Fixed income	◉	◉	◉	◉	◉	–
Real estate	◉	◉	◉	◉	◉	◉
Private equity	◉	◉	◉	◉	◉	◉
Hedge funds	◎	◉	◉	◎	◉	◎
Private debt	◉	◉	◉	◉	◉	–
Infrastructure	◉	◉	◉	◉	◉	◎
Commodity investments	◎	◉	◉	◉	◉	◎

◉ commonly used ◎ less commonly used – not relevant
[a] Some investors require additionality to classify their investments as impact investing.

approaches can be applied extensively across asset classes, although their level of use varies.

RI as a concept has evolved from investing in a few designated ESG investments into a more holistic implementation that covers all portfolio investments, across all asset classes. Increasingly, there are expectations that RI should not allow itself to be limited to how ESG risks and opportunities influence the risk–return profile of investments, but should include the investments' broader impacts on sustainable development and outcomes (i.e. positive and negative externalities). These demands are driven by international sustainability agendas and agreements such as the United Nations Sustainable Development Goals (SDGs) and the Paris Agreement.

Today, RI complements traditional financial analysis and portfolio construction techniques. A key driving force for this development has been the Principles for Responsible Investment (PRI) initiative. As a PRI signatory, an institutional investor undertakes to be an active owner and to include ESG criteria within the investment processes and investment decision-making. Signatories also commit to transparency by reporting on their RI activities and seeking appropriate ESG disclosure from the companies in which they invest. The PRI supports its signatories in these commitments by providing RI guidance and support on best practices in a broad range of asset classes as well as encouraging academic research.

With the mainstreaming of RI practices across asset classes and investment funds, investors are faced with the challenge of categorization. The EU's

Sustainable Finance Disclosure Regulation (SFDR) strives to assist investors in this challenge by providing technical classification requirements for funds and mandates, as laid out by Articles 6, 8 and 9. Article 6 funds are not promoted as having ESG factors or objectives; Article 8 funds promote E or S characteristics and follow good governance practices but do not position them as the overarching objective; while Article 9 funds have specific sustainable investment goals as their objective. Table 7.2 provides examples and a summary of RI opportunities in different asset classes.

7.1 Listed equity

Listed equity investment is an investment in a company undertaken by purchasing shares of that company on the stock exchange or another publicly available market. Listed equity investments can be made directly, in shares, or indirectly, through mutual fund and ETF units. Direct equity investors select the shares themselves and can include preferred ESG criteria in the decision-making. A direct equity investor can also exercise ownership rights at general meetings and engage with company management through dialogue as a shareholder. In the case of indirect fund investments, the fund's portfolio manager ultimately decides on the selection of investments. An indirect equity investor may invest in funds with specific ESG or thematic strategies and favour asset managers that follow RI approaches such as active ownership.

7.1.1 Direct equity investments

When investing directly in equities, an investor makes investment decisions independently, based on criteria which they view as important. The first step for the responsible investor can be to acquire ESG information on companies by reviewing corporate responsibility reports. Institutional investors may ask more specific ESG questions at company meetings to monitor the company's development. In addition to their internal research, some investors and asset managers purchase ESG information and expertise from service providers specializing in corporate responsibility and sustainability analysis (see Chapters 8 and 9 for more details on ESG data and ratings).

The investor can also take advantage of public and free corporate ESG assessments and listings, such as the Global 100, the Sustainability Yearbook and publicly available ESG company ratings. This information is mainly based on public sources, such as corporate responsibility reports. In addition, the investor can inquire about corporate responsibility, for example, from NGOs and follow media coverage. Chapter 5 explains more about different ESG themes and how they can be taken into consideration in investment decision-making.

As a direct shareholder, an investor has several ways in which to engage with companies. A standard right of shareholders is to be allowed to

Table 7.2 Examples of Responsible Investment in different asset classes

Asset class	Responsible Investment opportunities
Listed equity	• Invest in responsible companies based on internal and/or external ESG analysis • Invest in responsible and sustainable thematic funds, ESG index funds or exchange-traded funds (ETFs) • Favour asset managers with credible RI practices • Avoid investment in companies based on low ESG ratings, sector or norm-based screening, or other defined criteria • Practice active ownership by voting at annual general meetings (AGMs) • Engage with companies' management or asset managers in order to seek change in operations
Fixed income	• Invest in responsible bond issuers based on internal and/or external ESG analysis • Assess the corporate responsibility of the (deposit) bank • Invest in responsible and ESG-focused bond funds and ETFs • Favour asset managers with credible RI practices • Invest in green, social, transition and sustainability-linked bonds • Avoid investment in corporate and sovereign bonds based on low ESG ratings, sector or norm-based screening, or other defined criteria • Engage with companies, governments and asset managers in order to seek change in operations
Real estate	• Incorporate green building criteria in the design phase, construction, renovation and maintenance of buildings • Apply for green building certifications • Invest in responsible and ESG-focused real estate funds • Favour asset managers with credible RI practices • Engage with property designers, developers, suppliers, other owners, tenants and fund managers to promote responsible operations and green building • Participate in collaboration forums and initiatives that promote RI practices in the industry
Private equity	• Invest in responsible companies and funds based on internal and/or external ESG analysis • Invest in new business and sustainable innovations • Invest in companies and fund strategies seeking measurable impact • Favour asset managers with credible RI practices • Avoid investment in companies based on sector or other defined criteria • Engage with companies' management in order to seek change in operations and build a responsible corporate culture

...in funds that follow industry best practices for transparency and governance

- Assess the fund manager's ability to take ESG perspectives into account in the various asset class components of the investment strategy
- Invest in dedicated ESG and thematic funds
- Avoid fund strategies based on sector or other defined criteria
- Assess the fund manager's opportunities for active ownership and engagement practices
- Build a firm understanding of the fund's active trading strategies, including derivative use and short selling strategy, and their potential implications both on a fund and market level

Private debt
- Invest in responsible companies and funds based on internal and/or external ESG analysis
- Invest in debt instruments with specific allocation of proceeds to environmental or social outcomes, or with sustainability targets linked to the financing conditions
- Favour asset managers with credible RI practices
- Invest in companies and fund strategies seeking measurable impact
- Avoid investment in companies based on sector or other defined criteria
- Engage with companies and asset managers in order to seek change in operations

Infrastructure
- Integrate ESG perspectives into infrastructure project evaluation for the entire asset lifecycle
- Invest in infrastructure investments that provide solutions for social and environmental objectives
- Avoid investment in projects or funds based on sector or other defined criteria
- Engage with project management, developers, other contractors and asset managers in order to seek change in operations

Commodity investments
- Assess the ESG aspects of different commodities and related sectors
- Set ESG standards for real assets such as timberland and farmland
- Manage commodity derivative positions based on long-term fundamentals instead of price trends
- Avoid participation in agricultural futures market, fossil fuels or other defined criteria
- Favour commodity-linked investments that provide solutions for social and environmental objectives
- Engage with asset managers, index providers, commodity stock exchanges and traders in order to improve governance and transparency of investments and the market in general

Portfolio transparency
- Report regularly across asset classes on RI activities and outcomes, according to relevant frameworks such as:
  – PRI (Principles for Responsible Investment)
  – GRI (Global Reporting Initiative)
  – GRESB (formerly known as Global Real Estate Sustainability Benchmark)
  – TCFD (Task Force on Climate-related Financial Disclosures)
  – UN SDGs (Sustainable Development Goals)
  – Paris Agreement
  – Net Zero asset owner and asset manager initiatives
  – EU Taxonomy (2020/852) and SFDR (Sustainable Finance Disclosure Regulation 2019/2088)

participate in the decision-making at AGMs, and this can include making shareholder proposals. Other possible channels for engagement are corporate meetings, dialogues and investor initiatives. Chapter 6 describes active ownership and engagement practices in more detail.

7.1.2 Indirect equity investments

The ESG equity fund universe is very diverse (see Table 7.3). ESG equity funds tend to use multiple RI approaches side by side, and the strategies can be active or passive, with a specific regional, sectoral or thematic focus. RI approaches can include, for example, exclusions, engagement, and incorporation of ESG criteria into investment analysis using various methods. Furthermore, asset managers may apply several RI approaches and practices in a fund, without it being explicitly categorized as an ESG fund.

Sustainable and responsible equity funds consider ESG issues by means of a variety of approaches, tools and resources. Typically, these funds invest across different markets, in all or almost all sectors and often in large-cap companies. Often, these funds overweight companies that are assessed to have higher ESG standards than their peers, and likewise underweight sector laggards. The tools and resources behind the funds' ESG assessments can range from large internal RI teams with proprietary ESG databases to externally sourced ESG data or ratings. Many asset managers combine internal and external resources in their ESG practices. The degree of exclusion also varies widely between fund strategies. Some funds exclude companies only when their rigorous active ownership and engagement approach fails to reach its objectives. Other funds embark from an extensive exclusion list, as is often the case for ethical and faith-based strategies. From an SFDR perspective, sustainability- and ESG-categorized equity funds can be considered as Article 8 or 9 funds.

Table 7.3 ESG equity fund categories

ESG equity fund categories	Strategy and approach
Sustainable and responsible equity funds	A sustainability or ESG categorized fund that applies different RI approaches as part of its investment strategy. Can be classified as an SFDR Article 8 or 9 fund.[a]
Sustainability-themed funds	A fund that focuses on specific ESG themes or sectors as part of its investment strategy. Can be classified as an SFDR Article 8 or 9 fund.[a]
Responsible equity index funds and ETFs	A passive investment, such as an equity index fund or ETF, that applies different RI approaches and/ or replicates specific sustainability indexes. Can be classified as an SFDR Article 8 or 9 fund.[a]

[a] Applicable to products marketed in the EU only; provided that the other SFDR criteria are met.

There is also a growing number of *sustainability-themed funds* available that specifically focus on sustainability-related outcomes. These thematic funds concentrate on social and environmental shifts when making investment decisions, acknowledging the goal of a transition towards a more sustainable future. Sustainability-themed funds tend to operate with a global geographical focus, spreading among all company market cap sizes. Internationally, thematic funds are available for sectors and themes such as renewable energy, clean transport, low carbon, education, health and well-being, water, sustainable resource use and waste management. Some funds invest in line with selected UN SDGs.

Investors globally have access to a variety of *responsible equity index funds and ETFs* that are based on ESG research. These passive fund strategies can apply different RI approaches and/or replicate specific sustainability indexes. The world's largest index providers have proprietary sets of responsible equity indices. Passive equity investments are discussed in more detail in Section 7.1.3.

With RI becoming mainstream, asset managers are increasingly committing to developing RI practices and applying different RI approaches across their funds. These are not necessarily categorized as sustainability or ESG funds, but may still be of interest to responsible fund investors. Many of these funds can be classified as SFDR Article 8 funds.

With a broad spectrum of ESG equity funds and approaches available, investors need to consider these differences thoroughly to ensure that the investments are aligned with their own investment principles. In addition to traditional quantitative and fundamental fund analysis, a proper assessment of fund RI policies and practices helps investors make more informed investment decisions and avoid subsequent potential conflict situations regarding fund holdings. A proper understanding of the fund's ESG criteria – and how ESG-related incidents of investees are addressed – will decrease the risk of misunderstandings and negative media attention.

7.1.3 Passive equity investments and ESG

Passive investment is a core strategy for many investors, and the popularity of passive equity indices – and ETF investments in particular – is growing significantly. Passive investment strategies are used in various ways to either increase or decrease the portfolio's risk exposures. The most common passive product is a product that replicates a stock index as closely as possible, with the advantage of gaining exposure to up to hundreds of companies in a single transaction. Thus, the investor does not have to buy each company in the index separately, but quickly and cost-effectively obtains a comprehensive investment position in the desired market or group of companies.

A passive strategy does not depend on the portfolio manager's ability to interpret the market outlook, as the content and weightings methodologies of the portfolio are outlined in the fund strategy and prospectus. The company weights can be determined, for example, according to market capitalization, the number of companies or the desired risk exposure. Many investors believe that the stock market is so efficient that in the long run, it may be difficult or even impossible for an active strategy to overperform relative to the general market index after fees. In addition to listed equities, passive investment strategies are also used in other asset classes, such as corporate bonds and commodity investments, but not on the same scale as equity investments.

Enhanced equity index strategies are based on a selected market index (benchmark) and its content, but the strategy aims for a higher expected return than the benchmark index by increasing active risk to a certain level. Based on quantitative techniques, the enhanced strategy aims to optimize the benchmark index content cost-effectively. An enhanced strategy can include ESG factors and, for example, target ESG enhancements such as favouring companies with low carbon emissions. In addition, the fund strategy may exclude companies according to certain criteria. Often, the optimization process, particularly against ESG factors, results in fewer company names compared to the benchmark index.

A passive equity investor can be described as a universal owner because the investor holds a broad investment portfolio representing a small share of the global investment market. Due to this wide diversification and potential systemic risks, the passive index investor should have a financial interest in contributing to the long-term sustainability of the global economy – not just of individual companies. Therefore, global advocacy measures, such as promoting climate change preparedness among companies and decision-makers, eradicating corruption and increasing ESG reporting, are particularly relevant perspectives for the passive investor.

7.1.4 The rise of ESG in equity index strategies

With investor interest in passive equity investments growing, the industry's index providers and asset managers have in recent years responded effectively to investor demand by developing ESG stock indices and replicating funds for various markets. The growth rate of ETFs operating under ESG strategies, both in terms of number and AuM, has been particularly strong in recent years. The BlackRock US Carbon Transition Readiness ETF began trading in April 2021, making it the largest ETF launch to date, with US$1.25bn raised. iShares ESG Aware MSCI USA ETF, the largest ESG ETF globally, reached over US$20 billion in AuM in 2021.

The world's largest index providers, such as S&P Dow Jones Indices, MSCI, FTSE Russell and STOXX, are constantly bringing new responsible index strategies to the market as investor demand evolves. Positive from the investor's point of view is that the growth in ESG passive fund products has resulted in both lower fee levels and improved fund liquidity. It is becoming increasingly common for asset managers providing equity index funds to make some degree of ESG criteria additions to these funds. Equity index ESG strategies can include, for example, exclusion criteria related to different sectors, as well as cases of international norm violations. In addition, the ESG strategy may include a screening process or inclusion of companies based on their ESG ratings. A responsible investor may also choose index investments based on specific sustainability themes, such as climate change in the Carbon Disclosure Leadership Index (CDLI).

Asset managers are increasingly using active ownership and engagement in responsible equity index funds and ETFs. The fund can have internal processes or buy proxy voting and other engagement services from external service providers. As a universal owner, the asset manager may participate in sector- or market-specific engagement initiatives such as the Extractive Industries Transparency Initiative (EITI), the Carbon Disclosure Project or Climate Action 100+.

The EU Benchmarks regulation has recently introduced two new types of climate benchmarks: the EU Paris-Aligned Benchmarks (EU PAB) and the EU Climate Transition Benchmarks (EU CTB). The objectives of these are described in more detail in Table 7.4 (see also Table 3.2 in Chapter 3). The right to use EU PAB and EU CTB labels is strictly controlled, with failure to reach the (annual) objectives resulting in the loss of such a right.

Table 7.4 The EU climate benchmarks and their objectives

EU climate transition benchmarks (EU CTB)	*EU Paris-aligned benchmarks (EU PAB)*
• Voluntary labels designed to orient the choice of investors who wish to adopt a climate-conscious investment strategy and avoid greenwashing • The potential administrators of the benchmarks will have to provide an explanation of how the key elements of their methodology reflect ESG factors	
Based on the decarbonization of a standard benchmark. The underlying stocks will be selected based on their reduced carbon emissions, when compared to stocks constituting a standard benchmark.	A more ambitious version aligned with the objectives of the Paris agreement. The underlying stocks in this benchmark will be selected on the basis of their carbon emissions savings exceeding the stocks' residual carbon footprint. EU PABs are differentiated from EU CTBs by the following features. They: • Allow for a higher decarbonization of the investment relative to the underlying investable universe • Have additional activity exclusions • Have a stronger focus on opportunities with a significantly enhanced green share/brown share ratio

Source: EU Technical Expert Group on Sustainable Finance (2019)

The regulation also goes a step further, requiring all registered benchmark administrators based in the EU (or offering benchmarks within the EU) to disclose their methodology, including a statement explaining if and how ESG factors are reflected in the benchmark in a standardized and comparable way. Non-ESG-focused benchmarks have a non-disclosure option, but all benchmarks must include a disclosure on their alignment with the Paris Climate Agreement emissions reduction goals starting end of 2021.

Investors can also use ESG indices as a benchmark for their active investments. In this case, the investor generally selects stocks from an investment universe that has an inherently lower ESG risk profile than a traditional benchmark index. The return of these active investments is also compared to the return of the RI universe. Responsible indices can encourage companies not yet included to further develop their own operations and ESG reporting.

7.2 Listed fixed income

Fixed income refers to any type of investment security under which the borrower or issuer is obliged to make pre-determined payments on a fixed schedule to the investor. This section focuses on listed fixed-income investments in money market, corporate and sovereign bonds. Private debt investments are covered in Section 7.6.

A fixed-income investor is particularly interested in the ability of the investee, such as a company or government, to make interest payments and repay the principal. ESG analysis supports traditional interest rate risk analysis and helps the investor assess the repayment capacity of investments from a broader perspective – in terms of both ESG risks and longer-term operational opportunities. A fixed-income investor can take ESG issues into account regardless of the issuer or time horizon.

Traditional fixed-income investments are unsuitable for investors who use Islamic law (sharia) as a basis for investment decisions. For sharia investors, special financial instruments have been developed, such as sukuk bonds, which do not pay interest as such but instead refer to paying rent on capital. It is important to note that sukuk bond issuance is not just for Islamic countries or companies: non-Islamic issuers may want to expand their investor base by issuing sukuk bonds.

7.2.1 Money market

Money market investments are usually defined as short-term interest rate instruments with a duration of 12 months or under. Typical money market instruments include bank deposits, bank investment certificates, commercial papers and short-term government debt obligations. A responsible investor can evaluate issuers based on selected ESG criteria. In practice, by depositing money with a bank, the investor makes a loan to that bank, and the bank continues to use these assets in its operations and investments. The investor is therefore entitled to ask how the bank carries out its role as a responsible company – and as a responsible investor. The investor can evaluate banks' policies on corporate responsibility and sustainable finance and thereby select an appropriate bank. This evaluation process is also pertinent to other short-term debt issuers. Relevant questions to a deposit bank or issuer may include the following:

- How is good corporate governance ensured?
- What kind of remuneration systems are in place?
- What kind of personnel policy is pursued?
- What efforts are made to reduce the carbon footprint of operations and corporate clients?
- How is climate risk taken into account in business operations and lending – and, in these, what efforts to reduce climate risk are made?
- What is the contribution to the development and promotion of responsible industry practices?
- Are there voluntary commitments to initiatives such as the PRI, the Principles for Responsible Banking (PRB) or the Equator Principles?
- Is there lending to sustainable development projects?
- What is reported with regard to corporate responsibility, responsible lending and other investment activities?

7.2.2 Corporate bonds

Different RI approaches can be applied to corporate bond investments, using the same corporate ESG data as equity investors do. Based on positive and negative screening, the investor may favour providing financing to responsible companies, or avoid financing companies that operate in an environmentally unsustainable manner or have violated international norms such as human rights. ESG analysis allows the investor to form a more comprehensive picture of a company's bond value and identify potential factors affecting credit risk. The investor can conduct internal ESG analysis of companies and/ or purchase data from external service providers.

In recent years, credit rating agencies have begun to include corporate ESG data in their credit ratings. These agencies have been under a lot of pressure from responsible investors, among others, which has led to Moody's Investor Services, S&P Global Ratings and Fitch Ratings all publishing guidelines for the inclusion of ESG in credit ratings since 2015.

The corporate bond investor, like the shareholder, is interested in monitoring a company's financial operating conditions and thus engaging with regard to practices that may endanger the company's prospects. The bond investor does not have access to company general meetings, although bondholder meetings can be convened, the main purpose of which is updating bond issuance documentation as required. However, bond investors can engage with the company's management: for example, through dialogue or by participating in investor events organized by the company. ESG analysis and engagement is on the rise among corporate bond investors, which is a significant development from a company perspective, as for many companies the bond market is a more significant source of financing than the stock market. In practice, public equity markets provide corporate financing only through initial public offerings (IPOs) and new share issuances.

Through engagement, investors acquire more information about a company's state of affairs and how it intends to manage its ESG risks and opportunities. As the other party to this engagement, the company can build a better understanding of investor expectations. A carbon-intensive business model, disagreements with employees or a fraud case can turn into a credit risk for an investor as the company's cash flows dwindle, financial costs rise, regulatory oversight tightens and reputation suffers.

For corporate bond investors, opportunities for engagement depend on many things, such as the size of the loan, the company's refinancing needs, the situation in the debt market and interest rate levels and local and cultural factors. A lender usually has more influence if the size of the loan is significant or if there is limited competition among lenders in the debt market.

These days, there is a range of responsible alternatives available for corporate bond fund investors. The RI policy of many asset managers extends to fixed-income investments, and there are specialized ESG and green bond funds available in the market.

7.2.3 Government bonds

Government and government-related bond issuers account for up to 40% of the global bond market. A government bond investor finances and supports national government spending, and is thus entitled to assess the operations into which the issuing government channels the funds raised. An investor can apply positive or negative screening approaches within the asset class. For example, positive screening can use the Paris Climate Agreement and related nationally determined contributions (NDCs) as a basis for including or overweighting an issuer in the portfolio. Various sanctions lists from the UN, the Financial Action Task Force (FATF) or other relevant entities can form a basis for exclusion. Many countries have also defined their own sanctions lists. In addition, the investor may include or exclude specific issuers by examining the Freedom House organization's country ratings for the implementation of democracy and human rights, or Transparency International's Corruption Perceptions Index for individual countries.

International sanctions are the restriction or suspension of economic or trade cooperation and transport and communications links or diplomatic relations with a particular government or certain groups. As part of foreign policy, sanctions seek to influence the policies or activities of another government or group of people that are considered a threat to international peace and security. Such activities may include, for example, the proliferation of weapons of mass destruction, international terrorism or large-scale human rights violations.

According to Freedom House's *Freedom in the World 2021* report, 42% of the world's 195 countries are categorized as "Free" countries where certain political or civil rights are exercised; 30% are categorized as "Partly Free" and 28% as "Not Free." These statistics look rather different when viewed in terms of the global population: of the world's 7.8 billion people, only 20% live in "Free" countries, yet 38% in "Not Free" countries (see Figure 7.1).

The number of "Free" countries in the world has reached its lowest level in 15 years following a long period of global democratic decline, while the number of "Not Free" countries has reached its highest level. Dramatic declines in freedom have been observed in every region of the world. Europe has the overall highest proportion of "Free" populations (84%), while the Middle East and North Africa have the highest proportion of "Not Free" populations (85%). The lowest- and top-performing countries in Freedom House's report are listed in Figure 7.1.

Transparency International annually measures the level of public sector corruption in different countries and regions using a 0–100 scale, with the lowest scores indicating the most corruption. In 2021, the highest-scoring

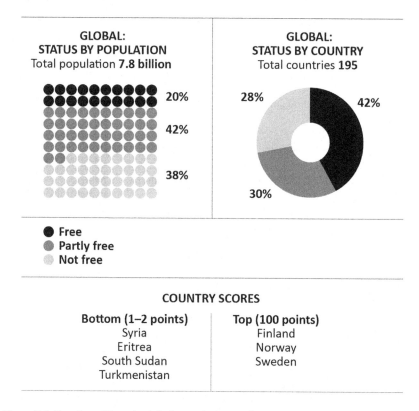

Figure 7.1 Freedom House's global population and country statistics
Source: Freedom in the World 2021

countries were Denmark, Finland and New Zealand (88 points), followed by Norway, Singapore and Sweden (85 points). The most corrupt countries were South Sudan (11 points), Syria (13 points), Somalia (13 points) and Venezuela (14 points). The low-performing countries in Transparency International's Corruption Perceptions Index are often also found on Freedom House's "Not Free" list.

In addition to using data from Freedom House and Transparency International, the investor can rate countries based on, for example, their compliance with international human rights and progress towards achieving the UN SDGs. Table 7.5 provides examples of possible government-related ESG issues that an investor might assess, and subsequently include or exclude countries based on their ESG ratings. Some investors will choose to reduce the weight in the portfolio of countries with a low ESG rating, while similarly increasing the relative weight of other countries.

Many government bond investors diversify their investments via investment funds. The global offerings of mutual funds include designated ESG funds for

Table 7.5 Examples of government-related ESG issues

Environment	Social	Governance	Ethical aspects
Biodiversity	Civil rights	Bribery and corruption	Death penalty
Climate change	Child labour	Efficiency of public administration	Development aid
CO_2 emissions	Gender equality	Political rights	Freedom of religion
Deforestation	Health care expenditure	Political stability	Military expenditure
Endangered species	Human Development Index (HDI)	Rule of law	Nuclear weapons
Environmental protection	Human rights		Use of nuclear power
Fertilizer use	Hygiene		
Fishery	Income distribution		
Nuclear power	Infant mortality		
Recycling	Labour standards		
Waste management	Unemployment		
Water use and management			

Ratification of international treaties

government bonds. The investment universe of government bonds is much narrower than, for example, that of the thousands of companies around the world and hence not all investors have been willing to reduce diversification opportunities by removing issuers according to ESG criteria. This may help to explain why investors have been slow to define and implement ESG criteria for government bonds. However, the situation has changed in recent years as government-related ESG criteria have been more broadly defined through frameworks such as the SDGs. Nonetheless, many investors in any case choose to avoid the risks of politically unstable countries, regardless of whether ESG criteria have been defined, which results in the weakest-rated countries (as designated by Freedom House or Transparency International, for example) commonly being excluded from the investment universe.

Engagement as an RI approach is gaining ground among government bond investors. Until recently, the general view has been that governments engage with one another, or through formal collaborations such as the UN. However, many bond investors are now engaging with government representatives and other country authorities: for example, to gain insight into fiscal and monetary policies. From an RI perspective, investors can use these meetings with sovereign representatives to address ESG issues that are important for their analysis and to encourage ESG data transparency and disclosure. A neutral starting point for discussions with issuers could be progress towards existing commitments, such as the SDGs and the Paris Agreement. Governments can, in turn, gain an improved understanding of investors' ESG expectations.

Engagement with sovereign bond issuers from both developed and developing countries should be considered when applicable. With the COVID-19 crisis increasing countries' public financing obligations, investors may engage with sovereigns on, for example, delivering sustainable recovery plans. Investors can also collaborate in engagement by joining investor initiatives for sustainable outcomes and sending co-signed letters to policy-makers globally.

Engagement with governments can be misinterpreted as lobbying, unsolicited advocacy or an unjust attempt to interfere in government policy and democratic processes. Transparent reporting by investors on engagement policies and activities reduces the risk of such misinterpretation.

7.2.4 *The rise of sustainable bonds*

Sustainable bonds with various themes such as "green" or "social" are increasingly becoming a part of investor portfolios. Sustainable bonds offer clear benefits to both issuers and investors. They can lower the issuer's financing costs and expand the investor base by providing better transparency and reducing perceived risk. Investors can benefit from greater openness and transparency of sustainable bonds because it supports risk management. The most significant difference from conventional bonds is the use of proceeds: the funds raised from sustainable bonds must be used to finance sustainable activities.

Sustainable bonds can be issued by governments, municipalities, supranational institutions or corporate or other organizations. To date, the largest issuers have been governments and supranational institutions such as the

European Investment Bank and the World Bank, the former issuing its first Climate Awareness Bond in 2007 and the latter issuing its first green bond in 2008. Corporate issuances began a little later, but now the corporate sustainable bond market is growing apace. In recent years, sustainability-linked bonds and climate transition bonds have emerged, further expanding the market for sustainable fixed-income issuances.

The Climate Bonds Initiative (CBI)'s statistics show that the total Q1–Q3 2021 volumes for sustainable fixed-income market issuance reached nearly US$780 billion. This total encompasses US$348.4 billion in green bonds, US$186.7 billion in social bonds, US$161.8 billion in sustainability-themed bonds, US$77.3 billion in sustainability-linked bonds (SLBs) and US$5.0 billion in transition bonds (see Figure 7.2). The CBI defines sustainability-themed bonds as having green and social benefits combined within one instrument. Cumulative sustainable issuance between 2017 and Q3 2021 reached US$2.3 trillion.

CBI has been including SLBs and climate transition bonds in its market tracking and forecasting since 2021. Unlike green, social and transition

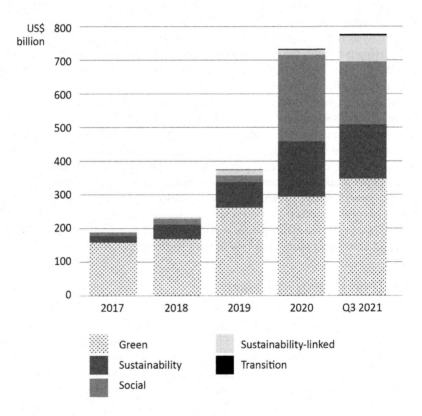

Figure 7.2 Five-year growth of sustainable fixed-income market issuance
Source: Climate Bonds Initiative, 2022

bonds, an SLB comes with no restrictions on the use of proceeds: rather, issuers of SLBs commit to improve their performance against specific ESG targets and the coupon paid to investors is linked to ESG performance. Some sustainable bonds also have a coupon step-up whereby the issuer must pay a higher coupon rate if predefined sustainability targets are not met. Starting in 2021, the European Central Bank has accepted these coupon step-up bonds as collateral, which should further increase their attractiveness to issuers.

Climate transition bond issuance is still developing and remains at a low level compared to other sustainability-labelled bonds. However, transition bonds are expected to enjoy rapid growth in the coming years as stakeholder and regulatory pressure mounts on companies and governments to transition away from assets and activities that are at risk of becoming stranded. With these bonds still at an early phase of development, expect more guidelines and principles to follow to prevent "transition-washing."

The creation of common standards and definitions is a key area for the development of the sustainable bond market. The International Capital Market Association (ICMA)'s Green Bond Principles (GBP) and Social Bond Principles (SBP) are broadly recognized and applied in the market. In 2018, ICMA unveiled its new Sustainability Bond Guidelines (SBG), which combine good-practice recommendations from both the GBP and SBP. Furthermore, in 2020 ICMA published both the Sustainability-Linked Bond Principles (SLBP) and the *Climate Transition Finance Handbook*.

The Climate Bonds Standards and Certification Scheme established by CBI is a global labelling scheme for bonds, loans and other debt instruments, and is used by bond issuers, governments, investors and the financial markets to prioritize investments that genuinely contribute to the goals of the Paris Climate Agreement to limit warming to under 2°C. This scheme incorporates both the GBP and the Green Loan Principles (GLP). In addition, it is aligned with the EU Green Bond Standard proposal and guidelines in China, ASEAN, Japan and India, among others. In July 2021, the EU Commission adopted the proposal for a European Green Bond Standard, which is specifically aligned with the EU Green Taxonomy. The EU is currently working on a social taxonomy which can be expected to have an impact on future bond standards. See Section 3.3.4 for more details on EU sustainable finance regulation.

7.3 Real estate

Real estate investing involves the purchase, management, development and rental or sale of real estate for profit. Real estate assets can be residential, such as apartments, commercial, such as office buildings, hotels or logistics centres, or even undeveloped land. Real estate developers are responsible for planning, designing, financing, selling and bringing in the partners who will construct and execute the building project. A real estate investor evaluates the market to find the best property for investment. In addition to direct investments, the investor can invest indirectly through investment funds or real estate investment trusts (REITs).

ESG is especially important in real estate investments. Construction and real estate link directly to energy consumption and greenhouse gas emissions, and thus to climate change. According to calculations by the United Nations Environment Programme (UNEP) and the International Energy Agency (IEA), buildings consume between 30% and 40% of the world's energy. One-third of the world's greenhouse gas emissions come from building use. The real estate industry therefore has an enormous role to play in reducing global emissions – and energy efficiency management is key.

The construction and real estate sector is also the world's largest user of natural resources, consuming several billions of tonnes of raw materials each year, accounting for about 40–50% of natural resource consumption worldwide. The built environment is also responsible for about 20% of the world's total water consumption.

Real estate has two intrinsic features which cannot be ignored when discussing ESG. The first is the long investment horizon: ESG issues are more likely to be material when assessed over longer periods. The second is the fixed geographical location: many ESG issues, such as physical risks as a result of climate change, play out at a local level. There is no easy option to "move operations," so identifying and managing ESG issues across investments is particularly important for protecting and enhancing investment value.

7.3.1 Sustainable real estate in practice

Sustainability in real estate means a building's overall ability to provide a comfortable, healthy and productive environment over the long term, without negatively impacting the environment. This is a reflection of how a building is planned, built, used and demolished. Green building is a concept that focuses specifically on the environmental aspects of real estate. Sustainable building as discussed in this section considers ESG aspects more broadly.

Sustainable building is most straightforward when it comes to new construction, as innovative solutions and lifecycle calculations can be brought in at the design phase. Location plays a key role in sustainable new construction. Good public transport connections are essential as are community and environmental considerations. Choices related to materials and building design can help reduce waste as well as water and energy consumption. Smart design also takes into account future renovation needs and extends the building's lifecycle.

High-quality construction also ensures a longer property lifecycle, and an investor or developer may require longer warranty periods from the construction partner in pursuit of quality. A construction partner's policy for addressing the grey economy and other relevant ESG issues should also be interrogated along with how it ensures the safety and well-being of site workers.

Comfort by design and good indoor air quality support either resident satisfaction or office workers' productivity. Innovative floor plan solutions improve the property's capacity to transform according to different user needs and thus extend its lifecycle.

New construction accounts for only a small percentage of the total building stock. Green and sustainable renovation is thus the key to developing the sustainability of buildings worldwide. This requires engagement and collaboration among a building's owners and/or investors, as well as the tenants and property users whose behaviour is instrumental in improvements in energy and water use and recycling. Mutually beneficial objectives can be achieved by knowledge-sharing among property users, or on a contractual basis by splitting energy and water costs. However, it may be difficult amending existing, long-term leases.

A sustainable building is considered a stable investment object with better payback due to, among other things, its energy savings and lifecycle planning. From a business perspective, sustainable buildings can increase productivity: a well-designed and functional work environment promotes comfort and reduces work-related health problems. Investment costs in sustainable buildings are estimated at a few percentage points higher than conventional properties, but operating costs are expected to be correspondingly lower, and they offer better returns. Facilities that serve the current customer and future expectations well have lower cash flow risk and thus a stronger long-term value development. Corporate users prefer such buildings because commercial locations both reflect the brand and form part of corporate responsibility objectives.

7.3.2 Indirect real estate investments

Many real estate fund managers are already considering ESG aspects in their investment decisions, even when the fund does not have a sustainability angle. A fund manager may well favour environmentally certified properties and may be reporting regularly on quantitative and qualitative ESG indicators. Some real estate investment funds and REITs specialize in green properties and construction, while others have social objectives, such as service housing for the elderly. In indirect real estate investments, an investor can engage with the fund manager to drive changes in pursuit of sustainability. It is common practice for real estate fund investors to add terms to an agreement to reflect this, i.e. a side letter about ESG aspects and active ownership.

Table 7.6 summarizes the common ESG issues to be evaluated in both direct and indirect real estate investments.

7.3.3 Green building certifications

From an international perspective, the construction industry is very fragmented with building regulations differing significantly from one country to another. Green building certifications are helping to harmonize construction practices. Green certifications allow investors, public authorities and building

Table 7.6 Examples of ESG issues to consider in real estate investments

Environmental	Social	Governance
• Biodiversity • Climate change • Energy consumption • Greenhouse gas emissions • Indoor environmental quality • Land contamination • Location and transportation • Materials • Pollution • Renewable energy • Resilience to catastrophe or disaster • Sustainable procurement • Waste management • Water consumption	• Accessibility • Community development • Controversial tenants • Human rights • Health and safety • Inclusion and diversity • Labour standards and working conditions • Occupier amenities and well-being • Social enterprise partnering • Stakeholder relations	• Anti-bribery and money laundering • Cyber security • Data protection and privacy • ESG clauses in leases • Fighting the grey economy • Legal and regulatory fines • Lobbying

Source: Based on PRI, An Introduction to Responsible Investment: Real Estate (2021)

users to compare, for example, the energy efficiency of buildings using uniform criteria. Third-party certifications can be used to verify a building's environmental performance transparently and independently.

The most widely used environmental certifications worldwide are Leadership in Energy and Environmental Design (LEED) and the Building Research Establishment Environmental Assessment Method (BREEAM).

LEED is a US-based, internationally comparable green property certification system. In order to obtain a LEED rating, a building must meet certain minimum requirements relating to, among other things, the building's location and its consumption of energy, water and materials. Certificates, which are awarded on a scale going from Certified, Silver and Gold up to Platinum, are valid for five years. The scheme encourages continuous improvement if an investor or developer wishes to maintain a building's certification level throughout its lifecycle.

BREEAM is a UK-based, green property certification scheme which examines the environmental impact of a building with reference to its management, energy and water consumption, materials used, transportation and land use, among other things. Certification is graded on a scale of "passed," "good," "very good," "excellent" or "outstanding," and is valid for three years.

There are also more regionally focused certifications and standards, such as the Green Building Initiative (GBI) and National Green Building Standard (NGBS) in North America, the National Australian Built Environment

Rating System (NABERS) and Green Star in Australia and the Comprehensive Assessment System for Built Environment Efficiency (CASBEE) in Japan.

7.3.4 ESG initiatives and policies

There are collaboration initiatives and forums that promote RI practice in the industry in which real estate investors and fund managers can participate. These include the European Association for Investors in Non-Listed Real Estate (INREV) and national Green Building Councils (all are members of the World Green Building Council). For reporting purposes, the Global Reporting Initiative (GRI) can be applied as a framework; or GRESB (formerly known as Global Real Estate Sustainability Benchmark) can be used – another common international reporting system for real estate and other real assets. In addition, many real estate investors commit to the PRI, which also backs climate-related reporting according to the Task Force on Climate-related Financial Disclosures (TCFD) recommendations, and Net Zero target setting in accordance with the Paris Agreement objectives and Science Based Targets (SBT).

Alongside real estate investor forums, governments have a key role to play in encouraging and promoting sustainable construction. The buildings and construction sector will need training and information to motivate and guide the various market players in developing their operations. Stakeholder pressure is a key driver for change in the sector. For example, the EU has established, through its Energy Performance and Buildings Directive (EPBD, 2010) and Energy Efficiency Directive (2012), a legislative framework to boost the energy performance of buildings. As an estimated two-thirds of the buildings that exist today will still be standing in 2050, there is much to be gained in retrofitting buildings for energy efficiency.

Construction and real estate is one of the sectors covered by the EU Taxonomy and its related technical screening criteria. For this sector, the criteria cover the reduction of primary energy demand, waste management, the use of sustainable technologies, controls around construction materials, the use of hazardous materials, and requirements for an environmental impact assessment where relevant.

7.4 Private equity

A private equity investor invests in non-listed companies directly or via investment funds. Typically, private equity investments target early-stage companies. The risk level of private equity investment is high, and the minimum investment required is usually considerable, so they mainly fit the investment profiles and plans of institutional investors and high-net-worth individuals. In recent years, crowdfunding, which allows participation by smaller investment, has become a more common source of financing among non-listed companies, especially for startups. Crowdfunding is still an evolving field, so this section will focus on more traditional forms of private equity investing.

Private equity investments are relatively illiquid. The holding period of an individual investment is typically between three and five years, and the term of an investment fund is around ten years. Investing through private equity funds is an effective way of diversifying risk between different investment objects and markets. The opportunities and approaches here for RI depend, among other things, on the private equity fund's investment strategy and sector focus, as well as the resources of the portfolio companies and their phase of development. Private equity investors are using ESG criteria not only to assess risks and identify opportunities for value creation but also to manage their portfolios to ultimately deliver a better investment at the exit.

7.4.1 *From compliance to value creation*

Ownership is generally very concentrated in non-listed companies, and the pursuit of majority ownership is often part of a private equity investor's strategy. A private equity investor will therefore likely have a much better opportunity to engage with a company than, for example, a shareholder of a publicly listed company. If a private equity investor is involved in building an early-stage business, they have the opportunity to actively create a responsible corporate culture and operating principles as the business scales up.

For indirect investments such as private equity funds, an investor must rely on reporting by the fund and on meetings with the fund manager rather than on direct access to the portfolio companies. Funds generally report their investments and results quarterly. However, the largest investors will typically get a seat on the fund's advisory board, where portfolio companies are discussed regularly and in more depth. An investor should always negotiate reporting content and the availability of advisory board seats before signing the subscription agreements. ESG issues in fund reporting might include new jobs created, human rights issues for employees, diversity, new technologies developed in portfolio companies, and environmental activities such as reduction of CO_2 emissions and waste. Investor-specific ESG acknowledgements and requirements can also be taken into account in a separate side letter.

In fund-of-fund (FoF) investments, an investor's engagement opportunities are more limited than in ordinary private equity funds. The FoF manager does not, in principle, have the capacity to influence the selection and evaluation of the target funds' portfolio companies. A responsible private equity fund investor will therefore incorporate RI and ESG aspects into the due diligence process of the investment. This might include questions about how ESG issues are integrated into the analysis and decision-making process and, if so, which ESG issues are assessed and what resources are deployed for this work, and how monitoring and reporting are conducted. Signing up for the PRI has become more widespread among private equity firms, and the investor may ask additional questions about PRI reporting and assessment.

Case study on private equity's ESG journey

The Global Private Equity Responsible Investment Survey (PwC, 2021) explored the views of general partners and limited partners in RI among global private equity firms. In all, 209 firms from 35 countries responded, the vast majority (81%) from Europe, and with 68% being PRI signatories. As the first survey was conducted back in 2013 and the previous one in 2019, this recent survey is able to offer a number of reflection points. One notable change is that ESG is commanding more attention at the board level, with 56% of firms saying that ESG features in board meetings more than once a year (35% in 2019), and 15% saying it was discussed at all board meetings (6% in 2019). Diversity and inclusion are also gaining momentum at the firm level, with 46% of survey respondents having set some form of gender, ethnic or racial diversity target.

According to the survey, the past few years have seen a fundamental shift in focus within private equity when it comes to ESG strategy and implementation: 66% of survey respondents rank value creation as one of their top three drivers of responsible investing activity (see Figure 7.3).

KEY DRIVERS FOR RESPONSIBLE INVESTMENT

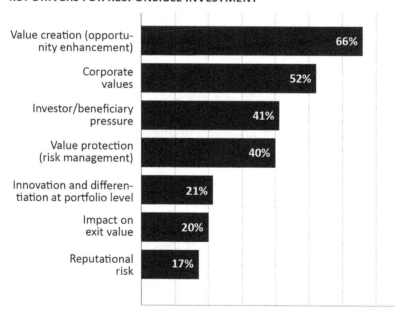

Figure 7.3 Key drivers for Responsible Investment activity among private equity investors

More than half of all respondents (56%) have either refused to enter an agreement with a general partner or turned down a potential investment on ESG grounds; 49% say they integrate material ESG issues into due diligence when making investment decisions. However, this is still on an ad hoc basis. The SDGs offer an outcomes-based framework for investors and companies, and 26% of firm respondents are using SDG-aligned KPIs.

Climate risk is a major topic in the market. However, merely 36% of survey respondents consider climate risk at the due diligence stage as a means of understanding and/or mitigating portfolios' exposure; 47% have not undertaken any work in understanding the climate risk exposure of portfolios, but more than half of those respondents say they intend to in the next year. Climate risk assessments are complicated and require a broad set of information related to the tools, methodologies and data. For the private equity sector, this implies stepping up their level of knowledge and sophistication over the coming years. This may be reflected in the survey results, where 89% are concerned about compliance with ESG regulation, and 56% say that more than half their investment team has received some formal ESG training.

The survey also included a parallel section for venture capital (VC). No significant differences were found between RI practices at pure-play VC firms and the practices of VC investment teams operating as part of a larger, diversified private equity house. The survey report contemplates whether this could reflect the significant growth in VC's focus on ESG and transition strategies.

Among the overall survey results, a growing interest in impact investing strategies was noted, with 17% of respondents already having a dedicated impact fund or saying they plan to launch one next year; 45% had no impact fund, but do consider the impact of their investments.

7.4.2 Supporting innovation and impact

The role of the private equity investor in financing and developing new business is significant. New companies create jobs, and the investor can support innovation by targeting investments in, for example, renewable energy, the circular economy, health services, education and clean technology companies. In addition, the private equity business and ownership model is well suited to engagement with investments and driving change. According to the GIIN Annual Investor Survey 2020, private equity is one of the most common asset classes for targeting impact investments and accounts for 17% of surveyed impact assets under management: 81% of private equity-focused investors seek market-rate returns for their impact investments.

Venture capital makes up 44% of impact strategies in the private equity asset class, followed by growth (35%) and buyout (21%), according to Phenix Capital Group's Impact Database. The most commonly targeted SDGs for private equity are (3) Good health and well-being, followed by (7) Affordable and clean energy, (9) Industry, innovation and infrastructure, (4) Quality education and (8) Decent work and economic growth.

Numerous regional venture capital associations provide guidance and recommendations for the development of responsible private equity investments. For its part, the PRI encourages responsible private equity investment by publishing studies on best practices in the field and developing reporting practices among signatories. Among the latest tools is a technical guide on implementing the TCFD recommendations for private equity general partners.

7.5 Hedge funds

Hedge funds generally aim to make an absolute return, i.e. to achieve a positive return on investments even when traditional equity and fixed-income markets are falling. By combining long and short positions, hedge funds can protect or "hedge" the portfolio from adverse price movements and reduce exposure to overall market fluctuations. Investors increasingly use hedge funds for diversification alongside traditional asset classes such as equities and fixed-income investments. Assets under management by global hedge funds were estimated at approximately US$4.3 trillion at the end of 2021 (Preqin, 2022). Since the hedge fund industry first took off in the 1990s it has experienced a rapid and steady growth.

To achieve their absolute return targets, hedge funds employ a variety of financial instruments and risk management techniques. A hedge fund can invest in all types of assets according to its mandate, but investments are made primarily in listed stocks, bonds, commodities, money markets and currencies including derivatives. The investment horizon of hedge funds varies from fund to fund, and each hedge fund has a unique strategy which will impact the investment risk, volatility and expected return profile.

7.5.1 Hedge fund characteristics and their relevance for RI

Key focus areas for responsible investors are the hedge fund's investment strategies, the fund domicile, its governance and market regulation and transparency.

7.5.1.1 Investment strategies

The flexible investment style and limited transparency of hedge funds pose several challenges for responsible investors. The most important task for the investor is to build a thorough understanding of the hedge fund's investment strategy and assess the implications from an RI perspective (see Table 7.7 for more details). By preparing the investment decision using a comprehensive

Table 7.7 Common hedge fund strategies and examples of Responsible Investment considerations

Hedge fund strategy	*RI considerations*
Fundamental selection, long/ short equity or credit	• Incorporating ESG in fundamental selection • Voting and engaging in equity and credit • Restricting the activity of borrowing shares for the purpose of voting • Shorting practices: avoiding strategies that involve large directional bets on a stock's decline or naked shorting (illegal practice; shorting without borrowing the stock that is being sold)
Relative value, arbitrage and volatility strategies	• Considering the wider market implications of the strategy, if no fundamental analysis opportunities • Understanding the types of information used by the hedge fund manager in strategies and whether they have explored the potential for ESG data to add value • Using ESG data for quantitative model optimization • Understanding high-frequency trading strategies used and the potential implications
Event-driven, corporate distressed, bankruptcy, restructuring	• Focusing on social and governance issues for distressed investing • Ensuring that no form of improper pressure or coercion is applied by the hedge fund manager in distressed investing situations • Considering social risk management for operational restructurings, which may involve job losses • Other areas of attention may be bankruptcy or restructuring strategies, and companies operating in residential foreclosures
Global macro, multi-strategy and global tactical asset allocation	• Using ESG data in the composition of equity and credit indices and in country risk analysis in macro strategies • Considering the use of derivatives • For multi-strategy funds, focusing on the main strategy (or strategies) and applying relevant RI practices as appropriate
Foreign exchange	• Considering the strategy's potential to affect the fortunes of an economy at a time of vulnerability if the strategy is widely pursued by a range of managers
Fixed income: government and supranational debt	• Avoiding investments in the bonds of a country subject to, for example, UN Security Council sanctions • Avoiding strategies that could be seen as exploiting the sovereign debt of developing countries
Mortgages, asset backed securities, specialized credit and financial services strategies	• Ensuring that hedge fund managers who actively participate in servicing and collection strategies in personal or mortgage debt comply with fair lending laws (including third parties providing these servicing and collection services) • Seeking full disclosure from the fund manager in relation to all parties involved in structuring securities • Avoiding traded life strategies, which create return on life insurance pay-outs of the original policy holders
Commodity strategies	• Understanding the ESG issues involved with exposure to commodities through real productive assets, debt or equity investments, physical commodities (direct or indirect) or commodity derivatives • Considering if and how physical and derivatives investments can impact the functioning of markets and the sustainable development of economies

Source: Based on PRI, Responsible Investment and Hedge Funds (2012)

due diligence process, the investor can understand the fund's investment strategy and the intrinsic risk and return profile. The PRI has prepared an RI-focused due diligence questionnaire, covering hedge fund investment policy, governance, investment process, monitoring and reporting. The questionnaire has been included in the member guidance of the Alternative Investment Management Association (AIMA), and the Standards Board for Alternative Investments (SBAI) also advances responsible standards in the hedge fund industry.

7.5.1.2 *Short selling*

Many hedge funds apply short-selling strategies. In a short sale, the fund borrows a financial instrument from a third party and sells it in the market. At a later date, the hedge fund buys back the instrument to return it to the third-party lender. Short selling is profitable if the instrument's value decreases during the loan period – but incurs a loss if the instrument appreciates in value. Hedge fund short-selling strategies have been criticized for disrupting market stability and increasing market volatility. Conversely, this activity is also perceived to improve market pricing mechanisms and support derivative trading and underlying market liquidity. Debate will undoubtedly persist about the correct and efficient use of short-selling strategies.

Confusion around these strategies has led some investors to question whether short selling is compatible with RI and long-term value creation. These investors may also question the loss of active ownership and engagement opportunities when shares are shorted or lend out. Some investors have brought in policies that prohibit securities lending during general meetings in order to use full ownership rights. Advocates argue that short selling can be an excellent tool for achieving several common goals of RI: mitigating undesired ESG risks and promoting better ESG outcomes while pushing the laggards to improve. Some activist short-sellers seek to fill the gaps when corporate governance, due diligence and regulators fail – by playing a role in identifying, uncovering and mitigating the effects of financial misconduct or greenwashing, for example. However, becoming a "short target" can have substantial impacts on companies, their related stakeholders and the market at large. Investors should consider the impact of the strategies that involve large directional bets on a stock's decline.

7.5.1.3 *Use of derivatives*

Hedge fund strategies often use derivative instruments, such as forwards, futures, swaps and options. Using derivatives allows the hedge fund to manage risk while striving for enhanced risk-adjusted returns. It can enable the instruments to be traded more efficiently, quickly and in a more liquid form than the underlying reference security or asset. This can sometimes even take place anonymously. Derivatives are traded via exchanges or bilaterally over the counter (OTC). Derivatives are normally cleared by independent market clearing houses, which require derivative investors to post collateral as a margin for fluctuations in the value of the derivatives. From an investor perspective, the hedge fund should be able to explain its counterparty risk management process on OTC products. It is also important for the investor to understand the hedge fund's main use of derivatives (substitution, risk control or arbitrage), the anticipated economic leverage involved, as well as how derivatives will be valued and monitored – including ESG within collateral used – and the estimated maximum potential loss as a result of leverage. Furthermore, a responsible investor can assess the ESG profile of the derivative's counterparty.

7.5.1.4 *Active trading*

Many hedge funds use active trading strategies to make use of short-term mispricing in the market. Investors need to understand the hedge funds' trading strategies, and the potential implications both at fund and market level (impacting other parts of the investor's portfolio). Taking positions in currencies or sovereign debt, especially if the same strategy is widely pursued by a range of other funds, can affect economies at a time of vulnerability. High-frequency trading has been criticized for increasing market volatility and creating a false illusion of liquidity provision or generating losses due to errors in trading algorithms.

7.5.1.5 *Fund domicile and governance*

Hedge funds commonly select an offshore structure or domicile that offers an equal legislative framework to investors regardless of their nationality. The selected jurisdiction might also be attractive to the fund, offering more freedom of action, less restrictive investment and disclosure requirements and opportunities for fiscal optimization. Investors can choose to exclude specific fund domiciles if they feel uncomfortable with the jurisdiction and want to avoid reputational risks. The EU list of non-cooperative jurisdictions for tax purposes, for example, may serve as a guideline for European investors. The purpose of the EU's list is to improve international tax governance by tackling tax-related fraud, evasion, avoidance and money laundering. Investors might still experience reputational risk from a broader group of jurisdictions, as media coverage can include areas not covered in official lists. A jurisdiction can also be added to these lists post-investment, making it difficult or prohibitively expensive to withdraw from investment contracts entered.

Fund governance approaches vary from jurisdiction to jurisdiction. Due to the limited transparency of hedge funds, governance issues are of particular importance. As part of due diligence, the investor should look into potential conflicts of interest between the hedge fund manager and other investors over fund policies. The due diligence may also include the background, role, contribution and oversight functions of the (independent) directors and the board governance model.

7.5.1.6　Regulation and transparency

Since the 2008 financial crisis, investment and financial regulation has tightened in both Europe and the USA (e.g. AIFMD, MiFID II, SMCR, EMIR and Dodd–Frank Act), and the special regulatory status of hedge funds has been regularly dismantled ever since. Increasing regulation on disclosure is a global trend. For example, the EU's Sustainable Finance Disclosure Regulation (SFDR) applies to all hedge funds domiciled or marketed in the EU.

As hedge funds can apply different investment strategies flexibly, it is vital for the investor to have sufficient transparency about the fund's underlying investments to enable proper due diligence, risk analysis and monitoring of portfolios. Reporting policies vary between hedge funds; hence, an investor should review the fund's policies before making a commitment. For example, the Open Protocol template, upheld by the Standards Board for Alternative Investments (SBAI), standardizes the collection, collation and representation of risk information of alternative investment funds. The Open Protocol working group expects this to be a monthly report, and typically it should be produced and distributed 15 business days after month-end. According to SBAI, hedge fund managers producing Open Protocol Reports managed US$2.18 trillion of assets as of February 2021. This accounts for over half of the global hedge fund assets under management.

7.5.2　Opportunities for a responsible hedge fund investor

While hedge funds may be diverse, with complicated drivers of risk and return, and use techniques such as short selling or derivative instruments, there are nonetheless many opportunities for investors to evaluate the ESG risks and opportunities associated with a hedge fund's strategy. This can be done by breaking the overall strategy into components and concentrating on the drivers of risk and return. No strategy as such is completely "ESG-neutral," as compliance with best-practice governance and transparency are standard requirements of most investors. However, some hedge fund strategies are likely to be better placed than others to integrate an RI policy.

Depending on the hedge fund strategy's components, RI approaches for traditional asset classes such as equities, credit and private equity can be applied to understand the impact of ESG factors on the fund investments. For a multi-strategy fund, the investor can focus on the main strategy or strategies and apply relevant RI approaches as appropriate. These approaches can include ESG integration, screening, active ownership and engagement.

The investor may evaluate the integration of ESG data into the fund's investment decision-making process. This is especially applicable when a hedge fund engages in a fundamental analysis and selection process. ESG data can also be relevant for quantitative models as well as macro strategies using passive index instruments. Exclusion criteria vary between investors, and these specific criteria may impose limits on the hedge fund strategies available.

For example, criteria on agricultural commodities or fossil fuels can disqualify investments in commodity and trend-following strategies. Hedge fund strategies that hold significant long equity positions for reasonable amounts of time might be expected to have voting policies in place. Engagement with corporate management can also be an investor expectation for equity and credit positions. Some investors may wish to avoid strategies that include large directional bets on a stock's decline or restrict the activity of borrowing shares for voting.

Hedge funds dedicated to ESG are not very common. However, constantly growing client demand and increasing regulation are expected to support the development of new ESG strategies. In practice, hedge funds dedicated to ESG can use one or a combination of RI approaches. These can range from long-only equity active ownership strategies to ESG screening-driven models, thematic climate focus and short-selling strategies of poor ESG performers. Thematic baskets can be a solution for fund strategies not trading single names. Thematic baskets can have as few as ten stocks or as many as a few hundred depending on the scope of the strategy. Thematic baskets and custom indices can offer long and short exposure to a specific business activity such as electric vehicles or renewable energy development. More niche ESG exposure can be provided for hedge funds via customized or structured products, with high specialization in themes such as reforestation or biodiversity.

As the sustainable bond market expands, more extensive and diverse issuance creates spread and yield curve trading opportunities for hedge funds with macro and fixed-income strategies. In return, hedge funds can supply the market with more liquidity and tighter bid offer spreads as the transactions increase. Carbon credits have become a tradable commodity beyond the practical requirements of utility companies and other heavy emitters, and some hedge funds trade on carbon pricing and regional arbitrage opportunities. These are not ESG strategies, but rather the fund participates in a market created to drive prices higher and trigger behavioural change.

As more hedge funds declare ESG integration strategies, it is up to the investor to evaluate how extensive and credible this practice is, and whether the fund's investment philosophy is sufficiently aligned with that of the investor.

7.6 Private debt

Private debt is a more recent asset class within the RI universe, covering a wide range of investment styles and strategies. Private debt typically refers to debt investments not financed by banks or issued or traded on the open market. Both listed and non-listed companies can seek private debt financing.

There are several factors behind the rapid growth in the private debt market. Alternative lenders began to emerge in reaction to the Global Financial Crisis (2007–2009), with the USA in the forefront. European banks, for example, reduced their lending at that time, especially to smaller private companies, in order to meet EU regulatory capital requirements. However, the financing needs of companies continued to develop as the global economy recovered after the crisis. These conditions led to the emergence of an attractive direct private lending market, where investors expect higher yields than public debt provides. Another contributing factor to the growth of private debt is that global investors are seeking new asset class diversification opportunities in a historically low-interest rate environment.

The global private debt market AuM crossed the US$1.2 trillion thresholds in 2021 (Preqin, 2022). The largest private debt markets are in the USA and Europe. The US market is larger and more mature than Europe. In Asia (including China), a swelling middle class has created growth in the SME (small and medium enterprise) market, which has inflated the demand for private debt. The most active investors in the private debt market are pension funds, foundations, endowments and insurance companies, which often diversify their investments by investing through private debt funds. Investors increasingly require private debt managers to follow the principles set out by the PRI and thus many of the world's largest private debt managers are already PRI signatories.

7.6.1 *Private debt characteristics and their relevance for RI*

A private debt investor's primary focus is on credit risk, meaning the possibility of a loss resulting from a borrower's failure to repay a loan, interest or meet other contractual obligations. ESG analysis can support traditional risk analysis by helping investors evaluate risk in a more holistic way and identify otherwise hidden drivers of risk that may impact a borrower's credit strength. The case for assessing long-term ESG issues becomes even more relevant when considering the relatively illiquid nature and hold-to-maturity approach for private debt investments. As private debt investors' focus is drawn to potential downside risks that may lead to a default, the ESG analysis tilts towards ESG issues as risk drivers rather than sources of opportunity (as for equity investors).

When conducting ESG analysis in private debt, the lack of publicly available data on companies is challenging if the issuer is not a publicly listed entity. This is simply because private, non-listed companies typically do not publish sustainability (nor financial) reports as their listed peers do. On the other hand, a non-listed company may provide detailed information directly to the investor upon request. This creates an opportunity for the investor to use different approaches to analyse and integrate ESG information into investment decisions. This will often require detailed primary research. Exclusions are usually more straightforward to implement, while positive screening and best-in-class comparisons are less practical due to the lack of ESG data and benchmarks for non-listed companies.

In the negotiation phase for private debt investments, there is generally some flexibility to agree on the terms around ESG reporting and specific ESG targets or standards, for example. The investor can seek ESG information from other stakeholders involved in the deal, such as private equity sponsors and banks, in order to broaden insight into the borrower's credit position. The scope for negotiation of terms often depends on the number of other lenders and their economic relevance.

Opportunities for lenders to engage with borrowers are determined by the level of access the lender has to senior management. This is often dependent on the number of lenders involved in the deal. As private debt financing is typically organized bilaterally or with a few syndication parties, private debt lenders have a better opportunity to drive terms (including ESG targets) than banks or bond financiers. Also, in some situations, the private debt lender is permitted an observer seat on the board.

The lack of publicly available data for non-listed companies – such as the small businesses that lack the resources to produce annual sustainability reports – can be addressed by means of ESG questionnaires, but beware of over-burdening borrowers with additional workload. However, borrowers' preparedness to respond to investor ESG inquiries is expected to improve as the asset class evolves.

Some investors include regular ESG reporting in the loan terms. There is a general expectation for more sizeable borrowers to be publishing some form of corporate sustainability policy and reporting on ESG issues.

7.6.2 *Impact and thematic investing opportunities*

There are many opportunities for thematic and impact investing for private debt investors. According to the GIIN Annual Investor Survey 2020, private debt is the most common asset class for targeting impact investments and accounts for over 20% of the impact assets under management in their survey. Impact investment is described in more detail in Chapter 6.

Debt instruments allow for the specific allocation of proceeds to environmental or social outcomes. For example, companies that are not inherently "green" can still raise debt to fund green projects through green bond issuance. The bulk of the private debt is used to fund infrastructure and real estate development, both sectors having great potential for positive outcomes considering their role in economic development, energy generation and use, and other essential public services. To ensure the consistency and credibility of loans labelled "green," "social" or "sustainable," the issuer needs to adhere to the relevant frameworks that qualify the processes and projects eligible for this label (see Section 7.2.4 on sustainable bonds for more details).

7.6.3 *Microfinance*

Microfinance is a traditional tool for impact investing and financial inclusion and seeks measurable financial, social and environmental outcomes.

Case study on ESG due diligence in private debt dealmaking: Churchill Asset Management (a majority-owned affiliate of Nuveen)

Asset manager
Area: US private equity-backed middle-market companies
AuM: $37billion in committed capital as of 1 January 2022

Churchill's investment team, in partnership with the Nuveen Responsible Investing team, has developed a proprietary ESG Ratings Template which leverages third-party frameworks to identify and assess material ESG risks and opportunities during due diligence.

The template uses the MSCI ESG materiality map, Institutional Limited Partners Association (ILPA) and Sustainability Accounting Standards Board (SASB) to inform the identification of material ESG factors by sector. It combines this with Verisk Maplecroft's data to determine location-based risk exposure. The risk exposure results in specific weights for each ESG factor. Each company is then assessed by its ability to manage the risk, which results in a score for each material factor, and aggregates into a weighted average overall ESG rating.

The output from the ESG Ratings Template is included in every investment memo presented to Churchill's investment committee for review. If the ESG rating or specific ESG risks identified during the due diligence of the proposed investment are not suitable, the investment committee may pass on the opportunity.

Churchill also assesses the sustainability impact of a company's products and services relative to the SDGs. Through a proprietary SDG logic model, industries are mapped to the goals, ultimately helping to communicate shared sustainability objectives with partners and stakeholders.

After closing, Churchill monitors the company's ESG rating over the course of the investment lifecycle and, at a minimum, the rating is reviewed on an annual basis. The initial rating that was assigned serves as the "baseline" against which subsequent performance is assessed and managed.

Recognizing the need for standardized disclosure, in 2021 Churchill partnered with a private equity firm to develop an ESG due diligence questionnaire which aggregates existing frameworks in the market with the aim of reducing data inefficiencies and asymmetries in disclosure. The questionnaire is expected to be launched in the first quarter of 2022 by PRI.

Source: Churchill Asset Management (2022)

It provides financial services to low-income individuals or groups who are typically excluded from traditional banking. The financial system has historically seen the low-income client segment as unprofitable and difficult to reach, especially in rural regions. Such individuals often do not have a permanent job or loan collateral, which disqualifies them from banks' traditional, often automized, credit risk assessments: manually conducted risk assessments and regular follow-ups are usually required.

According to the World Bank's latest Global Findex Database from 2017, an estimated 1.7 billion adults (2 billion in 2014) globally are financially excluded or "unbanked," and live without bank accounts, mobile money providers and credit. Most of these live in developing economies and often in low-income communities with few employment opportunities. Microfinance seeks to address their needs by providing core financial services which can offer both economic and social empowerment through self-reliance and economic sustainability. It especially targets marginalized groups, such as women or those in remote regions.

Microfinance institutions (MFIs) usually offer credit in the form of small working capital loans, also referred to as microloans or microcredit. Many MFIs also provide money transfers and insurance, and locally regulated microfinance banks can provide savings accounts. Mobile phone penetration is on the rise, and mobile banking innovations are providing new solutions for financial inclusion in developing markets. Mobile credit, savings, payment and e-wallets enable efficient access to financial services; and mobile solutions also serve as a tool to eliminate corruption.

Investments in microfinance can be made, for example, by investing directly in an MFI or through an intermediary such as a bank or cooperative. Microfinance investment funds are offered primarily to institutional investors. When evaluating an MFI, client protection is an important factor: these institutions should have robust responsible lending standards and policies to ensure that clients do not become over-indebted and are treated fairly and ethically.

7.7 Infrastructure

Infrastructure provides the services that are critical to the functioning of societies. Such activities and their ownership are often tightly regulated. Infrastructure investments typically include railways, ports, airports, water and power plants, energy distribution networks and (toll) roads. These investments are very illiquid in nature: airports or power plants are not sold on a daily basis and there is a limited number of potential buyers. They can be made directly or through funds, in public or private companies, and in the form of either equity or debt investments. Global private infrastructure assets under management were estimated at US$655 billion at the end of 2020 and are forecast to reach US$1.8 trillion by 2026 (Preqin, 2022).

Given that the definition of infrastructure is nothing less than a means of servicing a well-functioning society, it impacts human life in countless ways, from the water we drink to the way we travel to work and heat our homes. Infrastructure offers many positive solutions to sustainable development, but investors also need to proactively consider potential negative impacts caused by infrastructure projects. The construction of large infrastructure assets, such as railways and dams, can disrupt and displace communities and can have severe impacts on local biodiversity. Infrastructure construction and operation is also responsible for a large proportion of global greenhouse gas emissions. In order to be considered sustainable, infrastructure assets need to be carefully planned, designed, delivered, managed and decommissioned to minimize negative impacts and maximize positive impacts on the economy, society and the environment – throughout the asset's entire lifecycle. These considerations also help to protect the economic value of the infrastructure asset over its technical lifespan.

Active management of ESG and its impacts are essential for achieving sustainability and minimizing negative externalities. Several RI approaches can be applied in infrastructure investments. Screening can be used to exclude investments in specific sectors, such as coal-based energy production, or for a best-in-class selection. Thematic investments are possible – focusing on renewable energy, energy efficiency, sustainable waste management or social infrastructure, for example. ESG integration models can factor in physical climate risks such as flooding and drought. There are opportunities for investor stewardship through a direct shareholder or bondholder engagement, as well as engagement with, among others, infrastructure fund managers.

7.7.1 Closing the infrastructure gap

Infrastructure needs are rising rapidly as the world's population expands, urbanization accelerates and demand for services increases in emerging economies. In addition, existing infrastructure assets need updating; for example, in England and Wales alone almost 3 billion litres of water are lost daily due to leaking pipes. With climate change posing direct threats to infrastructure assets, through, for example, extreme weather events and rising sea levels, this necessitates the building or refurbishment of infrastructure that is resilient and sustainable. Resilient infrastructure plays a critical role, for example, in supporting and safeguarding energy and water systems, thereby helping societies survive and recover more quickly from environmental shocks.

Infrastructure is widely considered to have a positive societal impact, supporting economic, social and environmental development. Moreover, increased infrastructure spending is deemed to engender an economic multiplier effect. For example, public transport systems in cities increase social mobility and equality, making it easier for people to go to school, work and access health care services. In addition, the construction and operation of the infrastructure asset creates employment. Similarly, shifting from coal-fired power generation to renewables cuts greenhouse gases and reduces air pollution, thereby improving health and limiting demand for environmentally harmful mining activities. Infrastructure responds to many of the UN SDGs.

Governments' ability to invest in infrastructure in the traditional way using public finance may be further constrained in light of large COVID-19 stimulus packages, and private investor participation is increasingly needed to finance the global infrastructure gap. Public–private partnerships (PPPs) and blended finance structures, for example, can play an important role in facilitating the transition to decarbonized energy generation, updating existing assets such as water utilities, and building more sustainable transport solutions – both in developed and emerging markets. Blended finance refers to a combination of concessional financing (loans that are extended on more generous terms than market loans) and commercial funding.

The European Commission estimates that almost €500 billion per annum is needed in investments for the European transition to a greener and more sustainable model for transportation, energy production and waste recycling. However, these investments are currently not flowing into the overall greening of infrastructure, but focus mainly on renewable energy. According to a study conducted by Novethic (2021), this focus has its blind spots, such as insufficient investments into energy efficiency-related solutions. This means that, in their current form, investment strategies for green infrastructure may ultimately be inadequate to meet EU environmental objectives. In the USA, the Build Back Better legislation plan was expected to increase incentives for new infrastructure investments and for programmes reducing the effects of climate change. However, by early 2022, the legislation plan had not been passed in its current form.

7.7.2 *Managing material risks and delivering value*

Infrastructure investments tend to have a particularly long lifecycle, which emphasizes the benefits of adding ESG issues into the investment analysis. Relevant issues here include physical impacts of climate change, changes in environmental legislation, demographic trends, resource depletion, social crises and conflicts. Each infrastructure project has its own ESG-related challenges and opportunities to be evaluated, but understanding these issues can enable a more comprehensive assessment of the infrastructure project. Due diligence assessment is particularly important for an infrastructure investor, and it requires extensive expertise across projects. Alongside risk management, ESG can help infrastructure investors identify and take advantage of opportunities, via the influence they exercise, for value preservation and creation. These opportunities may include reducing the asset's carbon footprint, finding resource efficiencies, retaining staff, supporting biodiversity and driving further innovation. High ESG standards will make it easier to find potential buyers for the infrastructure asset in future.

The challenges for a responsible infrastructure investor include identifying and assessing key ESG issues in different geographical areas, different sectors and different investment periods. New infrastructure or so-called greenfield projects may offer opportunities for positive societal impact, but stakeholder management from an early stage is key in obtaining and maintaining the legal and social licence to operate, as the development phase of the asset tends to have significant effects on the surrounding environment and communities. Similarly, existing brownfield assets need to maintain a social licence in their ongoing operations, and this includes reconstruction and expansion projects. Another challenge is to ensure that ESG standards are addressed at all the various stages of implementation, i.e. how partners, such as developers and other contractors, comply with these standards. ESG standards should also extend to subcontractors and supply chains.

Case study on investing in a just transition: Quinbrook Infrastructure Partners

Asset manager
Area: UK, developed market portfolios
AuM: $2.3billion

Delivering a just transition is as important as achieving Net Zero and the goal of decarbonization. To create a genuine drive toward a more equal, community centred and international shift to Net Zero, infrastructure investors have a key role to play.

Building fair work opportunities in local, decarbonizing communities

Investment in clean energy infrastructure can create a significant opportunity for local workers, particularly in rural and regional areas where assets are typically sited. Coal mines, smelters or landfill sites are examples of potentially retiring infrastructure that can provide interconnection capacity for new renewable energy projects. In the UK, Quinbrook has targeted re-powering opportunities at older landfill gas and coal mine methane sites. The intention is to install co-located solar and battery storage at underutilized grid connections. Furthermore, Quinbrook is in the process of commissioning a new-build critical grid support project on a brownfield site, reducing the use of arable or greenfield land.

Historically, Quinbrook has partnered with government projects to provide apprenticeships, training and upskilling in regional communities or to provide opportunities to those without school qualifications. These partnerships have also sought to develop projects in communities that have limited access to affordable energy because of local economic disadvantages, or have previously been reliant on coal, to directly support both fair, safe work and deliver local economic benefits.

Modern slavery and human rights in supply chains

Quinbrook has implemented an extensive human rights assessment and engagement process to address potential human rights risks in modern and complex global supply chains. The assessment and engagement process includes:

- Risk assessment of suppliers and contractors
- Requests for information during tendering – on corruption, environmental, safety and human rights track records, policies, breaches and incident resolution
- Extensive auditing of supply chains
- Implementation of modern slavery terms in contracts, such as termination rights
- Influencing change directly by engaging with suppliers
- Avoiding certain risks: for example, by using batteries that do not contain minerals such as cobalt with a high risk of being produced by child labour
- Supporting end-of-life processes such as local recycling of metals and equipment.

Source: Quinbrook Infrastructure Partners (2022)

In general, no public data is available for private infrastructure projects. Some infrastructure projects are quite sizeable, but most of the market remains very granular, with limited mandatory public disclosure or reporting requirements. This lack of standards has led many managers to build their own dedicated ESG assessment approaches for infrastructure strategies – for example, applying the SDGs. One formal environmental and social risk management framework is the Equator Principles, which was developed for the banking sector. Banks committed to the Equator Principles initiative will only lend to development projects in developing countries that meet its social and environmental criteria.

Infrastructure asset operators, fund managers and investors that invest directly in infrastructure can use GRESB to measure the ESG performance of the portfolio or asset. Investors can use the GRESB data and fund reports to monitor the ESG-related risks, opportunities and impacts of their investment managers. The GRESB data can also function as a basis for further manager engagement dialogues, and investors may encourage new managers to join this reporting benchmark. The GRESB assessment framework is updated annually to provide new data and analytical tools covering, among other things, the EU Taxonomy, the SGDs and TCFD recommendations.

There is an increasing need for both positive and negative impact indicators for infrastructure investments. Expectations are high about the contribution that the EU Taxonomy regulation will make, which will require reporting according to the "Do No Significant Harm" principle. This principle could help to initiate the needed impact measurement that will improve the infrastructure market's contribution to environmental and social objectives.

7.8 Commodity investments

Although commodity trading has a long history, the broader investor interest in commodity investments is more recent. One contributing factor is the liberalization of the derivative market for commodities, especially with the US Commodity Futures Modernization Act of 2000 which allows investors, not just traditional hedgers and insurers, to trade commodity futures. In general, investors seek diversification opportunities and inflation protection by investing in different commodity investments.

There are several ways for an investor to seek commodity exposure. Trading with commodity futures is a typical way of participating in commodity markets, and generally preferred over physical commodity trading; and it offers the possibility of opting out of physical storage and deliveries. Investments in real assets, such as timberland and farmland, are gaining more interest among investors. Commodity-linked investments such as equities, represent another way of gaining commodity-factor exposure. The different types of commodity investment each have their own ESG-related challenges and opportunities.

Responsibility in commodity investing has many facets. Natural resource depletion, biodiversity loss and climate change are posing challenges in a world where demographic and lifestyle changes are leading to increased resource consumption. Growing resource demand for technological solutions, electrification and low-carbon transition affects commodity prices, which creates both new investment opportunities and risks for the investor. There are also many challenges in the production and trade of commodities with ESG implications, such as labour and human rights issues and the environmental impact of production. These challenges pose a significant financial and reputational risk to the investor.

7.8.1 Commodity futures

Commodity futures is one of the main forms of commodity investment, and also the one that presents the largest challenges from an RI perspective – both in terms of the structural effect on commodities markets, and the limited opportunities to become informed about the origin and production of the commodity or to enter into an engagement to wield influence.

Although investors have an essential role to play in bringing liquidity to commodity markets, the financialization of commodities markets has impacted the market's structure and price movements. Increased investor demand can influence the price signals in the derivatives market and can thus have a bearing on producers' decisions and the commodity's price level. Wider speculative activity in the derivatives market may disrupt that market's original function as a pricing and risk diversification tool for farmers and producers. Large investment inflows in commodity indices, ETFs and hedge funds can increase activity in the market that is not based on real commodity demand. Investors also monitor commodity price trends and may through their actions strengthen the direction of the trend. As investment returns decline in the most significant commodity markets, investors may move to increasingly smaller and illiquid commodity markets, where the impact of trading on price volatility is even larger. Speculative investors can "play" with physical deliveries and storage of commodities, thus impacting supply and demand, and this forces market participants to maintain high stock levels, which raises prices.

The 2008 Food Price Crisis triggered a debate about the role of investor speculation in food-related commodities. Academic research reached mixed conclusions because food prices were simultaneously impacted by other factors such as extreme weather, first-generation biofuel production, and rising energy and fertilizer prices. As a concrete outcome of the crisis, many institutional investors withdrew from agricultural futures markets. Investor initiatives, such as the PRI, compiled best-practice guidelines for derivative investments in commodities. The guidelines included, among other things, managing commodity positions based on long-term fundamentals instead of price trends, setting limits on trading prices and volumes, and limiting trading on less liquid markets. The guidelines also addressed the need to engage with managers, index providers, commodity stock exchanges and traders to improve governance and transparency of investments and the market in general. The Food Price Crisis pushed many investors to further evaluate the ESG aspects of different commodities and related sectors more broadly.

7.8.2 Real assets

Real assets provide the most direct opportunities to integrate ESG aspects into an investment. As an owner of real assets, such as timberland and farmland, an investor is directly involved in management and production and is thus in a better position to take ESG aspects into account. The investor can pursue positive social and environmental benefits by, for example, developing local environmental conditions, food production and expertise. As an owner of real assets, the investor also bears responsibility for any direct risks associated with the investment. Principles for responsible agricultural investment have been developed by the UN in cooperation with the World Bank.

The investor can either set specific ESG standards for the real assets or apply for sustainable production certification and ask local market participants and intermediaries to consider best practices when managing the assets. A proactive discussion should be held with the local community if production is likely to affect them or if there is conflicting information about property rights. If no best practices are in place locally, the investor can engage and develop standards together with local actors. Continuous policy development and transparency is key to managing reputational risks. In this regard, the PRI has developed responsible investor guidelines related to investments in both forestry and farmland. Institutional investors often invest through diversified investment funds, shifting the focus to the responsibility of the asset managers.

7.8.3 Commodity-linked companies

A commodity investor can also invest in commodity-linked companies through equity or bond instruments. Commodity-linked companies can be defined as those with operations that focus on the production and distribution of commodities. Commodity-linked investments may not give the portfolio diversification benefits or the direct access to commodity prices that some investors are seeking, but they can increase the commodity-factor exposure of the portfolio. In addition, taking ESG-related aspects into account is more straightforward compared to futures investments: the investor can conduct a sector-specific ESG company analysis and further engage with companies on their operations (see more on responsible equity and fixed-income investments in Sections 7.1 and 7.2). The next section explores commodity sectors in more detail.

7.8.4 ESG considerations in commodity sectors

Commodities will continue to play a vital role in the future economy. Investors, regulators and consumer preferences can all drive the minimization of the negative ESG impacts of commodities production and processing. ESG aspects and potential investor actions vary across the different commodity sectors, i.e. fossil energy, metals, agricultural products and timberland (see Table 7.8 for a summary).

7.8.4.1 Fossil energy

Coal, oil and gas are considered unsustainable sources of energy. Today, thermal coal mining companies are increasingly excluded from responsible investor portfolios as there are minimal opportunities from a sustainability angle. Oil and gas extraction and refining processes have a high negative impact on the environment, and various pollutants are released during use. As a reliance on oil and gas persists during the global transition to a low-carbon economy, some investors have decided to stay invested and engage with these companies to achieve more sustainable practices. Alternatively, investors may favour companies that are in transition and committed to a credible development of renewable fuels.

7.8.4.2 Metals

The mining and processing of nonprecious metals such as steel, zinc, lead, tin and copper have considerable negative environmental impacts. Most smelting processes burn coking coal, with high carbon emissions. The mining sector is characterized by challenges related to poor labour rights and safety issues, especially in small-scale, artisanal mining in emerging markets. It is estimated that the global demand for metals will continue at a high level, not least as an integral part of a low-carbon future, with the rising demand for electric vehicles and batteries requiring metals such as lithium and copper. Rapid technology development and software updates do not support the extension of product lifecycles, smartphones being a salient example.

Gold mining is marked by similar environmental and social challenges. Some regulatory efforts, such as the Dodd–Frank Act in the USA, have been made to ensure accredited sourcing for gold. A Fairtrade certification is also available.

Rare-earth metals are widely used in modern ICT devices, clean energy solutions, and aerospace and defence-sector instruments. And virtually all of them are mined and processed in regions, which are not known for prioritizing health, safety or environment. As these extraction and processing companies represent a fairly limited investable universe, a responsible investor's focus should be turned to the vast number of companies that use rare-earth metals.

From an RI perspective, the investor can focus on companies that recycle metals or aim to make more resource-efficient products with recycling-friendly designs, or those that seek more sustainable substitutes. Recycling cannot fully replace the primary production of metals, but it does reduce demand. Other possible actions for a responsible investor are engagement with companies on the adoption of best practices and supporting ethical sourcing initiatives. Initiatives such as the Extractive Industries Transparency Initiative (EITI) and the Initiative for Responsible Mining Assurance (IRMA) support the mining sector by setting standards for good governance and providing certifications for responsible mining.

7.8.4.3 Agricultural products

The unsustainability of current global food systems is widely acknowledged. The expansion of animal farming and farmland replaces forests which function as carbon sinks and as ecosystems supporting biodiversity. Also, many crops require irrigation and are being grown in environments where water is already scarce. Inefficient supply chains and logistics represent a further barrier to sustainability: as much as 30% of world agricultural production never reaches the food market, either remaining unused in the ground or rotting in transit due to poor or non-existent storage facilities and transport networks. In developed economies, the majority of food waste occurs in trade or after reaching the consumer. For these and other reasons, despite economic growth and increased agricultural productivity, extreme hunger and malnutrition remain a huge barrier to development in many countries.

The UN points to underinvestment in the world food system and agriculture in recent decades. It is estimated that, by 2050, the world will need to produce some 50–70% more food than it does today in order to meet the demands of the growing population. There is a limit to the amount of potential arable land, so innovative solutions are needed to increase yield. Genetically modified organisms (GMOs) have already been used to improve crop yields, but some investors avoid GMO-related investments for different, sometimes ethical, reasons. Technological innovations can increase yield and confer other benefits, such as more water-efficient irrigation systems. The International Fund for Agricultural Development (IFAD) sees small-scale farming as solving many problems: by serving domestic food demand, improving local income by providing jobs and because of its inherent knowledge of local ecosystems. One way this can be supported is through dedicated impact investment funds.

The challenges of the global food systems are complex, and the sector is in dire need of investments. From an RI perspective, an investor can look to innovative producers or infrastructure and technology to improve agricultural productivity and a more efficient use of resources.

Demand for plant-based and other non-meat proteins grows as consumer dietary preferences and values are changing, largely due to an increased understanding of how individuals can make an impact through their choices. This brings investment opportunities into innovations in the food sector. However, jurisdictions each have their own rules and regulations when it comes to food production and safety and these differences can prevent innovations from reaching new markets.

The Farm Animal Investment Risk & Return (FAIRR) Initiative is a fast-growing investor network focusing on ESG risks in the global food sector, driving change in the animal agriculture space in particular. FAIRR produces and analyses data from the world's largest protein producers and manufacturers, thereby supporting investors' decision-making and joint engagement efforts in the sector.

7.8.4.4 Timberland

Forests play an important role in climate change mitigation, binding CO_2 from the atmosphere and acting as carbon sinks. At a global level, deforestation – due mostly to construction, mining, expansion of agriculture and increased

Table 7.8 ESG issues and possible actions for responsible investors in different commodity sectors

Commodity	ESG issues	Responsible action
Fossil energy Coal Oil and gas	• Finite, unsustainable resource • Pollution • Accelerating climate change	• Divest or exclude • Engage with companies for transition to a low-emission future and more sustainable practices • Invest in renewables
Metals	• Environmental damage from extraction • Deforestation • Pollution and toxic by-products • Health and safety • Carbon cost of purification	• Engage with company to ensure best practice • Invest in recyclers and support research • Support ethical sourcing initiatives • Engage with companies on resource-efficient, recycling-friendly products and substituting materials • Divest or exclude
Agricultural products Crops Livestock	• Speculative futures impact on food prices • Deforestation • Biodiversity loss • Water scarcity • Inefficient crop production and use of land • Food waste • Unequal access to land	• Exclude commodity futures • Invest in innovative producers • Invest in plant-based and other non-meat protein alternatives • Invest in infrastructure and technology to improve agricultural productivity and efficient use of resources • Support small-scale farming
Timberland	• Unsustainable forest management • Climate change mitigation • Biodiversity loss	• Invest in sustainably managed forests • Ensure sustainable end-product use • Support afforestation

Source: Based on Mercer LLC, "Investing Responsibly: The Use of Commodities" (2020)

forest fires – is one of the main sources of greenhouse gas emissions. From a sustainability perspective, the end use of timber is critical. Using timber as fuel removes the benefit of carbon capture, as the combustion process releases CO_2 back in the atmosphere.

A responsible investor should focus on timberland investments in which the end product will have a more sustainable use. Growing high-quality timber means that its carbon will be stored in products that are as long-lasting as possible (carbon storage effect), such as construction materials. An indirect substitution effect is achieved, too, if wood products displace those with higher fossil greenhouse gas emissions, such as steel, cement, plastics or cotton textiles (avoided emissions). In addition, sustainable forest management can improve the carbon balance of timberland investments. The better the forests grow, the more they bind CO_2 from the atmosphere. Forest certifications such as that of the Forest Stewardship Council (FSC) help to ensure responsible forest management and the preservation of biodiversity.

Classifying timberland as a "green" investment is not self-evident. Considering the purpose is to increase the carbon sink effect of forests, tree growth should exceed tree removal. In practice, this requires regular forest growth and carbon sequestration calculations. Afforestation is considered the most efficient method of increasing carbon capture in this sector.

Forest carbon offset markets offer an additional income source for timberland investors. However, it should be noted that the purpose and use of carbon offsets are considered controversial, and there is as yet no tailored guidance for investors. Net Zero investment frameworks, such as the Paris Aligned Investment Initiative, indicate that offsets should be used as a last resort, once all measures to reduce emissions directly have been exhausted. Furthermore, the availability of offsets is finite, as there is not enough available land for everyone to rely on afforestation. This effectively means that carbon offsets should be reserved for activities such as heavy industry, where direct decarbonization solutions do not yet exist at scale. Carbon offset schemes also face criticism around the issues of additionality and double counting.

Chapter 7 key Q&As

Here are the answers to the key questions posed at the start of this chapter.

Can Responsible Investment be implemented in all types of asset classes?

RI can be taken into account in all asset classes and in both direct and indirect investments. A responsible investor does not have to exclude individual asset classes from the investment portfolio.

In practice, how can ESG be taken into account in different asset classes?

Each asset class has its own challenges and opportunities to be considered from an RI perspective. The asset class's specific characteristics determine how different RI approaches can be applied. Most approaches, such as ESG integration, screening and engagement, can be applied extensively across asset classes, although the level of use may still vary between asset classes. Table 7.2 summarizes RI opportunities for different asset classes.

Can a passive investor be a responsible one?

Passive investment is a key strategy for many investors, and the popularity of passive equity index and ETF investments in particular is growing significantly. With this growth, index suppliers and asset managers have in recent years responded effectively to investor demand by developing ESG indices and replicating investment funds and ETFs covering different geographical markets. Passive investment products can apply active RI approaches such as voting, engagement and thematic investments.

Bibliography

Alternative Investment Management Association (AIMA). (2020, 17 July). "Short Selling and Responsible Investment." Retrieved 20 February 2022 from https://www.aima.org/sound-practices/industry-guides/short-selling-and-responsible-investment.html

Baraniuk, C. (2020, 18 August). "Tracking Down Three Billion Litres of Lost Water". *BBC News*. Retrieved 21 February 2022 from https://www.bbc.com/news/business-53274914

BNP Paribas. (2020, October). *Hedge Funds and ESG: Finding their Place on the ESG Spectrum*. Retrieved 20 February 2022 from https://securities.cib.bnpparibas/app/uploads/sites/3/2021/04/ss-files-2020-hedgefunds-esg-report.pdf

Boston College Institute for Responsible Investment. (2009). *Handbook on Responsible Investment across Asset Classes*. Retrieved 18 February 2022 from https://iri.hks.harvard.edu/files/iri/files/iri_handbook_on_responsible_investment_across_asset_classes.pdf

Bproperty.com. (2021, 2 May). "Differences between Real Estate Developer and Investor". Retrieved 20 February 2022 from https://www.bproperty.com/blog/real-estate-developer-real-estate-investor

Building Research Establishment Environmental Assessment Method. (2021, 19 August). "What Is BREEAM?" Retrieved 20 February 2022 from https://www.breeam.com

CDP (Carbon Disclosure Project). (2022). "The A List 2021". Retrieved 19 February 2022 from https://www.cdp.net/en/companies/companies-scores

Churchill Asset Management. (2022). Personal Communication with the Authors, 15 February 2022.

Church Pension Fund (Finland). (2021, 17 June). *Climate Strategy of the Church Pension Fund*. Retrieved 20 February 2022 from https://evl.fi/documents/1327140/48902395/Climate+Strategy+of+the+Church+Pension+Fund.pdf/58a2df4e-5811-c7dc-5d9f-71c99c56492f?t=1630311986002

Climate Bonds Initiative (CBI). (2021). *Sustainable Debt: Global State of the Market 2020*. Retrieved 19 February 2022 from https://www.climatebonds.net/files/reports/cbi_sd_sotm_2020_04d.pdf

Climate Bonds Initiative (CBI). (2022, 11 January). "Certification under the Climate Bonds Standard". Retrieved 19 February 2022 from https://www.climatebonds.net/certification

Climate Bonds Initiative (CBI). (2022, 17 January). "Q3 Briefing". Personal Communication with the Authors, 17 January 2022.

Comprehensive Assessment System for Built Environment Efficiency. (2022). "CASBEE". Retrieved 20 February 2022 from https://www.ibec.or.jp/CASBEE/english

Corporate Knights. (2021, 30 August). "2021 Global 100 Ranking". Retrieved 19 February 2022 from https://www.corporateknights.com/rankings/global-100-rankings/2021-global-100-rankings/2021-global-100-ranking/

Economist Intelligence Unit. (2019). *The Critical Role of Infrastructure for the Sustainable Development Goals.* Retrieved 21 February 2022 from https://content.unops.org/publications/The-critical-role-of-infrastructure-for-the-SDGs_EN.pdf?mtime=20190314130614

Equator Principles. (2022). "The Equator Principles". Retrieved 19 February 2022 from https://equator-principles.com

European Association for Investors in Non-Listed Real Estate. (2022). "About INREV". Retrieved 20 February 2022 from https://www.inrev.org/about-inrev

European Central Bank (ECB). (2020, 22 September). "ECB to Accept Sustainability-Linked Bonds as Collateral". Retrieved 19 February 2022 from https://www.ecb.europa.eu/press/pr/date/2020/html/ecb.pr200922~482e4a5a90.en.html

European Commission (EC). (2019, 18 June). *TEG Report on EU Green Bond Standard.* Retrieved 19 February 2022 from https://ec.europa.eu/info/files/190618-sustainable-finance-teg-report-green-bond-standard_en

European Commission. (2019, 18 June). *TEG Interim Report on EU Climate Benchmarks and Benchmarks' ESG Disclosures.* Retrieved 19 February 2022 from https://ec.europa.eu/info/files/190618-sustainable-finance-teg-report-climate-benchmarks-and-disclosures_en

European Commission. (2019, June). *Report on Benchmarks, EU Technical Expert Group on Sustainable Finance.* Retrieved 19 February 2022 from https://ec.europa.eu/info/sites/default/files/business_economy_euro/banking_and_finance/documents/190618-sustainable-finance-teg-report-climate-benchmarks-and-disclosures_en.pdf

European Commission. (2022). "EU Taxonomy Compass: Construction and Real Estate". Retrieved 20 February 2022 from https://ec.europa.eu/sustainable-finance-taxonomy/activities/sector_en.htm?reference=7

European Commission. (2022). "Energy". Retrieved 20 February 2022 from https://energy.ec.europa.eu/index_en

European Council. (2021, 5 October). "Taxation: EU List of Non-cooperative Jurisdictions". Retrieved 20 February 2022 from https://www.consilium.europa.eu/en/policies/eu-list-of-non-cooperative-jurisdictions

European Union. (2019, 27 November). Regulation (EU) 2019/2088 of the European Parliament and of the Council on Sustainability-Related Disclosures in the Financial Services Sector. Retrieved 18 February 2022 from https://eur-lex.europa.eu/legal-content/EN/TXT/?uri=celex%3A32019R2088

Extractive Industries Transparency Initiative. (2022). "The Global Standard for the Good Governance of Oil, Gas and Mineral Resources". Retrieved 20 February 2022 from https://eiti.org

FAIRR Initiative. (2020, 30 June). "The World's Fastest-Growing Investor Network Focusing on ESG Risks in the Global Food Sector". FAIRR. Retrieved 20 February 2022 from https://www.fairr.org

Fiastre, P. (2019, 28 January). "ESG: The Foundation of Responsible Infrastructure Investment". IPE Real Assets. Retrieved 21 February 2022 from https://realassets.ipe.com/infrastructure/esg-the-foundation-of-responsible-infrastructure-investment/10029601.article

Financial Action Task Force (FATF). (2022). "Financial Action Task Force". Retrieved 19 February 2022 from https://www.fatf-gafi.org

FINCA International. (2020, 21 September). "What Is Microfinance?". Retrieved 20 February 2022 from https://finca.org/our-work/microfinance

Food and Agriculture Organization (FAO), International Fund for Agricultural Development (IFAD), United Nations Conference on Trade and Development (UNCTAD) and World Bank Group. (2010, 25 January). *Principles for Responsible Agricultural Investment that Respects Rights, Livelihoods and Resources.* Retrieved 20 February 2022 from https://openknowledge.worldbank.org/bitstream/handle/10986/24101/Principles0for0s000extended0version.pdf

Food and Agriculture Organization (FAO) of the United Nations. (2009, 13 October). *Global Agriculture towards 2050. High Level Expert Forum.* Retrieved 20 February 2022 from https://www.fao.org/fileadmin/templates/wsfs/docs/Issues_papers/HLEF2050_Global_Agriculture.pdf

Forest Stewardship Council (FSC). (2022). "Forest Management Certification". Retrieved 20 February 2022 from https://fsc.org/en/forest-management-certification

Freedom House. (2021). *Freedom in the World 2021: Democracy under Siege.* Retrieved 19 February 2022 from https://freedomhouse.org/sites/default/files/2021-02/FIW2021_World_02252021_FINAL-web-upload.pdf

Fund EcoMarket. (2022). "Sustainable, Responsible and Ethical Fund Styles Explained". Retrieved 19 February 2022 from https://www.fundecomarket.co.uk/help/sri-styles-directory

Global ESG Benchmark for Real Assets (GRESB). (2021). *2021 Infrastructure Asset Assessment Framework.* Retrieved 11 December 2021 from https://documents.gresb.com.s3-website.eu-central-1.amazonaws.com/generated_files/infrastructure/2021/asset/assessment/complete.html

Global Impact Investing Network (GIIN). (2020, June). *2020 Annual Impact Investor Survey.* Retrieved 20 February 2022 from https://thegiin.org/research/publication/impinv-survey-2020

Global Sustainable Investment Alliance. (2021). *Global Sustainable Investment Review 2020.* Retrieved 18 February 2022 from https://www.gsi-alliance.org/wp-content/uploads/2021/08/GSIR-20201.pdf

Green Building Council Australia. (2022). "What Is Green Star?" Retrieved 20 February 2022 from https://new.gbca.org.au/green-star/green-star

Green Building Initiative. (2022). "Green Globes Certification". Retrieved 20 February 2022 from https://thegbi.org

Hatshima, H., & Demberel, U. (2020, 27 January). "What Is Blended Finance, and How Can It Help Deliver Successful High-Impact, High-Risk Projects?" Independent Evaluation Group. Retrieved 21 February 2022 from https://ieg.worldbankgroup.org/blog/what-blended-finance-and-how-can-it-help-deliver-successful-high-impact-high-risk-projects

Hyrske, A., Lönnroth, M., Savilaakso, A., & Sievänen, R. (2020). *Vastuullinen sijoittaja.* Helsingin kauppakamari.

Imbert, D., & Knoepfel, I. (2011, September). *The Responsible Investor's Guide to Commodities.* onValues Ltd. Retrieved 20 February 2022 from https://d306pr3pise04h.cloudfront.net/docs/issues_doc%2FFinancial_markets%2FCommodities_Guide.pdf

Initiative for Responsible Mining Assurance (IRMA). (2021, 10 March). "About Us". Retrieved 20 February 2022 from https://responsiblemining.net/about/about-us

International Capital Market Association (ICMA). (2015, May). *Standard Aggregated Collective Action Clauses ("CACS") for the Terms and Conditions of Sovereign Notes Governed by English Law*. Retrieved 19 February 2022 from https://www.icmagroup.org/assets/documents/Resources/ICMA-Standard-CACs-Pari-Passu-and-Creditor-Engagement-Provisions---May-2015.pdf

International Fund for Agricultural Development (IFAD). (2020, 16 December). "Five Reasons IFAD Is Putting Small-Scale Farmers at the Forefront of Food Systems Transformation". Retrieved 20 February 2022 from https://www.ifad.org/en/web/latest/-/story/five-reasons-ifad-is-putting-small-scale-farmers-at-the-forefront-of-food-systems-transformation

KPMG in Finland. (2020, 10 June). *EU Sustainable Finance Explained: Takeaways Related to Key Climate Benchmarks and the Benchmarks' ESG Disclosures*. Retrieved 19 February 2022 from https://home.kpmg/fi/fi/home/Pinnalla/2020/05/eu-sustainable-finance-explained-climate-benchmarks.html

Leadership in Energy and Environmental Design. (2022). "LEED Rating System". Retrieved 20 February 2022 from https://new.usgbc.org/leed

Lou, X., & Karpoff, J.M. (2009). "Short Sellers and Financial Misconduct". *SSRN Electronic Journal*, 65(5), 1,879–1,913. https://doi.org/10.2139/ssrn.1443361

Mackenzie, M. (2021, 8 April). "BlackRock Secures Largest-Ever ETF Launch as Green Investing Wave Builds". *Financial Times*. Retrieved 19 February 2022 from https://www.ft.com/content/43b757a3-306d-4567-b6db-69ab226500e2

Mercer LLC. (2020). "Investing Responsibly: The Use of Commodities". Retrieved 20 February 2022 from https://www.mercer.us/our-thinking/wealth/investing-responsibly-the-use-of-commodities.html

Mittal, A. (2009, June). *The 2008 Food Crisis: Rethinking Food Security Policies*. G-24 Discussion Paper Series No. 56. UNCTAD. Retrieved 20 February 2022 from https://unctad.org/system/files/official-document/gdsmdpg2420093_en.pdf

MSCI ESG Research LL. (2021, April). *The Top 20 Largest ESG Funds – Under the Hood*. Retrieved 19 February 2022 from https://www.msci.com/documents/1296102/24720517/Top-20-Largest-ESG-Funds.pdf

Nareit. (2022). "REITs & ESG: Environmental, Social & Governance". Retrieved 20 February 2022 from https://www.reit.com/investing/reits-sustainability

National Australian Built Environment Rating System. (2022). "What Is NABERS?". Retrieved 20 February 2022 from https://www.nabers.gov.au

National Green Building Standard. (2022). "What's a National Green Building Standard (NGBS)?". Retrieved 20 February 2022 from https://www.ngbs.com/the-ngbs-green-promise

Nauman, B. (2020, 24 October). "Short-sellers Step Up Scrutiny of ESG Stocks". *Financial Times*. Retrieved 20 February 2022 from https://www.ft.com/content/b8c91561-b44c-43cf-9810-7aeff9c377a8

Novethic. (2021, January). Infrastructure Funds Facing the European Green Recovery. Retrieved 21 February 2022 from https://www.novethic.fr/fileadmin//Novethic_2021_Infrastructure-Funds-Facing-the-European-Green-Recovery.pdf?_ga=2.91826842.1287079141.1638556038-2095493334.1615542398

Paris Aligned Investment Framework. (2021, March). *Net Zero Investment Framework Implementation Guide*. Version 1.0. Retrieved 20 February 2022 from https://www.parisalignedinvestment.org/media/2021/03/PAII-Net-Zero-Investment-Framework_Implementation-Guide.pdf

Phenix Capital Group. (2021, February). *Impact Report: Deep Dive on Private Equity Funds*. Retrieved 20 February 2022 from https://www.phenixcapitalgroup.com/private-equity

Preqin. (2021, 4 February). *2021 Preqin Global Infrastructure Report: Sample Pages*. Retrieved 21 February 2022 from https://www.preqin.com/insights/global-reports/2021-preqin-global-infrastructure-report

Preqin. (2022, 12 January). *2022 Preqin Global Infrastructure Report: Sample Pages*. Retrieved 21 February 2022 from https://www.preqin.com/insights/global-reports/2022-preqin-global-infrastructure-report

Preqin. (2022, 12 January). *2022 Preqin Global Private Debt Report: Sample Pages*. Retrieved 20 February 2022 from https://www.preqin.com/insights/global-reports/2022-preqin-global-private-debt-report

Preqin. (2022, 12 January). *2022 Preqin Global Hedge Fund Report: Sample Pages*. Retrieved 20 February 2022 from https://www.preqin.com/insights/global-reports/2022-preqin-global-hedge-fund-report

Preqin. (2022). "Private Debt". Retrieved 20 February 2022 from https://www.preqin.com/academy/lesson-4-asset-class-101s/private-debt

Principles for Responsible Investment (PRI). (2012). *Responsible Investment and Hedge Funds: A Discussion Paper*. Retrieved 20 February 2022 from https://www.unpri.org/download?ac=4155

Principles for Responsible Investment (PRI). (2016). *Sustainable Real Estate Investment. Implementing the Paris Climate Agreement: An Action Framework*. Retrieved 20 February 2022 from https://www.unpri.org/download?ac=3006

Principles for Responsible Investment (PRI). (2017, 9 May). "Responsible Investment DDQ for Hedge Funds". Retrieved 20 February 2022 from https://www.unpri.org/hedge-funds/responsible-investment-ddq-for-hedge-funds/125.article#policy

Principles for Responsible Investment (PRI). (2018). *ESG Engagement for Fixed Income Investors: Managing Risks, Enhancing Returns*. Retrieved 19 February 2022 from https://www.unpri.org/download?ac=4449

Principles for Responsible Investment (PRI). (2018). *Primer on Responsible Investment in Infrastructure*. Retrieved 21 February 2022 from https://www.unpri.org/download?ac=4141

Principles for Responsible Investment (PRI). (2019). *Spotlight on Responsible Investment in Private Debt*. Retrieved 20 February 2022 from https://www.unpri.org/download?ac=5982

Principles for Responsible Investment (PRI). (2019, 11 February). "Private Debt Overview". Retrieved 20 February 2022 from https://www.unpri.org/private-debt/an-overview-of-private-debt/4057.article

Principles for Responsible Investment (PRI). (2020). *ESG Engagement for Sovereign Debt Investors*. Retrieved 19 February 2022 from https://www.unpri.org/download?ac=12018

Principles for Responsible Investment (PRI). (2020). *TCFD for Private Equity General Partners*. Retrieved 20 February 2022 from https://www.unpri.org/download?ac=10436

Principles for Responsible Investment (PRI). (2020). *Technical Guide: ESG Incorporation in Hedge Funds*. Retrieved 20 February 2022 from https://www.unpri.org/download?ac=11344

Principles for Responsible Investment (PRI). (2021). *An Introduction to Responsible Investment: Real Estate.* Retrieved 20 February 2022 from https://www.unpri.org/download?ac=10287

PwC. (2021). *Private Equity's ESG Journey: From Compliance to Value Creation. The Global Private Equity Responsible Investment Survey.* Retrieved 20 February 2022 from https://www.pwc.com/gx/en/private-equity/private-equity-survey/pwc-pe-survey-2021.pdf

Quinbrook Infrastructure Partners. (2022). Personal Communication with the authors, 14 February 2022.

Science Based Targets. (2022). "How it Works". Retrieved 20 February 2022 from https://sciencebasedtargets.org/how-it-works

S&P Global. (2022). *The Sustainability Yearbook 2022.* Retrieved 19 February 2022 from https://www.spglobal.com/esg/csa/yearbook

Standards Board for Alternative Investments (SBAI). (2022). "Open Protocol". Retrieved 20 February 2022 from https://www.sbai.org/toolbox/open-protocol.html

Task Force on Climate-Related Financial Disclosures. (2020, 22 September). "Recommendations". Retrieved 20 February 2022 from https://www.fsb-tcfd.org/recommendations

Transparency International. (2022). *Corruption Perceptions Index 2021.* Retrieved 19 February 2022 from https://images.transparencycdn.org/images/CPI2021_Report_EN-web.pdf

United States Congress. (2000, 14 December). H.R.5660 – 106th Congress (1999–2000): *Commodity Futures Modernization Act of 2000.* Retrieved 20 February 2022 from https://www.congress.gov/bill/106th-congress/house-bill/5660/text

White House. (2021, 28 October). "President Biden Announces the Build Back Better Framework". Retrieved 21 February 2022 from https://www.whitehouse.gov/briefing-room/statements-releases/2021/10/28/president-biden-announces-the-build-back-better-framework

World Bank. (2017). *Global Findex Database.* Chapter 2: "The Unbanked". Retrieved 20 February 2022 from https://globalfindex.worldbank.org/sites/globalfindex/files/chapters/2017%20Findex%20full%20report_chapter2.pdf

World Green Building Council. (2013). "The Business Case for Green Building: A Review of the Costs and Benefits for Developers, Investors and Occupants". Retrieved 20 February 2022 from https://www.worldgbc.org/news-media/business-case-green-building-review-costs-and-benefits-developers-investors-and-occupants

World Green Building Council. (2022a). "Our Green Building Councils". Retrieved 20 February 2022 from https://www.worldgbc.org/our-green-building-councils

World Green Building Council. (2022b). "What Is Green Building?" Retrieved 20 February 2022 from https://www.worldgbc.org/what-green-building

8 ESG data

Key questions in this chapter

- Where does ESG data come from?
- How can ESG data be categorized?

All Responsible Investment (RI) approaches in all asset classes require information. There are many ways in which the necessary information can be gathered and organized for RI purposes. This chapter describes them more in detail.

Individual environmental, social and governance (ESG) data points for companies – such as the percentage of women in the company's top management – offer only limited insights when looking at companies' sustainability risks and opportunities from an investment point of view. As a result, data points are usually combined to form a more holistic, often company-specific, ESG indicator, ESG factor or ESG rating. To be clear on the terminology: an ESG data point is a single data point that can be read from company filing; an ESG indicator is created when ESG data points are combined, often by external observers such as a company that provides ESG ratings; an ESG factor is a standardized and normalized quantitative value describing how well a company is performing in a particular ESG issue; and, finally, an ESG rating is a combination of ESG indicators or factors which describes how well a company is performing across a series of ESG issues.

This chapter focuses on ESG data and ESG indicators (see Figure 8.1). ESG factors and ESG ratings are described in more detail in Chapter 9.

8.1 Where does ESG data come from?

The majority of the ESG data in recent ESG analysis comes from the companies themselves, who disclose their policies, strategies and performance data points, with relevant context, as part of their routine reporting. As a result, most current ESG rating systems are based on public company reporting, complemented by surveys, questionnaires and other types of interaction with companies.

DOI: 10.4324/9781003284932-9

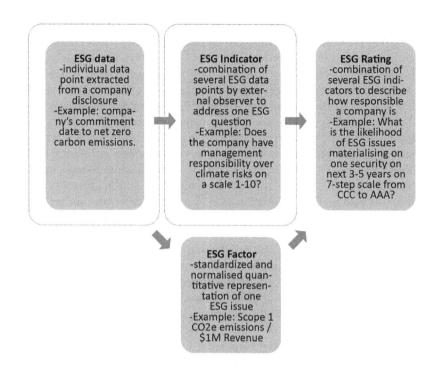

Figure 8.1 From ESG data and indicators to ESG ratings and factors (see chapter 9)

8.1.1 *Corporate responsibility reporting frameworks as a source of ESG data*

There are several frameworks guiding companies in their corporate responsibility reporting. The Global Reporting Initiative (GRI) was established in 1997 as a multi-stakeholder initiative comprising companies, NGOs, labour unions and investors. Its ambition was to provide a framework for all companies regardless of size, sector or domicile within which to report on the ESG issues they face and how they address them. Other frameworks have emerged recently to complement the GRI.

The Sustainability Accounting Standards Board (SASB) was founded in 2011 as an investor-driven reporting framework with a predefinition of materiality to help investors more precisely identify the ESG issues likely to impact companies' financial performance. This focus on materiality has made SASB popular, particularly among responsible investors who use the ESG integration as a RI approach (see Chapter 6), as well as companies seeking advice about issues to address. The Value Reporting Foundation's "Integrated Reporting" is a means of integrating forward-looking financial and sustainability/corporate responsibility information. Several topic-specific initiatives and reporting frameworks have risen in popularity as well. The Task Force on Climate-related Financial Disclosures (TCFD) and CDP (known initially as Carbon Disclosure Project) both aim to guide companies' climate disclosure. Other reporting frameworks are based on themes, such as human rights, specific industries (e.g. hazardous chemicals) or countries and regions.

In the EU, selected large investors must report on various sustainability characteristics of their investment portfolios at entity and fund levels, and provide a so-called Principle Adverse Impact (PAI) statement and report on the PAI indicators. While these are not company reporting requirements per se, investors will likely prefer the companies to report these specific data points themselves rather than investors or their service providers estimating them.

These frameworks all overlap with each other to some extent, but they do have individual characteristics. Both companies and the investment communities would prefer, in theory at least, a unified framework for reporting: scattered indicators and frameworks ramp up the costs of producing and consuming the said report. For perspective, financial accounting frameworks took decades to converge. The process started in the 1950s when international trade started to pick up after the war, and today there are still two dominant diverging frameworks: the International Financial Reporting Standards (IFRS) and the Generally Accepted Accounting Principles (GAAP).

In September 2020, five leading reporting framework and standard-setting organizations – CDP, CDSB (Carbon Disclosure Standards Board), GRI, IIRC (International Integrated Reporting Council) and SASB – announced a shared vision for a comprehensive corporate reporting system that includes financial accounting and sustainability disclosure, connected via Integrated Reporting. In November 2021, the IFRS Foundation announced the formation of the International Sustainability Standards Board (ISSB), which aims to develop a comprehensive global baseline of high-quality sustainability disclosure standards to meet investors' information needs. Given the IFRS's role in consolidating and overseeing the financial accounting standard, most practitioners (including existing framework organizations) agree that IFRS can play a decisive role in creating a unified framework around ESG disclosure worldwide. The IFRS initiative has also been supported by G7 finance ministers and the International Organization of Securities Commissions (IOSCO).

8.2 The characteristics of sustainability data reported by companies

In corporate responsibility reporting, numerical ESG indicators like carbon emissions require many assumptions and estimations, regardless of the company. Putting a figure on carbon emissions is partially based on the reporter's fuel and electricity use and is intuitively reasonably straightforward. In practice, most large companies do not possess a neat depository of electricity bills to add together and calculate their annual electricity use and then translate it to carbon emissions. Most companies have a wide variety of facilities. They might share facilities with other companies, or be in more than one country, with the amount of carbon in the electricity bought from the grid differing from one to another, not to mention the low-carbon or other renewable energy contracts in the mix. And energy utilities' billing dates might not tally with the company's financial year. If it is a company whose industrial activities involve raw materials and fuel, the amount of effort required will grow exponentially. This complexity is evident when looking at the Greenhouse Gas Protocol's guidance on their website.

Companies generally have an incentive to communicate with their (potential) investors. High-quality investor relations have been linked to more consistent earnings forecasts, greater institutional ownership, good media coverage, a better price-to-book ratio, and increased liquidity, leading to a lower cost of capital. A company's transparency in financial reporting reduces information asymmetry, which further reduces bid-ask spreads, benefiting the company. In theory, the same should apply to ESG data: the higher the quality of ESG information produced by a company, the better the ESG investment decisions – and everybody should be better off.

In practice, companies' corporate responsibility reporting does not always accurately reflect their sustainability risks and opportunities. The difference between perceived and actual ESG risk might be unintentional, as companies might not see their sustainability risks in the same way as the ESG rating provider or ESG data user. Companies can also knowingly downplay the importance and materiality of ESG risks, and simultaneously overstate their sustainability credentials. As an example of this, in January 2020 an Italian oil company was fined €5 million by the Italian Competition and Markets Authority for misleading marketing. The company advertised their palm oil-based biodiesel as green, while palm oil sourcing was contributing directly to deforestation. Palm oil-based biodiesel has a lower carbon footprint than traditional diesel based on prevailing calculation methodologies, and thus the company's claims have some merit.

Companies are also slow and conservative in describing or reacting to changes in circumstances or to their failures. Former corporate responsibility employees of a multinational technology company published a report in January 2021 which alleged that, while the company committed itself to zero tolerance on child labour, it knowingly continued business with a supplier for which such issues were a matter of record. The report alleges that this was down to the strategic importance of the supplier, which, again allegedly, trumps sustainability in this company's decision-making, and these priorities were not disclosed by the company. Supply chains, particularly in electronics, tend to be secretive for commercial reasons relating, for instance, to the security of supply and the price of critical components. In this specific example, the only way the issue could have come to light was by people with first-hand knowledge blowing the whistle. But NGOs and investigative journalists have relatively few tools to expose these kinds of issues, at least systematically. Therefore, responsible investors rely on companies' disclosure of data and issues in a truthful, timely and coherent fashion. The ESG ratings cannot accurately reflect companies' ESG risks and opportunities without accurate corporate responsibility reporting.

8.3 ESG information on companies from sources other than the company

Although the ESG data published by companies is essential, it is also possible to assess a company's sustainability using sources outside the company. While social media tends to create noise and sometimes inaccurate accounts of events, the phenomenon has nonetheless proved largely positive for ESG analysis. Analysts can now read local newspapers online anywhere globally, which can be auto-translated if necessary. Social media gives local communities and activists a platform to get their stories out. Machine learning enables natural language processing to winnow through the information flow and separate out company-specific news items for investors' attention. This is particularly useful with regard to social controversies like conflicts with local communities or disputes between a company and its workforce. Such issues are unlikely to be reported by the company or receive international media attention; by contrast, they are very likely to be found on local and social media. However, the open nature of social media will always raise a question mark over the accuracy of any such allegations.

Nonetheless, the broad sentiments that can be inferred from social media posts can be understood as part of a company's brand and therefore be very material. Companies can try with all their might to influence public opinion, but ultimately it is not up to the company to decide how sustainable it is. The true measure is to be found in the combined opinion of all the company's stakeholders. As such, the media-based ESG signal can be regarded as creating a more authentic picture of a company's sustainability credentials than anything based on company disclosure ever will.

ESG information on company operations can be built up using surveys, like employee surveys, for example. Employee survey sites collect thousands of anonymous reports from company employees who report their salary levels in exchange for knowledge of the salaries paid for comparable job descriptions by both their employer and competitors. These sites then provide anonymized responses as bulk data for third parties, including investors and ESG raters. This data can reveal employee-related aspects that the company might be reluctant to disclose, such as the gender pay gap.

Satellite imaging has already been used by some investors to gather ESG information. The most famous example is of it being used to discern the amount, and even the type, of cars on retail parking lots to infer the retail company's level of sales. Methane emissions can also be discerned from satellite images; this instance of remote sensing is interesting because fugitive methane emissions from oil and gas wells are not visible to the naked eye. So investors can observe methane leaks before the companies owning the wells are aware of them or prepared to disclose them.

The UN and various UN-affiliated institutions gather a wealth of sustainability-related data globally, often originating from UN member countries. These include for example economic information (unemployment), environment (greenhouse gas emissions), education (average years of schooling), health (access to health care) and governance (proportion of women in the parliament). Similarly, global indices encompassing various facets of sustainability are gathered by multiple international NGOs, including Transparency International (TI), which maintains its Corruption Perceptions Index (CPI) measuring the prevalence of corruption in each country, and the International Union for Conservation of Nature (IUCN) with its Red List of threatened species. These country-level lists can be used to measure companies' exposure to, for example, corruption and biodiversity loss.

A predictor for risk of corruption is a company's reliance on government licensing on account of its industry (e.g. fossil fuels or telecom) reckoned against the corruption of the host country (as calculated by TI's CPI). Similarly, a company's exposure to biodiversity loss can be modelled using its sector (e.g. mining or cement manufacturing) and its exposure to biodiversity-sensitive areas (based on IUCN's Red List). Country-level data, particularly from UN-affiliated institutions, tends to be more reliable and accurate than company data. There are fewer countries than there are companies, data gathering has a long history, and often the data will be scrutinized more closely by civil society and media than company-specific data is. For these reasons, corporate-level ESG data or ESG data combining issuer and country-level data can be less reliable than country-level data alone.

Academic research can make a significant contribution to ESG data sets, mainly by weeding out false and possibly outdated assumptions, creating new methodologies, and identifying and creating new data points. Subtleties around ESG issues can often be linked to cultural and even individual contexts. As a result, there is no shortage of opinions when assessing how sustainable (or not) any economic activity is. The scientific method can significantly contribute to the body of knowledge around different issues and how they interact with financial markets. At the same time, RI practitioners (ESG rating providers and ESG dedicated asset managers) might have access to data and information that academic researchers do not. Also, robust scientific studies typically require a long time series of data, which a rapidly evolving industry struggles to provide. As a result, practitioners will typically develop products based on perceived best practices and ideas complemented by scientific evidence.

Machine learning can also be applied in academic research from an ESG analysis point of view. At the time of writing, some startup companies have introduced commercial products that uncover the sustainability of different products and services based on machine learning methods applied to a corpus of academic evidence.

8.4 A hierarchy of ESG data

A common myth in ESG analysis is that the ESG data lacks quality, coverage and comparability. As this chapter has demonstrated so far, there is certainly no shortage of data. Instead, the question is how to categorize all the different bits and pieces of ESG information for quality control in preparation for its use. The hierarchy of ESG data can be described with the ESG data hierarchy model (Figure 8.2). The model starts from context, followed by policy and strategy, and concludes with outcomes.

8.4.1 Context

Context refers to changes in a company's operating environment which it will have little ability to influence, especially in the short term. For example, climate change affects companies' physical environment and emissions regulation. Changing demographics changes consumer behaviour, and rapidly evolving technologies change how companies position themselves in their value chain. These factors influence companies' responses and lay the foundation for how companies understand, behave and ultimately perform from an ESG point of view. These can also be understood through the megatrends lens, as described in Chapter 5.

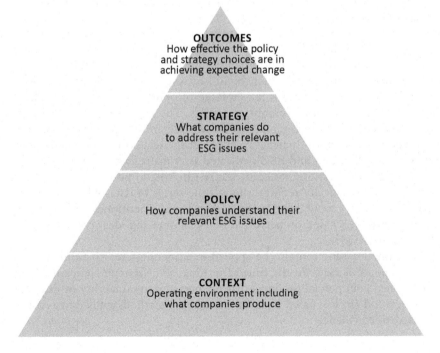

Figure 8.2 ESG data hierarchy model

8.4.1.1 *What do companies produce?*

A company's context is often understood through its products and services and where it operates rather than its operational performance. The products and services, in particular, reveal most of the risks and the opportunities to which it is exposed. Based on revenue (i.e. the revenue-based system), a basic understanding of this exposure can be acquired by assigning a company to a specific industry, like energy or financials. The breakdown can be made more granular by, for example, dividing financials into corporate, retail and investment banking and financial services. Most professional investors use comprehensive cascading tree industry classifications, of which there are several commercially available. Many governments and international associations also run industry classification systems. Table 8.1 lists some commonly used commercial and governmental industry classification systems.

All industry classification systems are broadly similar and comparable, but there are some crucial differences. For example, commercial systems tend to respond faster to changes, while government-run systems tend to be updated roughly every five years.

The most accurate classification trees have thousands of branches and provide a good starting point for ESG analysis. These systems, however,

Table 8.1 Examples of industry classification systems

Abbreviation	Full name	Nature	Owner
GICS	Global Industry Classification System	Commercial	MSCI
ICB	Industry Classification Benchmark	Commercial	FTSE Russell/ London Stock Exchange Group
BICS	Bloomberg Industry Classification System	Commercial	Bloomberg
RBICS	Revere Business Industry Classification System	Commercial	Factset
NAICS	North American Industry Classification System	Governmental	Mexico's Instituto Nacional de Estadística y Geografía, Statistics Canada, and the United States Office of Management and Budget
NACE	Nomenclature statistique des activités économiques dans la Communauté européenne	Governmental	European Union
ISIC	International Standard Industrial Classification	Governmental	United Nations

depend on companies' disclosure and their willingness to accurately disclose revenue from their product lines. There are also differences among regions. The Nordic markets expect company disclosure to be quite detailed, and, as a result, Nordic companies are comfortable providing a significant amount of detail. Asian companies often disclose their revenues at relatively superficial levels, making it more difficult for investors to assess the sustainability of revenue streams. Pharmaceutical companies, for example, might disclose their revenue as simply "pharmaceutical," while the differences in ESG risk and impact between, say, malaria medicine and fillers used in cosmetic surgery are immense. Similarly, companies are usually quite active and open in disclosing revenue from products that are perceived to be positive for society, like education or water purification; they tend to be more obtuse when discussing, for example, weapons manufacturing or coal mining.

The revenue-based system can be extended to cover companies' supply chains if data availability permits. Similarly, revenues can be augmented by capital expenditure and operational expenditure to add a more forward-looking flavour to the effectively backward-looking accounting data represented by revenue alone.

8.4.1.2 Where do companies operate?

As with companies' product/service mix, their geographic reach may also dictate the magnitude of certain ESG risks. As explained earlier, companies with products and services that need government concessions (such as oil and gas exploration, mining or telecom) and operate in countries with high corruption rates are exposed to an elevated risk of corruption. Companies can take steps to mitigate this risk, but, as a baseline, understanding the context is a crucial component in getting the ESG analysis right.

A geographical analysis relies on company disclosure, a legal requirement in most jurisdictions, at least at a most basic level. After years of debate, the EU agreed on country-by-country reporting in terms of taxes beginning in 2024. The US Securities and Exchange Commission (SEC) currently requires a breakdown between domestic (i.e. USA) and international (i.e. anything other than USA), but country-by-country reporting for tax purposes is also in the process of being legislated.

Companies use various buckets to report their revenue (or assets or employees). But they can also report their revenue precisely per country. Tables 8.2 and 8.3 present a hypothetical example of a company's reporting.

These percentages can be tied to a country-level indicator of a specific ESG issue, such as corruption, water scarcity, biodiversity, etc. For corruption, the CPI provides a score ranging from 0 (most corrupt) to 100 (least corrupt). The calculation in Table 8.3 shows that the company has an elevated corruption risk (a score of 55) compared to a company that conducts all of its business in France (which has a CPI score of 69). This does not mean that the company in Table 8.3 is more corrupt than its counterpart operating only in France. What it does mean is that, if companies are otherwise comparable (i.e. their product and services mix is the same, and they address corruption risk in a similar way), the company with a lower CPI value is more exposed to corruption risk.

Country exposure is not always negative. Table 8.3 gives "Access to clean water" as a percentage of the population that has access to basic drinking water services in rural areas in 2020, as listed in the SDG Indicators database maintained by the UN. If this example company was a water utility, it would be better positioned to help with the SDGs because it provides critical water services in Malaysia and the Philippines, compared to its counterpart in France, where all citizens already have access to clean water.

The same logic can be applied using the company's distribution of employees or asset base. Companies' revenue distribution is widely available and a reasonable proxy for the distribution of employees and assets. But if the employee or asset distribution differs from revenue distribution, and is available, using employees or assets might make more sense. Employee base would be more accurate when assessing employee health and safety, for example, and asset base would be more important to note when looking at local environmental impact like biodiversity.

Table 8.2 Example of a company's geographical revenue breakdown

Country	Percentage of revenue
France	46%
Malaysia	27%
Philippines	15%
Indonesia	12%

Table 8.3 Example of scoring based on a company's geographical revenue breakdown

Country	Percentage of revenue	CPI Score	Access to clean water
France	46%	69	100
Malaysia	27%	51	90
Philippines	15%	34	91
Indonesia	12%	37	86
Weighted average		55	94.3

8.4.2 Policy, strategy and outcome indicators

Companies' policy and strategy indicators reveal how they identify, mitigate and adapt to certain risks. From a responsible investor point of view, it is more straightforward to influence companies' policy and strategy (how they operate) than their context (what they produce and where they operate).

8.4.2.1 Policy

Policy analysis refers to the company's acknowledgement of certain ESG risks or opportunities. These policies are most often written and available in company materials like websites. The most formal policies are often stand-alone documents with titles such as "Environmental Policy" or "Human Rights Policy." These can be available as an individual document, signed by the company management, or part of a company's formally available documents like the annual report. The quality and coverage of these statements can be scored, although it is essential to note that this is difficult to do objectively and might lead to biases. Policy analysis can evaluate whether the company understands and accepts a specific named risk.

It is also important to realize that the absence of a publicly available policy document does not necessarily mean that the company is not aware of or is not addressing the risk. The availability of formal policies also depends on the openness of the capital market in the company's domicile and its regulatory structure. A Western company might routinely publish dozens of policy documents, whereas its Asian counterpart might be more reluctant to do so. However, increasing disclosure requirements are bridging the gap.

8.4.2.2 Strategy

Strategy analysis builds on top of policy analysis, which strives to identify and assess the measures that a company has taken to capture a specific ESG risk or opportunity. Evaluating the appropriate strategy for each risk is a subjective matter, and, as a result, an objective strategy analysis for a large group of heterogeneous companies is nearly impossible to conduct. But it can be quite valuable if the specific strategy issues are formalized and are assessed for a comparable group of companies. Specific strategy questions may include the following:

- Is there board-level or senior management responsibility for the specific ESG issue, e.g. climate?
- Is the risk identified and addressed stringently?
- Does the company engage or partner with external organizations on the specific issue?
- What is the amount of time and money spent on training? Is such training specified for a job function?
- Regarding the quality and reach of the management system – is the management system certified? Does it have built-in feedback loops enabling

the company to learn from mistakes and shortcomings? Does this feed-back loop enable reporting of near misses and analysis of accidents that almost happened as well as those that did?

Assuming the policy questions successfully capture how well a company un-derstands the ESG risks and opportunities and its role in society, the strategy questions should then interrogate how adept the company is at mitigating these risks or capturing these opportunities.

8.4.2.3 Outcomes

Outcome indicators are quantitative indicators that measure whether the pol-icy and strategy choices are achieving the expected effects in the long term. Outcomes are, in many ways, the cherry on top of the ESG data hierarchy. None of the signals from the policy and strategy layers alone creates a holistic picture of a company's sustainability.

A benefit of outcome indicators is that they are often observable externally and verifiable by auditors. Outcome indicators also tend to be quantitative by nature, lending themselves more easily to investment decision-making. Quantitative outcome indicators are also easier to observe and compare uni-formly over time and over a larger group of companies.

But outcome indicators have shortcomings, too. They tend to be context-specific, so comparing carbon emissions from one industrial company to another might not be relevant if the underlying industrial processes are dissimilar. Assessing the percentage of women in manage-ment and comparing Nordic with East Asian banks will lead to biases because of the cultural context. Some outcome indicators also fluctuate naturally. For example, a utility company's carbon emissions might vary depending on rain patterns. After a rainy year, a company might use more of its carbon-light hydro assets than after a drier year when it relies more on carbon-heavy fossil fuel assets. Disregarding such natural variation will lead to false conclusions.

Chapter 8 key Q&As

Here are the answers to the key questions posed at the start of this chapter.
Where does ESG data come from?
Most ESG data comes from companies. It is increasingly available due to regulatory demands, but companies also disclose a lot of information vol-untarily following a few well-established frameworks, which themselves are consolidating rapidly. A commonly used analogy among RI practitioners is that of financial accounting principles, which have had hundred years of it-erative improvement, while ESG data frameworks are in their infancy. Re-search and experience show that financial accounting quality improves over time, and this seems to be the case with the data quality of ESG reporting.

The quantity of ESG reporting, regardless of framework, is certainly increasing over time. This improvement is partly expected, given the cross-border nature of trade and capital-raising. Still, reporting frameworks have certainly played a role, too, and hopes are high, especially for the IFRS unification process in creating a clear pathway in the future, further improving both quantity and quality of ESG reporting globally.

How can ESG data be categorized?

ESG data is increasingly quantitative but requires context, policy and strategy indicators to provide background and complement outcome indicators that directly describe the societal outcomes companies are generating. ESG data provided by companies can be categorized using the ESG data hierarchy. The ESG data can also be complemented by data using other sources, like NGOs or academic research, as long as the sources are well vetted and fit for purpose.

Bibliography

Brennan, M.J., & Tamarowski, C. (2000). "Investor Relations, Liquidity, and Stock Prices". *Journal of Applied Corporate Finance*, 12(4), 26–37. https://doi.org/10.1111/j.1745-6622.2000.tb00017.x

Bushee, B.J., & Miller, G.S. (2007). "Investor Relations, Firm Visibility, and Investor Following". *SSRN Electronic Journal*. https://doi.org/10.2139/ssrn.643223

European Union. (2021). Directive (EU) 2021/2101 of the European Parliament and of the Council of 24 November 2021 Amending Directive 2013/34/EU as regards Disclosure of Income Tax Information by Certain Undertakings And Branches (Text with EEA Relevance). Official Journal of the European Union, Document 32021L2101. Retrieved 23 February 2022 from https://data.europa.eu/eli/dir/2021/2101/oj

Farraghe, E.J., Kleiman, R., & Bazaz, M.S. (1994). "Do Investor Relations Make a Difference?" *The Quarterly Review of Economics and Finance*, 34(4), 403–412. https://doi.org/10.1016/1062-9769(94)90023-x

Government of India, Ministry of Corporate Affairs. (2021). Frequently Asked Questions (FAQs) on Corporate Social Responsibility (CSR) -reg (CSR-05/01/2021-CSR-MCA). Retrieved 23 February 2022 from https://www.mca.gov.in/Ministry/pdf/FAQ_CSR.pdf

Greenhouse Gas Protocol. (2004, March). "Corporate Standard". Retrieved 23 February 2022 from https://ghgprotocol.org/corporate-standard

Transparency International. (2019, 14 October). Corruption Perceptions Index 2020. Transparency.org. Retrieved 23 February 2022 from https://www.transparency.org

United Nations, Department of Economic and Social Affairs. (2020). SDG Indicators Database. Retrieved 23 February 2022 from https://unstats.un.org/sdgs/unsdg

United States Congress (2021, 8 June). H.R.3007 – 117th Congress (2001–2002): Disclosure of Tax Havens and Offshoring Act. Retrieved 23 February 2022 from https://www.congress.gov/bill/117th-congress/house-bill/3007

9 ESG ratings

Key questions in this chapter

- How can ESG data be structured?
- What is an ESG rating, and how is it constructed?
- Where do ESG ratings come from?

Once the environmental, social and governance (ESG) data has been gathered for the selected investment universe (European or US large-cap companies, for example) and is organized into a usable form, the next question is how to combine and structure the individual data points to make them functional in investment decision-making or communication (see Figure 9.1). The approaches to this combination can be roughly divided into two primary schools of thought: ESG factors and ESG ratings. This chapter describes ESG ratings and their characteristics, how the ratings are compiled; it describes some existing ESG rating mechanisms and ESG rating providers and explains how they use ESG data.

9.1 Factor thinking in ESG analysis

ESG data points can be normalized and standardized and thereby expressed in a factor format. This format is comparable to how financial factors like momentum, value or liquidity are expressed in mainstream investment analysis. Each factor describes one characteristic of a particular security. They are expressed in a simple numerical form and can all be objectively defined, understood, read from the financial markets disclosures and replicated by market participants.

GHG emissions, for example, can be captured as:

$$\sum_{n}^{i} \left(\frac{current\ value\ of\ investment_i}{investee\ company's\ enterprise\ value_i} \times investee\ company's\ Scope\,(x)\ GHG\ emissions_i \right)$$

Equation 9.1 Formula to calculate GHG emissions as ESG factor
Source: EU Joint ESA Final Report on Draft Regulatory Technical Standards

DOI: 10.4324/9781003284932-10

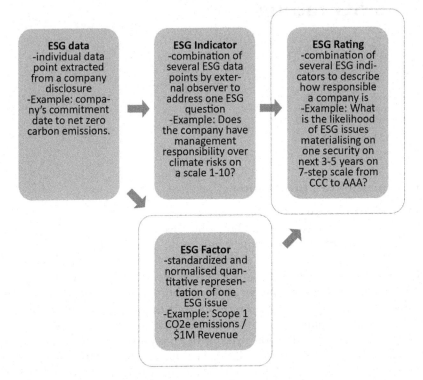

Figure 9.1 From ESG data and indicators (see chapter 8) to ESG ratings and factors.

Various ESG issues can be expressed as a factor, i.e. a continuous numerical value for each dimension, with unique characteristics. Table 9.1 describes various ESG factors that can be used independently or combined with other investment management factors.

As Table 9.1 demonstrates, ESG factors can be defined in various ways. Some factors, like carbon efficiency, are becoming reasonably well established. Some involve a certain amount of subjectivity: for example, when defining what products and services qualify as environmental and social goods.

Once the ESG data is expressed in a factor format, it can be used much like financial factors. An investor can screen companies in and out of the portfolios, optimize the individual company weights in portfolio construction, use the factors in traditional risk management and modelling, and communicate with clients, prospects and stakeholders on factors for a single company in the total portfolio. Portfolio-level reporting based on factors is discussed in Chapter 10.

9.2 Anatomy of an ESG rating or ESG score

ESG ratings are somewhat similar to credit ratings. The purpose of a credit rating is to evaluate the likelihood of a credit event, one that forces the issuer

Table 9.1 Examples of commonly used ESG factors

Factor name	Definition	Comment
GHG emissions	Tonnes of GHG emissions expressed in CO_2e per enterprise value	Included in the SFDR PAI and TCFD frameworks
Waste efficiency	Tonnes of waste generated per $1 million revenue	–
Water efficiency	Freshwater used per $1 million revenue	Included in the SFDR PAI framework
Gender equality	Percentage of women on boards and in top management	–
Executive pay	The ratio of executive-level pay to average employee pay	Included in the SFDR PAI framework
Board independence	Percentage of independent board members	–
Environmental good	Revenue from environmental products or services	Subjective; can be defined in various ways. The EU Taxonomy provides a standard.
Environmental harm	Revenue from environmentally harmful products or services	Subjective; can be defined in various ways
Social good	Revenue from socially beneficial products or services	Subjective; can be defined in various ways
Social harm	Revenue from socially harmful products or services	Subjective; can be defined in various ways
Economic development	Operations in the least developed countries	–
Avoiding water scarcity	Operations that are potentially in conflict with local communities over scarce water resource	–
Employment	Number of jobs created	–
Tax gap	Taxes paid compared to company's statutory tax rate	–
Non-renewable energy consumption and production	Share of non-renewable energy consumption and non-renewable energy production of investee companies from non-renewable energy sources compared to renewable energy sources	Included in the SFDR PAI framework
Activities negatively affecting biodiversity-sensitive areas	Share of investments in investee companies with sites/operations located in or near to biodiversity-sensitive areas where activities of those investee companies negatively affect those areas	Included in the SFDR PAI framework. Subjective as no international standards exist yet. TNFD is currently working on methodologies.

(Continued)

Factor name	Definition	Comment
Gender pay gap	Average unadjusted gender pay gap of investee companies	–
Violations of UNGC Principles or OECD Guidelines	Share of investments in investee companies that have been involved in violations of the UNGC Principles or OECD Guidelines for Multinational Enterprises	Included in the SFDR PAI framework. Partially subjective as the significance and impact of the violation can be interpreted in many ways.
Processes to monitor compliance with UNGC Principles and OECD Guidelines	Share of investments in investee companies without policies to monitor compliance or grievance/complaints handling mechanisms to address violations of the UNGC Principles or OECD Guidelines	Included in the SFDR PAI framework. Partially subjective as the scope and the coverage can vary.
Implied temperature score	Percentage change of companies' carbon emissions (trajectory) compared to percentage change of chosen scenario translated into temperature rise usually stated as celsius degrees?	Partially Included in the TCFD framework as part of scenario analysis
Physical climate risk	Physical climate risk by facility size for each company	Included in the TCFD framework

CO_2e, carbon dioxide equivalent; GHG, greenhouse gas; PAI, principal adverse impacts; SFDR, EU Sustainable Finance Disclosure Regulation; TCFD, Task Force on Climate-related Financial Disclosures; TNFD, Taskforce on Nature-related Financial Disclosures
Source: EU SFDR Regulatory Technical Standards, PAI indicators, TCFD and Impact Cubed

to default on their debt obligations. Similarly to credit ratings, most ESG ratings express the risks and likelihood of ESG issues (both positive and negative) materializing over a certain period. Some ESG ratings measure companies' sustainability compared to their peers, while others analyse their reputation. As a result, different ESG ratings and ESG rating methodologies do not automatically measure the same thing. To successfully use an ESG rating, the user needs to be familiar with the methodology and its purpose.

Problems can arise if several ESG rating frameworks are used side by side and the differences between the methodologies are not accounted for. At the time of writing, it has become fashionable to criticize how different ESG ratings do not correlate. An immediate response to that is: why should different ESG ratings correlate if they don't aim to answer the same question?

9.2.1 *What do ESG ratings measure?*

A typical ESG rating starts by defining the question to which the rating aims to provide an answer. ESG ratings that mimic credit scores typically try to answer the question "What is the probability of both negative ESG risks as

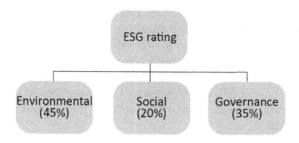

Figure 9.2 Illustrative example: the first weightings to be made in establishing an
    ESG rating

well as positive ESG opportunities materializing for the rated entity in the
next few years?" ESG ratings can also be broader in definition and consider
not only those issues that are financially material but also those important
to a more comprehensive set of stakeholders or society at large. It should be
noted that definitions of what qualify as material issues in the rated entity
are not standardized. Some frameworks, like the Sustainability Accounting
Standards Board (SASB), provide guidance on material issues for sectors, but
there are no widely accepted definitions of what issues are material for each
company, sector or region. Therefore, the choice between a focus on either
material or broader societal issues typically has considerable overlap. To com-
pute the ESG rating, different branches of E, S and G in the rating tree need
to have subjective relative weights as described in the example in Figure 9.2.

9.2.2 What ESG issues to include in an ESG rating

The process continues by defining what specific ESG issues should be considered. As there is no universally accepted definition of materiality, it is crucial
to define these issues carefully when establishing an ESG rating. Table 9.2
provides an example list of potentially material ESG issues.

Table 9.2 Potentially material ESG issues

Environmental	Social	Governance
• Air and water pollution • Biodiversity • Climate change and carbon emissions • Deforestation • Energy efficiency • Waste management • Water scarcity	• Community relations • Customer satisfaction • Data protection and privacy • Employee engagement • Gender and diversity • Human rights • Labour standards	• Audit committee structure • Board composition • Bribery and corruption • Executive compensation • Lobbying • Political contributions • Whistleblower schemes

Note that the list of ESG issues will not be exhaustive, meaning that a company may have material ESG issues other than those used in the rating. Different sectors also tend to have drastically different material issues.

Furthermore, ESG issues are often interlinked, and it can be challenging to classify an ESG issue into just one category – i.e. environmental, social or governance. While ESG issues can often be easily defined and measured (e.g. a company's labour standards), it is not so straightforward to determine how material they are in reality (e.g. what effect the poor labour standards have on the company).

9.2.3 Defining the relative importance of the ESG issues included

Having defined what issues are material, it is helpful to determine their relative importance. Table 9.3 provides an example of relative E, S and G weights.

Figure 9.3 shows the weight of waste management as a component of an ESG rating tree.

Table 9.3 Illustrative example: relative weightings among various ESG issues

Environmental (45%)	*Social (20%)*	*Governance (35%)*
• Biodiversity (15%)	• Data protection and privacy (5%)	• Board composition (15%)
• Deforestation (5%)	• Employee engagement (5%)	• Bribery and corruption (10%)
• Waste management (25%)	• Labour standards (5%) • Local community relations (5%)	• Executive compensation (10%)

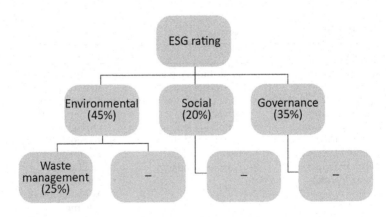

Figure 9.3 Illustrative example: relative weights of ESG issues focusing on waste management

The weightings of what are fundamentally different issues is a very subjective matter. ESG rating providers might change their weightings over time. Such changes might be automated – referred to as dynamic weighting – for example, by following global news flows and adjusting according to relative amounts of column inches and airtime. However, dynamic weighting seems to be quite rare among the popular commercial ESG rating applications and could in any case prove challenging from an ESG rating user's point of view.

9.2.4 Establishing the list of indicators and weights for each ESG issue

The next step is to establish definitive indicators for each ESG issue. Most ESG rating systems use a hierarchical approach (described in more detail in Chapter 7): they choose a few indicators from each policy, strategy and outcome category and then weigh them accordingly. Taking the waste management issue in Figure 9.2, it can be measured and weighted as shown in Table 9.4. Here, the 25% weight allocated to waste management is broken down into policy, strategy and outcomes indicators, and given weights of 30%, 30% and 40%, respectively. These weights are further broken down into two different indicators. This is also shown as a tree diagram in Figure 9.4.

The weighting depicted in our example in Table 9.4 and Figure 9.4 is difficult to do objectively. Some ESG ratings put more emphasis on policy indicators, for example; others emphasize actual outcomes – i.e. waste reduction and the lack of incidents in the past – over other indicators. Another difficulty is the lack of indicator-level disclosure: does such a thing imply insufficient reporting or is it a sign of lack of action, board oversight and delegation? Some jurisdictions have legal requirements for board-level responsibility and reporting; rating frameworks that do not account for differences in legal requirements between countries might unintentionally favour companies with mandated board-level responsibilities.

Table 9.4 Illustrative example: weighting of selected indicators within waste management

Category	Indicator	Scale	Weight
Policy (30%)	Does the company have board-level responsibility for waste management?	Y/N	50%
	Does the company have a publicly available policy covering waste?	1–10	50%
Strategy (30%)	Does the company have a certified environmental management system?	Y/N	40%
	Does the company invest in waste reduction?	1–10	60%
Outcomes (40%)	Do the reported amounts of waste generated decrease over time and against peers?	1–10	80%
	Does the company have serious pollution incidents in the past?	1–10	20%

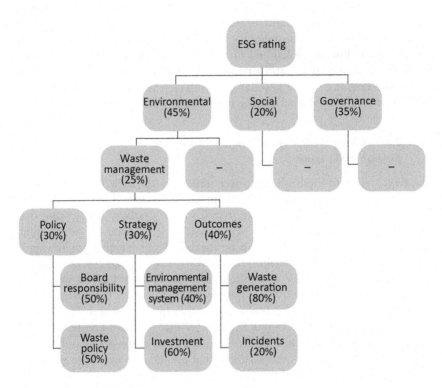

Figure 9.4 Illustrative example: full breakdown of an ESG rating

Each indicator will ideally have a relatively small weight as a fraction of the total ESG rating. In our waste management example in Figure 9.4, multiplying the weights going up the tree (50% × 30% × 25% × 45% for example) shows us that each indicator comprises less than 4% of the weight of the company's total ESG rating. A collection of low figures is desirable, since it shows that no single issue determines a majority of the total rating. On the other hand, using an average can hide material ESG risks in a particular issue if the overall ESG rating is positive.

9.2.5 All indicators and issues are rated and combined into the final ESG rating

Towards the end of the process, all the indicators for all the issues are rated, which produces a single value – for example, a numerical value between 1 and 100 – for each company. To adjust for sectoral, regional or possibly cultural biases, each company score is normalized against a universe of comparable companies, which might comprise thousands of names depending on the ESG rating provider's coverage. The normalizing process first groups companies together, often according to industry, and can then be further refined, perhaps geographically, so that Asian companies, for instance, are compared to their Asian peers rather than their global counterparts, removing potential cultural bias.

Once the grouping method is established and scores within that group have been normalized, companies can be assigned their final ESG rating, which can use letters, such as a scale of CCC to AAA, mimicking credit ratings. The normalization of the score can be presented quite simplistically: for example, by labelling the worst-performing companies "high risk". But it could also be statistically more complex and granular, awarding scores based on how many standard deviations each company is from the peer-group mean, for example.

9.3 Characteristics of ESG indicators

The rating method discussed in the previous section assumes that ESG indicators are all alike and each in a similar way captures the importance (the materiality) of an issue. There are several reasons why this is a rash and misleading assumption.

Indicators do not necessarily measure ESG risk and opportunity symmetrically. Some ESG issues might pose material risks, but just because a company manages them better than their peers does not necessarily mean that it gains a considerable advantage.

ESG indicator data can be perceived as normally distributed when it might be pretty lopsided in practice. For example, accident statistics are often factored into employee health and safety-related issues. The indicator might include a company that had one accident among a peer group that had none at all. Against a zero baseline like this, the unfortunate company looks considerably worse than its peers despite suffering only the one incident.

Some ESG ratings put a lot of emphasis on adverse events, like past environmental accidents, thereby awarding a low score to a company with an accident history. Other ESG ratings might look at the same company and the same data and conclude that the company has learned from its mistakes and give it a higher ESG rating than its peers.

ESG indicators also correlate with one another. If a company has a policy to address climate change, it is likely to have management systems and strategies for climate change, too. Nitrogen and sulphur oxides, and other local air emissions correlate heavily with carbon emissions. Measuring both issues independently will result in higher scores for companies that likely have the same policy and strategy to address both. This pairwise correlation tends to happen with other issues as well. If a company is diligent in training its employees, its health and safety is probably at a reasonable level, too. If a company has a lot of independent board members, its executive compensation tends to be more cautious.

Some indicators do not change much over time. Suppose a company has seven independent board members out of a total of ten. It is unlikely that the proportion of independent board members will fall outside the 60–80% range in the following year. Board member rotation is annual, and it is in companies' interest not to change too many at a time.

9.4 Characteristics of ESG ratings

The correlations between ESG ratings can be examined in multiple ways. One typical approach is presented in Table 9.5. In this approach, the E, S and G scores from three different ESG providers were collected, and a simple correlation was established with the corresponding E, S and G scores in a sample of the 1,200 biggest companies in the world by market capitalization. The pairwise correlations, in which a score of 1 indicates perfect correlation, only average out at 0.13. Therefore, the individual E, S, and G scores differ substantially among providers.

These low levels of correlation are to be expected, as the ratings from different providers are not necessarily trying to ask the same question. While "How probable is it for an ESG issue to materialize for this company?" sounds similar to "How sustainable is this company?", they are different questions and require different technical choices at a methodology level. Another reason for the rating differences are the choice of indicators and the dynamics in the weighting scheme, which vary considerably between providers.

ESG issues are often qualitative, and it is not easy to compare the risk or societal importance of various abstract matters related to sustainable development against each other. Climate change is a significant issue for every industrial company, but is it more important than employee health and

Table 9.5 Correlations of selected ESG scores of three ESG rating providers

	E1	E2	E3	S1	S2	S3	G1	G2	G3
E1									
E2	0.28								
E3	-0.14	-0.07							
S1	0.13	0.31	-0.11						
S2	0.62	0.17	-0.07	0.10					
S3	0.05	0.21	0.17	0.01	-0.07				
G1	0.10	0.26	-0.03	0.05	0.17	-0.11			
G2	0.73	0.30	-0.11	0.10	0.52	-0.08	0.21		
G3	0.21	0.24	0.13	0.05	0.13	0.07	-0.01	0.23	

safety? Of course, the issue can be debated, and people can agree to disagree in an informal setting. But ESG rating methodologies require a number or a quantitative outcome of some sort. An equal weighting implies that the likelihood of two adverse events happening is similar. Assigning a higher weighting to climate change implies that a negative climate change impact is more likely to occur than an adverse employee safety event, and yet the company might have good policies, strategies and outcomes to mitigate climate risks.

The weights and by extension the importance of ESG issues can vary over time. A decade ago tax payment and tax planning were rarely seen in the early ESG rating frameworks because this was seldom regarded as a sustainability issue. But nowadays tax transparency and fair payment of corporate taxes are a much more common part of corporate responsibility discussions and are therefore more likely to feature in ESG ratings. But, because the perceived importance of tax payment has not been consistent over time, different ESG rating mechanisms may assign different weights at any given point in time.

ESG rating necessitates grouping companies so that the indicators can be compared. There is no definitive method of constructing these groups; even the size of the group is a matter for debate. Let us imagine an electric utility company with 60% production capacity in various renewables like wind and solar and the remaining 40% in fossil fuels like gas and coal. One ESG rating system includes all electric utilities from one geographical region in one group. Under this rubric, the company is rated very well in climate (which tends to be a significant issue for electric utilities) since most of its generation is from renewables. But another ESG rating system has a separate industry group for utilities that specialize in renewables. In this group, our utility is the poorest performer simply because it still relies to a significant extent on fossil fuels.

ESG rating mechanisms also differ in the way they weigh indicators within an issue. Some ESG rating mechanisms can be policy- and strategy-driven and assign more weight to publicly available policies and efforts to mitigate a specific ESG risk. Other systems can be more outcome-driven and emphasize outcome indicators, paying less attention to publicly available policies. Cultural factors might come into play, too.

There is no one correct way to balance these issues. And, as a result, a range of ESG ratings can all be factually correct while simultaneously differing drastically. Ultimately, the diversity of the ESG ratings can be regarded as beneficial, providing a broader range of views. Investors can therefore look for an approach that best fits their needs.

9.5 Commercial players in ESG ratings and the data sector

The ESG data and research market have grown by an average of 20% annually over the past decade. In 2021, the size of this market was estimated at US$1 billion and it is forecast to grow to US$5 billion by 2025. The first

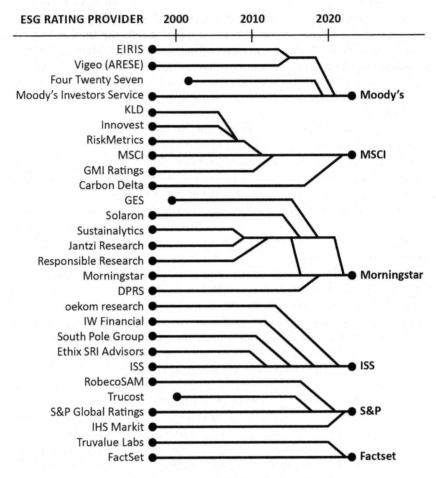

Figure 9.5 Consolidations and mergers of ESG rating providers: selected examples

thing one notices about how the industry is developing is its tendency to consolidate (Figure 9.5 shows how a number of ESG rating providers have consolidated over two decades). There are several likely reasons for this. The rapid growth in demand has driven more prominent traditional financial services companies to serve a sizeable market. These same companies might face stakeholder demands to provide products and services linked to sustainable development in ESG data. The financial data industry enjoys considerable economies of scale, and one salesforce can service the same set of clients with a wider product range. Also, users of ESG data might prefer to get all their data – financial and ESG – from one "shop".

The majority of the large ESG rating providers tend to be generalists maintaining a flagship ESG rating for a sizeable investable universe and offering specific data and analytics services alongside these flagship products. These include services for particular uses, like norm-based screening and theme-based analytics, e.g. climate analytics. Alongside the more prominent ESG service providers, a vibrant community of smaller players and startups has emerged, typically providing more specialized data and services.

Chapter 9 key Q&As

Here are the answers to the key questions posed at the start of this chapter.

How can ESG data be structured?

ESG data can be structured as ESG factors or as ESG ratings, which each have their pros and cons and suitable applications. ESG factors are based on fewer assumptions and are often more quantitative. They are also better, especially for large investment universes, in screening specific issues, portfolio construction and risk management, much like financial factors. ESG ratings are similar to credit ratings. They answer a more holistic question and combine several issues into one communicable rating.

What is an ESG rating, and how is it constructed?

ESG ratings have a lot of data ingredients. They are typically combined with weighted averages, which, by nature, involve quite a few subjective assumptions. The ESG ratings are easy to use, but the differing assumptions and variety of applications potentially make them less comparable among one another. This lack of comparability is sometimes seen as a shortcoming of ESG ratings. However, the diversity of opinions can also be considered a strength.

Where do ESG ratings come from?

Several commercial players provide ESG ratings. The ESG rating market has consolidated over the past decade due to economies of scale and requirements for wide-scale distribution, which has made it increasingly difficult for smaller players to maintain their specific products for market niches.

Bibliography

European Supervisory Authorities. (2021, February). Final Report on Draft Regulatory Technical Standards. Retrieved 23 February 2022 from https://www.esma.europa.eu/sites/default/files/library/jc_2021_03_joint_esas_final_report_on_rts_under_sfdr.pdf

Impact Cubed. (2020). Retrieved 23 February 2022 from https://www.impact-cubed.com

Substantive Research. (2021, 17 September). ESG Data Marketplace Survey. Retrieved 8 January 2022 from https://substantiveresearch.com/matter/substantive-research-completes-survey-of-the-evolving-esg-data-marketplace

Task Force on Climate-related Financial Disclosures (TCFD). (2020, 21 September). Retrieved 23 February 2022 from https://www.fsb-tcfd.org

10 Assessing the responsibility of asset managers and funds

Key questions in this chapter

- What questions should an investor ask about the responsibility of asset managers and investment funds?
- What tools can investors use to assess the responsibility of investment funds and their underlying holdings?

This chapter provides practical ideas for questions that an investor can use to assess an asset manager's Responsible Investment (RI) credentials and how these are manifested in the investment funds and other products. Such an assessment will broadly strive to answer the following key fundamental questions: does the asset management company address its general corporate responsibility well? Is its RI policy adequate, and how is it implemented? Does the fund and its underlying holdings demonstrate the required ESG qualities?

This chapter addresses these questions separately, but investors should consider them as a whole in deciding between different funds and their handling of environmental, social and governance (ESG) issues/ topics/ indicators. The answers to these questions will not necessarily correlate with one another: an asset manager that addresses its corporate responsibility well might not apply high ESG standards to all the funds it manages. Similarly, an asset manager that is not vocal on these issues or known for its company-wide ESG credentials might provide very high-quality ESG funds.

10.1 Evaluating asset managers' corporate responsibility

Asset managers range from large multinational, often bank-affiliated, companies, with a wide range of investable products in various asset classes, to small boutique firms providing services to a specific niche market. Asset managers are fiduciaries for assets trusted upon them, but they also have corporate responsibilities like any other company. The 2008 financial crisis and the ensuing regulatory developments have drawn further attention to the industry's social responsibilities and economic impact, and its obligations to provide proper advice to customers and manage risks at the entity, portfolio

DOI: 10.4324/9781003284932-11

and individual investment levels. The following questions can help an investor assess how an asset manager is addressing corporate responsibility.

---

1. How do asset managers report on their corporate responsibility?

Typically, large asset managers use the GRI (Global Reporting Initiative) reporting framework, Integrated Reporting (which can also be a GRI report), SASB (Sustainability Accounting Standards Board) reporting, or a combination of these in their corporate responsibility reporting. Smaller asset managers may prefer to report on corporate responsibility as they best see fit according to their size.

2. How do asset managers address compliance?

Asset managers have legal requirements and a fiduciary duty related to operating and marketing, disclosure and prohibition of fraudulent activities. Despite the regulation, some asset managers still fall short in ensuring that clients understand the nature of risks taken in investment strategies. Failure to provide accurate advice may lead to litigation and diminished client trust. To avoid the worst, investors might usually look at their asset managers' disclosure with regard to: provision of adequate information, the regulatory violation records of employees, and the number and amount of associated fines and settlements. Asset managers also need to follow complex and sometimes inconsistent rules relating to performance, conduct, and disclosure on insider trading and tax evasion. Investors can ensure asset managers' regulatory compliance by reviewing the policies and processes related to internal controls.

3. How do asset managers manage employee-related issues?

Asset managers are in stiff competition for the best employees, while the industry has relatively low levels of diversity, even compared to other knowledge-based industries. Companies can likely reduce their employee turnover and improve operational efficiency by ensuring gender and racial diversity, which would ultimately benefit asset management companies and investors alike. To ensure that asset managers understand and properly address the issue, investors can investigate asset managers' employee-related policies, processes and disclosure on employee age, gender and ethnic diversity.

10.2 Evaluating asset managers' Responsible Investment activities

Many investors use so-called traditional (i.e. not labelled as ESG) investment funds in their portfolios. The asset managers of these funds may have an RI process even if they have no designated ESG or RI funds in their product offering. The following questions can help an investor assess the extent to which an asset manager is applying RI practices in general.

---

1. Have you signed the PRI?

By signing the Principles for Responsible Investment (PRI), an asset manager commits to developing RI activities, as well as publicly reporting on this work on an annual basis. In practice, this means that investors can expect from a PRI signatory readiness for responsible investing. PRI commitment also means having an RI policy covering more than 50% of the assets under management (AuM), dedicated resources and RI reporting. The PRI publishes annually the reports of all signatories ("Transparency Reports") on its website. A separate PRI Assessment Report, prepared for every signatory, is not public by default, but investors can ask the asset manager directly what scores they received from the PRI, or ask to see the report itself.

2. Do you have an RI policy?

There are no credible means of making Responsible Investments without a policy or guiding documents of some sort. In principle, all PRI signatories must have well-articulated RI policies or principles as a minimum requirement.

3. Why do you invest responsibly? What does responsible investing mean in practice in your investment activities?

Responsible investing should not simply be a greenwashing exercise or part of an asset manager's charitable activities. It should seek improved risk management and increased return opportunities for positive societal impact. This thinking should be reflected in the asset manager's response, and it should preferably cover all investment decision-making, not just the marketing of individual investment products. The investor wants to know what key ESG issues are influencing the asset manager's investment decision-making, e.g. climate change, human rights, good governance, etc.

In ESG analysis, the asset manager assesses the investees' responsibility using a variety of methods, leading to either inclusion or exclusion. ESG analysis can be conducted by the asset manager's internal investment team or purchased from an external service provider. The key factor is how the ESG information is incorporated into the investment process and decision-making.

The investor can engage with asset manager to ask for more ESG integration or conduct more active ownership. For example, asset managers may attend annual general meetings (AGMs) of portfolio companies or engage with them through dialogue – or they may use a service provider for these activities. The asset manager should maintain AGM attendance and voting records and document any other engagement processes with company management. A minimum level of active ownership activity could be part of the asset manager's mandate on behalf of the investor.

4. What dedicated resources for responsible investing do you have?

An investor needs to know if an asset manager has the necessary resources and skills to carry out the promised RI activities. How many people work in RI? Who bears ultimate responsibility for the success of the chosen RI approaches? An investor might also want to know who is actually carrying out the ESG analysis of investee companies and engaging with them. The portfolio manager and the investment team will make the practical investment decisions for the mandate portfolio or fund, so they should consequently have broad knowledge and expertise on ESG issues. Investment decisions can be supported by internally generated ESG analysis, or the necessary information and data can be purchased from an external service provider. As a potential motivating factor, the investor might inquire about ESG-linked remuneration systems for portfolio managers.

5. Can you elaborate on situations or provide case studies where ESG issues have influenced your investment decisions?

Concrete examples will give an investor a better picture of the asset manager's practices. Examples will also prove whether the activity has been carried out in practice.

An investor wants to know how an asset manager monitors incidents in the investee companies. Monitoring should be frequent, comprehensive and cover all the portfolio companies. Predefined and transparent operational processes and governance structures should be in place to ensure each incident is adequately addressed.

6. How do you report on your RI activities?

An investor wants to know how regularly and in what form an asset manager reports on its RI activities. This can be demonstrated, for example, by providing a sample report. The aim is for the investor to monitor the progress of the asset manager while also reporting forward about RI activities to its own stakeholders. In addition to all regulatory RI reporting, voluntary RI reporting can include, for example, the carbon footprint of investments, ESG scores, impact or examples of engagement dialogue.

10.3 Evaluating the responsibility of a particular investment fund

In recent years, various tools have become available to investors for assessing and rating the responsibility of mutual funds. A cost-conscious investor does not have to buy them all: in fact, free assessment tools are available, which can still afford a comprehensive picture of a fund's level of responsibility. RI fund labels are also free to utilize by investors, although an annual license fee is, paid by asset managers seeking the certification. Topline ESG ratings and ESG factors are also available for free from a number of sources, although in-depth analysis is only available commercially. Regardless of cost, using external tools implies an understanding of ESG assessment methods and the underlying criteria being used. This section discusses these three kinds of tools in more detail.

10.3.1 RI fund labels

The use of ESG labels has grown alongside the growth of the industry. Almost 1,800 ESG-labelled funds were distributed in Europe alone at the end of 2021, representing more than €1,300 billion in AuM (Novethic, 2022).

Currently, the labels and their attribution are local in scope, defined and promoted by national bodies. Because of this, they differ in their requirements, some being dedicated to specific environmental issues, for example, and others being more general. Table 10.1 lists a few commonly used European ESG fund labels.

10.3.2 ESG ratings-based analysis for funds

Some commercial data providers, e.g. MSCI, Morningstar, ISS and Refinitiv, deliver holdings-based fund ratings for large fund universes. These ratings can help investors choose between different funds and approaches and also help asset managers develop and communicate their funds' ESG credentials. Each fund-level ESG rating provider has its own unique methodology. Despite the challenges around differing rating methodologies, the fund-level ratings provide valuable information for clients looking at several comparable funds.

One example of ESG ratings-based fund analysis comes from Morningstar, which introduced the first responsibility rating for funds in March 2016. The classification is based on company-specific ESG data, and the rating requires at least 67% of the fund's holdings to have a company-specific rating. The fund rating consists of two stages. In the first, the fund is assigned a responsibility rating based on the normalized ESG scores of the fund's holdings, less the impact of any controversial events. Morningstar normalizes company-specific ESG ratings to make them comparable to industry benchmarks to score diversified funds.

In the second stage, Morningstar divides the funds into five groups with a normal distribution by comparing the fund's responsibility rating to Morningstar's funds in that fund category, such as equity funds investing in large European companies. These five classification groups are known as "Globe

Table 10.1 Examples of common European ESG fund labels

Label and country	Scope	Governance	Key ESG criteria
Label ISR (France)	Listed equity and fixed-income funds; annual licence fee	Stakeholder committee, supported by the French Ministry of Finance	ESG screening of more than 90% of the portfolio and 20% reduction of the investable universe based on ESG scores, or "significantly" better average ESG score than the initial universe
Towards Sustainability (Belgium)	Listed equity and fixed-income funds; annual licence fee	Dedicated not-for-profit organization	100% ESG screening, exclusion of weapons, tobacco, fossil fuels (with revenue thresholds), electricity generation over carbon intensity threshold, and screening against Global Compact principles
FNG Siegel (Germany, Austria, Switzerland)	Listed equity and fixed-income funds; annual licence fee	Dedicated not-for-profit organization	100% ESG screening of the portfolio, exclusion of weapons, coal, non-conventional oil/gas, nuclear (with revenue thresholds) and screening against Global Compact principles
Nordic Swan Ecolabel (Nordics)	Listed equity and fixed-income funds; annual licence fee	Nordic Eco-labelling Board, supported by Nordic governments	Exclusion of human rights and environmental violations, fossil fuels, uranium, arms and tobacco, ESG analysis covering at least 90% of holdings and selecting minimum 50% high ESG performers, active ownership through voting and engagement

Ratings," with one globe meaning low performance and five globes designating high, and they are based on companies' public disclosure. Funds invested in large-market-capitalization companies tend to receive better ratings as their disclosure level is higher than small- and mid-cap companies.

10.3.3 ESG factor-based analysis for funds

An analysis based on ESG factors shows the exposure of the underlying fund holdings to selected ESG issues (factors), and this exposure can be modelled and displayed in different ways. The ESG factors can be derived, for example, from the UN Sustainable Development Goals (SDGs) and their objectives. Factor-based analysis provides the investor with more detailed insight into specific ESG issues and characteristics in the fund, compared to only a single overall ESG rating.

Figure 10.1 gives an example of such an analysis. The model has been constructed to compare an equity portfolio to its benchmark using 15 ESG factors (these ESG factors are described more in detail in Section 9.1).

Figure 10.1 Example of an ESG factor analysis and model to compare an equity portfolio to its benchmark

Source: Impact Cubed

The model shows how the portfolio holdings contribute to the selected
ESG factors, either positively or negatively. In the figure, the darker symmetrical line represents the benchmark to which the portfolio is compared
independently in each of the 15 ESG factors. The fund values further out
from the darker symmetrical line are better than the benchmark, and those
nearer the centre are worse: for example, in the portfolio companies there are
fewer women in management (gender equality) and fewer independent board
members (board independence) compared to the benchmark.

Chapter 10 key Q&As

Here are the answers to the key questions posed at the start of this chapter.

*What questions should an investor ask about the responsibility of asset managers and
investment funds?*

There are several areas for investors to consider when assessing the responsibility of an asset manager or the ESG qualities of their investment funds.

First, does the asset manager address its overall corporate responsibility well? Second, does the asset manager have a comprehensive RI policy? Third, does the investment fund have a satisfactory ESG profile? And, finally, do the fund holdings reflect the asset manager's RI policy and the chosen RI approach?

What tools can investors use to assess the responsibility of investment funds and their underlying holdings?

Fund investors have an increasing amount of tools at their disposal when looking at the ESG qualities of a given fund. There are several labelling schemes whereby a third party certifies the level of ESG in a fund. When comparing investment funds, investors can also use readily available commercial solutions that aggregate ESG factors or ESG ratings to a fund level.

Bibliography

FNG Siegel. (2022). Retrieved 23 February 2022 from https://fng-siegel.org

Impact Cubed. (2022). Retrieved 23 February 2022 from https://www.impact-cubed.com

Label ISR. (2022). Retrieved 23 February 2022 from https://www.lelabelisr.fr

Morningstar. (2016). The Morningstar Sustainability Rating. Retrieved 23 February 2022 from https://www.morningstar.co.uk/uk/news/148119/the-morningstar-sustainability-rating.aspx

Nordic Swan Ecolabel. (2022). Retrieved 23 February 2022 from https://www.nordic-ecolabel.org

Novethic. (2022). Market Data Sustainable Labels December 2021. https://www.novethic.com/sustainable-finance-trends/detail/market-data-sustainable-labels-europe-december-2021.html

Novethic. (2022). Retrieved 23 February 2022 from https://www.novethic.com

Principles of Responsible Investment (PRI). (2022). "Public Signatory Reports". Retrieved 23 February 2022 from https://www.unpri.org/signatories/reporting-and-assessment/public-signatory-reports

Towards Sustainability Initiative. (2022). Retrieved 23 February 2022 from https://www.towardssustainability.be

11 Responsible Investment reporting

Key questions in this chapter

- Why is it important to report on Responsible Investment activities?
- Who should report on their Responsible Investment activities?
- What are the key elements of Responsible Investment reporting?

Reporting on investment activities is comparable to corporate responsibility reporting. It is a way of communicating the policy, governance and activities relating to Responsible Investment (RI) to stakeholders. The key stakeholders of an institutional investor, such as bank clients or pension fund beneficiaries, want to know how their investments are being managed. It is vital to report regularly on RI implementation, as it highlights the concrete actions taken and increases trust, transparency and also comparability between different investors.

Clients and beneficiaries expect the investment activities to reflect the values of the investor's organization. Employees and potential employees are also increasingly looking for employers that share their values. Communicating these values and how they affect investment activities can strengthen the relationship between an organization and its stakeholders.

Typically, RI reporting is not regulatory based, although this is starting to become more common. For example, Principles for Responsible Investment (PRI) reporting is required only from those investors who have voluntarily signed up to the initiative. In some jurisdictions, regulatory-based reporting includes RI and sustainable finance measures. In the EU, for example, the promotion of sustainable finance is part of the EU's Sustainable Development Action Plan and the implementation of the Paris Climate Agreement. As part of the EU action plan, institutional investors face obligations relating to sustainability in their investment processes and reporting. Various jurisdictions have also included Task Force on Climate-related Financial Disclosures (TCFD) recommendations in its guidelines for companies when reporting non-financial information.

DOI: 10.4324/9781003284932-12

11.1 Who is responsible for Responsible Investment reporting?

The board and management are responsible for developing and overseeing the activities of the investment organization, including monitoring and reporting on RI activities. Usually, they simply sign off ready-to-publish RI reports, which are in fact compiled by the institutional investor's staff – usually the environmental, social and governance (ESG) team or equivalent – and sometimes with the support of the communications team or an external service provider. Sometimes additional input is needed from investees. Institutional investors often collect information about RI activities across the whole portfolio using surveys, for example. As well as for reporting purposes, the survey results can be used to compare managers against peers or over time.

11.2 How to report on Responsible Investment?

RI can be reported annually, quarterly, monthly, weekly or even daily. The reporting frequency depends on its specific use. Institutional investors report on the progress of responsible investing at least once a year, usually in connection with the annual or corporate responsibility report. Many investors also maintain up-to-date information about their operations on their websites. An increasing number of asset management companies are also adding ESG indicators to their monthly fund reports. Investors can also use frameworks such as the PRI, Sustainability Accounting Standards Board (SASB) and TCFD for their reporting, as described below.

Standardized reporting models and metrics would save investors time and effort and improve comparability between RI reports, but these are only beginning to emerge. As with corporate responsibility reporting, guiding principles for RI reporting include materiality, reliability and accuracy.

11.2.1 Principles for Responsible Investment

Many institutional investors have signed up to the UN-supported PRI. One of the principles (Principle 6: the signatory undertakes to report on its activities and the progress of RI) concerns the transparency of RI and its reporting. Once a year, the signatory must report on its RI activities to the PRI, which publishes the transparency reports of all signatories on its website.

Although the PRI reporting framework has changed over the years and will continue to evolve in the future, the transparency reports give an idea of the history and development of each reporter's RI practices. The PRI also provides all signatories with an annual assessment of how well they are performing in their RI activities compared to other signatories.

This annual assessment is an excellent sparring tool to help investors develop their practices. Although the report is not public by default, an investor can choose to publish it or perhaps its stakeholders will request it for their use.

Asset owners are increasingly using PRI reports to monitor their external asset managers and compare asset managers' RI practices.

PRI reporting requires some commitment of resources from the investor, which means that small institutional investors might find being a PRI signatory burdensome. The more extensive the investment portfolio, and the more direct investments an investor has, the more comprehensive the reporting required by the PRI. Alongside the PRI, there are the Principles of Responsible Banking (PRB) for banks and the Principles for Sustainable Insurance (PSI) for insurers. These initiatives also require annual reporting.

11.2.2 Sustainability Accounting Standards Board

The SASB was established in 2011 to provide companies with ESG reporting tools. Its goal is to combine financially relevant ESG variables with traditional accounting. Unlike many other reporting frameworks, it limits the amount of variables, making an SASB report a concise package. The reporting is not intended to serve all stakeholder groups: it is a reporting model explicitly designed for investors' needs. Any changes to the framework or the indicators to be reported will only be made following extensive consultation to ensure only the most economically significant variables are included. The organization itself does not produce any classification or index based on the reporting framework, but investors and service providers might independently develop products, analyse companies or use the information as part of their advocacy processes.

11.2.3 Task Force on Climate-related Financial Disclosures

The TCFD is a working group of international financial experts which has developed recommendations for investors on managing and reporting on climate risk. TCFD's reporting recommendations cover an investor's climate change efforts related to governance, strategy, risk management, measurement and target setting. The TCFD principles are incorporated in the European Commission's guidelines for reporting on climate and are also embedded in the EU sustainable finance regulation and practical guidance given by the European Central Bank and European Banking Authority to European banks. Institutional investors worldwide are currently preparing to meet the TCFD reporting requirements.

11.3 What gets reported?

RI reporting content varies from investor to investor. Some initiatives, such as the PRI, have particular reporting formats. The content often depends on how far the investor is along the path to RI and what resources are available.

RI reporting content can be roughly divided into three different sections:

A.   A description of the general approach
B.   Portfolio-level information (across asset classes/products)
C.   Practical examples of RI activities

11.3.1 Description of the general approach

In periodic reporting, an investor can briefly describe the responsible investing principles outlined in the RI policy and any changes made during the reporting year. It may reveal new resources acquired or new RI approaches, a description of work done in managing climate risk, ESG criteria, or participation in investor initiatives. Annual or more frequent reporting usually follows up on violations of international norms and how engagement processes with non-compliant companies are developing.

It can also include information on regularly exercised ownership rights and results obtained over the past year. There might be information about attendance and voting in general meetings, other types of engagement with companies or participation in investor initiatives. Generally, an investor's website will provide more information on the general practice of responsible investing.

11.3.2 Portfolio-level information

Investors can report the ESG characteristics of their investments at the overall portfolio level, by asset class or by fund. The reporting may at the same time link with a particular RI approach, such as portfolio-level reporting on thematic or impact investments. Regular RI reporting is becoming more common as investors incorporate internally or externally retrieved ESG information into their portfolio management systems. As a result, the investor may then include in its official monthly reporting the ESG ratings or distributions of the portfolio's or fund's investments.

Reporting on an investment portfolio's carbon footprint is becoming more common. This is supported by institutional investors' commitments to initiatives aiming for Net Zero greenhouse gas emissions by 2050 or earlier. Some investors report the carbon footprint of their investments more frequently than just once a year. When reporting portfolio emissions investors should use global standards, broadly approved recommendations and market practices such as PCAF or TCFD.

11.3.3 Practical examples of Responsible Investment activities

By reporting practical RI examples, investors concretize their work. Websites and annual RI reports are natural places to publish useful information on how RI is practised across asset classes and funds.

Chapter 11 key Q&As

Here are the answers to the key questions posed at the start of this chapter.

Why is it important to report on Responsible Investment activities?

Reporting on RI activities is an important tool in communicating policy, governance and RI activities to stakeholders. Clients and beneficiaries expect the investment activities to reflect the values of the investor's organization. Employees and potential employees are also increasingly looking for employers who share their values.

Who should report on their Responsible Investment activities?

The board and management are responsible for developing and overseeing the activities of the investment organization, including monitoring and reporting on RI activities. They are usually supported by the ESG team or its equivalent and are sometimes supported by the communications team or an external service provider.

What are the key elements of Responsible Investment reporting?

Some initiatives, like the PRI, have particular reporting formats, but in practice RI reporting varies from investor to investor.

RI reporting content can be roughly divided into three different sections:

A. A description of the general approach
B. Portfolio-level information (across asset classes/products)
C. Practical examples of RI activities

Bibliography

Paris Aligned Investment Initiative. (2021). "Net Zero Investment Framework Implementation Guide." Retrieved 23 February 2022 from https://www.parisalignedinvestment.org/media/2021/03/PAII-Net-Zero-Investment-Framework_Implementation-Guide.pdf

Principles for Responsible Investment (PRI). (2022). Retrieved 23 February 2022 from https://www.unpri.org

Sustainability Accounting Standards Board (SASB). (2022). Retrieved 23 February 2022 from https://www.sasb.org

Task Force on Climate-related Financial Disclosures (TCFD). (2022). Retrieved 23 February 2022 from https://www.fsb-tcfd.org

United Nations Environment Programme Finance Initiative (UNEP FPI). (2022a). "Principles for Responsible Banking". Retrieved 23 February 2022 from https://www.unepfi.org/banking/bankingprinciples

United Nations Environment Programme Finance Initiative (UNEP FPI). (2022b). "Principles for Sustainable Insurance". Retrieved 23 February 2022 from https://www.unepfi.org/psi

Epilogue

This book has set out to provide clear definitions of responsible investing and related terminology and show how to incorporate environmental, social and governance (ESG) issues within various asset classes. The intention has been to show that any organization or individual can consider ESG in investing and financing across an entire portfolio, and can benefit from it via a better risk–return ratio and more sustainable outcomes. There is no single universal way to be a responsible investor; rather, there is a myriad of possible combinations. This is why it is possible to find a solution that fits the needs of every organization or individual. An appropriate analogy would be a cooking one: using the same ingredients but coming up with different recipes according to taste.

Investors can use different Responsible Investment (RI) approaches and tools as they see fit. Some might concentrate on historical screening data, others on active ownership, or they might base their investment decisions on forward-looking data points, including future trends or megatrends. Most often, investors will combine approaches and tools, as requirements can vary both within and between asset classes. The main message from this book is: start from the overall investment strategy and build an RI policy to support it via the selection of appropriate RI approaches and tools. Also important are practical implementation, progress monitoring and transparent reporting, which should all support learning-by-doing, building trusted relationships with stakeholders and minimizing reputational risks.

The book has also described the origins of RI and its development, which points to innovation continuing to advance the incorporation of ESG into investment processes and decision-making. Expectations of stakeholders will continue to increase, and systematic RI policies, processes and target setting will need to increase alongside them. Whatever the drivers, we can be sure that the quantity and quality of ESG data and tools will continue to grow. Perhaps in the (near) future, we will no longer be discussing responsible investing as a separate function from overall investments. Maybe the few remaining organizations or individuals who still fail to see the benefits of incorporating ESG into investment decision-making will be required to explain why they are not behaving like mainstream responsible investors?

Responsible investments as described in this book are clearly mainstream now. This does not mean that we have seen all that RI has to offer. As much as it has evolved over the last two decades, we will continue to see further innovation and plenty of research. Maybe the RI future will be linked more with planetary boundaries, planet stewardship and the creation of wider societal good? This would require stringent target setting and robust reporting based on a clearly defined set of mandatory requirements – including the "do no significant harm" principle. Irrevocable damage to the planet and its habitants can no longer be justified by financial gains or some other positive outcomes.

One alternative future scenario or "the next (r)evolution" in Responsible Investment could be *planetary investing*. This is a new concept developed by the authors and is built on their own experience and on the concepts of planetary boundaries and "planetarism."[1] The authors of this book have taken the liberty of using this new concept to help express their future thinking.

Planetary investing is not philanthropy or charity. The requirement for a positive return is an absolute must, as is the need to demonstrate the environmental and societal benefits created through the investment activity. The benefits are not assessed from the individual investor's viewpoint but from the perspective of the wider community. The investor uses responsibility objectives derived from a societal agenda rather than individually chosen investment strategies, approaches and benefits. Planetary investing is a long-term investment philosophy, based on making investments that support the planet in the long run while creating positive returns for the investor.

The baseline principles for planetary investing are, at a minimum:

- Respecting the environment and human rights beyond basic screening
- Active ownership for all (relevant) asset classes
- ESG integration throughout the entire portfolio
- Meaningful impact measurements
- Transparent and comparable reporting and communication
- Ambitious and robust target setting.

Investors still have choices over how to implement planetary investing. It will not drive all investors to invest in a similar way using the same asset and geographical allocations, nor to use the same benchmarks. The following examples shed some light on how to align investment activities with the baseline principles for planetary investing:

- **Respecting the basic requirements on environmental and human rights issues** is a cornerstone of planetary investing. It is a way of verifying that the investment activities are not causing significant harm to others. Norm-based screening with additional biodiversity and impact analysis would fulfil this principle.

- Through **active ownership**, investors can advance sustainable development and the implementation of responsible policies by companies and externally managed funds. Active ownership should also be a key function within passive products. Objectives and activities relating to voting and engagement should be clearly reported in detail.

- **ESG integration** is important: it guarantees that ESG is incorporated into all investment decision-making. ESG specialists can provide valuable information and support portfolio managers in their work, but it is equally important that ESG issues are embedded in valuation models.

- Planetary investing requires investors to **measure impacts**. Taking the double materiality principle – i.e. impacts created by the investments and impacts affecting the investments – into account is a mandatory feature within planetary investing. These measured impacts need to include relevant positive and negative indications using a third-party-assured method or reporting. There are already several international frameworks to help investors with impact measuring, which include the Task Force on Climate-related Financial Disclosures (TCFD), the UN Sustainable Development Goals (SDGs), the Taskforce on Nature-related Financial Disclosures (TNFD) and net impact calculations.

- Investors need to provide **transparent and comparable reporting** on the activities and impacts they have brought to bear. Reporting must include how planetary boundaries are factored into investment strategy and allocation. Clients, beneficiaries and other stakeholders need to be able to comment and provide feedback in a systematic manner.

- **Target setting** is important: the investor must state publicly what future outcomes it is aiming for. These outcomes include both return and impact aspects. Net Zero or Paris alignment by a certain point in time is a minimum requirement. In addition, targets should be set for social dimensions and wider ecological aspects. Disclosure on progress in achieving the set targets is a key component via annual (or more frequent) reporting.

Satisfying the mandatory planetary investment principles will require an investor to follow similar steps to those described in Chapter 4 (developing policies, implementing, monitoring and reporting). It also requires multidisciplinary data – lots of it – and the ability to analyse it and utilize it in investment decision-making. In the end, investors want to generate returns – and investment is a data business. Whoever can effectively gather, understand and use data will be able to create positive net impacts and also beat market returns.

Note

1 Planetarism is a philosophical model introduced by Dr Ele Alenius (2005), combining rational thinking and a common-sense approach to development which
respects our planet.

Bibliography

Alenius, E. (2005). *Planetarismi maailmankehityksen rationaalisena perustana*. Edita.

Appendix

List of global megatrends and global issues for selected entities

Agenda2030 – Sustainable Development Goals. United Nations, 2015.

1	No poverty
2	No hunger
3	Good health and well-being
4	Quality education
5	Gender equality
6	Clean water and sanitation
7	Affordable and clean energy
8	Decent work and economic growth
9	Industry, innovation and infrastructure
10	Reduced inequalities
11	Sustainable cities and communities
12	Responsible consumption and production
13	Climate action
14	Life below water
15	Life on land
16	Peace, justice and strong institutions
17	Partnerships for the goals

A safe operating space for humanity: Planetary boundaries. Rockström et al., 2009.

Biodiversity loss
Biogeochemical flow boundary: nitrogen cycle and phosphorus cycle
Climate change
Ocean acidification
Change in land use
Global freshwater use
Atmospheric aerosol loading (not yet quantified)
Chemical pollution (not yet quantified)
Stratospheric ozone depletion

The Global Risks Report. The World Economic Forum, 2022.

Economic	Asset bubble bursts in large economies Collapse of a systemically important industry Debt crises in large economies Failure to stabilize price trajectories Proliferation of illicit economic activity Prolonged economic stagnation Severe commodity shocks
Environmental	Biodiversity loss and ecosystem collapse Climate action failure Extreme weather events Human-made environmental damage Major geophysical disasters Natural resource crises
Geopolitical	Collapse of a multilateral institution Fracture of interstate relations Geoeconomic confrontations Geopolitical contestation of strategic resources Interstate conflict State collapse Terrorist attacks Weapons of mass destruction
Societal	Collapse or lack of social security systems Employment and livelihood crises Erosion of social cohesion Failure of public infrastructure Infectious diseases Large-scale involuntary migration Pervasive backlash against science Pollution-driven harms to human health Severe mental health deterioration Widespread youth disillusionment
Technological	Adverse outcomes of technological advances Breakdown of critical information infrastructure Digital inequality Digital power concentration Failure of cybersecurity measures Failure of technology governance

Index

Note: **Bold** page numbers refer to tables; *italic* page numbers refer to figures.

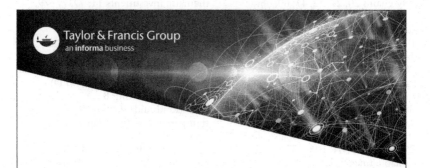

Printed in the United States
by Baker & Taylor Publisher Services